Official TOEFL iBT ® Tests, Volume 1

Using the Digital Resources

Authentic TOEFL iBT test questions are used in this book. When you take the actual TOEFL iBT test, you may notice some variations in how the questions are presented to you on-screen.

Installation

First, go to **www.mhprofessional.com/totvol1**. Once on the site, you'll be prompted to enter your access code. You can find your unique code in an envelope at the end of the book, or in your ETS account. Please note that this code is redeemable only by you and a maximum of four times.

Once you enter your access code, a download will automatically begin. This download will contain the audio files you need as well as files that contain the tests in both PC and Mac® format.

Main Menu for Practice Tests

When you launch the program, the following screen will appear.

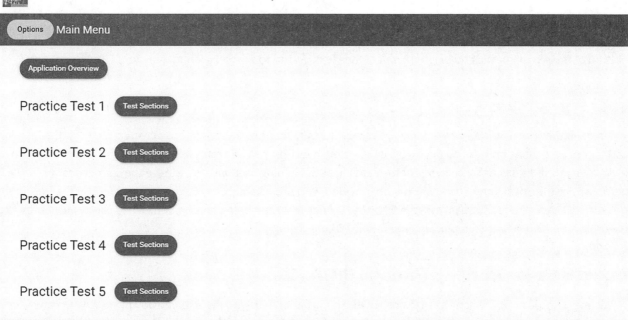

 Official TOEFL iBT® Tests Volume 1, 5th Edition

Options Main Menu

Application Overview

Practice Test 1   Test Sections

Practice Test 2   Test Sections

Practice Test 3   Test Sections

Practice Test 4   Test Sections

Practice Test 5   Test Sections

Taking TOEFL iBT Tests on Your Computer

From the **Main Menu**, choose Test 1, 2, 3, 4, or 5. Then select the test section you wish to take: **Reading, Listening, Speaking**, or **Writing**. Note that you can take each section more than once.

When you open a test section, you will first be provided with instructions for that section. A timer on the screen shows how many minutes and seconds you have left for that section. You can hide the timer if you find it distracting.

If you wish to take a break during the test, select **Main Menu** at the top of the screen. This will take you back to the main menu. When you are ready to resume, open the test section again and select the **Continue** button. Your work will not be lost, and when you resume, you will begin exactly where you left off. The timer clock will stop while you are on your break and will restart immediately when you resume the test. Breaks are not permitted during the actual test.

Answering Questions

To answer the questions in the Reading and Listening sections, select the best answer or follow the instructions given. For some questions, you will need to select more than one answer. Select the **Next** button to move forward to the next question. In the Listening section, the **Next** button is only enabled after you select an answer choice or choices. In the Reading section, you can select the **Next** button at any time to move forward to the next question, and you can select the **Back** button to move back to the previous question.

For the Speaking section, you should record your response to each question using a recording device after you hear the instruction telling you to begin speaking. Stop recording once the response time expires.

For the Writing section, write your response to each question in the space provided within the time allowed.

When all the questions in a section have been answered, select the **Next** button to complete the section.

Playing Audio Tracks

In the Listening, Speaking, and Writing sections, you will listen to audio tracks. Audio controls are available at the bottom of the screen. At the end of a track, select the **Next** button to start answering questions.

Your Performance

On the **Main Menu**, select any test you have taken. The percentage of questions answered correctly for the Reading and Listening sections only will be displayed. By selecting a test section and then selecting **Review**, you will be able to review the questions from that section. For the Reading and Listening sections, you will see the correct answer for each question. For the Speaking section, you will be provided with important points for each question. Use the important points to evaluate your performance on the Speaking Section. For the Writing section, you will be given topic notes. Use the topic notes to evaluate your performance on the Writing section.

Audio Files for Working Through the Tests in the Book

You may choose to work with the tests printed in the book rather than with the tests you download to your computer. If so, you will still need to listen to the audio tracks. Once you download the folder named "Audio Files" to your computer, you can select the audio tracks by number as you proceed through the book. As you work through the tests in the book, a headphones symbol 🎧 will indicate each time you need to play a track. Select the number of the track as instructed in the book.

Official
TOEFL iBT® Tests

VOLUME **1**

FIFTH EDITION

1 2 3 4 5 6 7 8 9 LON 29 28 27 26 25 24

Domestic Edition
ISBN   978-1-265-47907-7
MHID   1-265-47907-0

e-ISBN 978-1-265-48019-6
e-MHID   1-265-48019-2

ETS, the ETS logo, MYBEST, SPEECHRATER, TOEFL, and TOEFL iBT are
registered trademarks of Educational Testing Service (ETS) in the United
States of America and other countries throughout the world. TOEFL
GOLEARN! and the T logo are trademarks of ETS in the United States and
other countries.

McGraw Hill books are available at special quantity discounts to use
as premiums and sales promotions or for use in corporate training
programs. To contact a representative, please visit the Contact Us pages
at www.mhprofessional.com.

McGraw Hill is committed to making our products accessible to all learners.
To learn more about the available support and accommodations we offer,
please contact us at accessibility@ mheducation.com. We also participate
in the Access Text Network (www.accesstext.org), and ATN members may
submit requests through ATN.

Contents

Introduction

About the TOEFL iBT Test

More than 12,000 universities, agencies, and other institutions in more than 160 countries—including Australia, Canada, New Zealand, the United States, the U.K., and countries all across Europe and Asia—accept TOEFL iBT scores as part of their admissions criteria, making the TOEFL iBT test the most widely accepted English-language test in the world.

Each TOEFL iBT test contains four sections: Reading, Listening, Speaking, and Writing. The questions in these sections measure how well you **read, listen, speak, and write in English**. They also measure how well you use these skills together, so in some cases you will be asked to integrate your skills. For example, you may read a passage or listen to a lecture and then write or speak about what you learned. Here are brief descriptions of each section, including what the section measures and the types of questions it contains.

Reading Section

This section measures your ability to understand academic passages in English. The passages are excerpts from textbooks and other books suitable for use in introductory university courses.

You do not need any background knowledge about the topics contained in the passages in order to successfully answer the questions. All the information you need to answer the questions can be found in the passages. The questions measure your ability to understand stated information, make inferences, and distinguish main ideas from less important information.

Here are the types of Reading questions, with an explanation of each type:

Basic Comprehension questions	
Factual Information	These questions ask you to identify factual information that is explicitly presented in the passage.
Negative Factual Information	These questions ask you to distinguish information that is true from information that is not true or is not included in the passage.
Vocabulary	These questions ask you to identify the meanings of individual words or phrases *as they are used in the passage.*
Reference	These questions measure your ability to identify relationships between ideas mentioned in the passage and expressions that refer to the ideas. For example, an idea could be presented and another sentence could refer to "This idea." A question might ask what the phrase "This idea" refers to.
Sentence Simplification	These questions ask you to choose a sentence that has the same essential meaning as a particular sentence from the passage.
Inferencing questions	
Inference	These questions ask about information that is implied but not explicitly presented in the passage.
Rhetorical Purpose	These questions ask about the rhetorical function of specific information presented in a passage. These questions ask *why* or *how* the author mentions or includes a specific piece of information in the passage. Some questions of this type ask how an author organized information in the passage.

Insert Text	These questions provide a new sentence and ask you to place that sentence into the passage where it would best fit.
Reading-to-Learn questions	
Prose Summary	These questions ask you to identify major ideas from the passage and distinguish them from minor ideas or from ideas that are not presented in the passage. To select the correct answers, you need to both understand the relative importance of various pieces of information from the passage and identify the combination of answer choices that cover the major ideas presented in the passage. This question is always the last question in a Reading set. This question is worth up to 2 points. Test takers receive 2 points if all three correct answers are selected, and 1 point if only 2 correct answers are selected.

Listening Section

This section measures your ability to understand conversations and academic lectures in English.

You will listen to two conversations. One conversation takes place in a professor's office and may include discussion of academic material or course requirements. The other conversation takes place on a university campus and includes discussion of nonacademic content that is related to university life. Each conversation is followed by five questions.

You will also listen to three lectures on a variety of topics. In some lectures, only the professor speaks. In others, students contribute to the discussion; the professor may ask students questions about the topic being discussed or may answer students' questions. Each lecture is followed by six questions.

Each conversation and lecture is heard only once. Each contains a context photograph depicting the speaker(s). Some conversations and lectures contain other visuals, such as blackboards that present technical vocabulary or uncommon names.

Here are the types of Listening questions, with an explanation of each type:

Basic Comprehension questions	
Gist-Content	These questions ask you to identify the main idea of a lecture or conversation.
Gist-Purpose	These questions ask about the main purpose of a lecture or conversation.
Detail questions	These questions ask about important details from a lecture or conversation.
Pragmatic Understanding questions	
Function or Purpose	These questions ask you to identify a speaker's purpose in making a statement or how a statement functions in a lecture or conversation.
Speaker Attitude	These questions ask you to identify a speaker's attitude, opinion, or degree of certainty.
Connecting Information questions	
Understanding Organization	These questions ask you about the organization of information in a lecture.
Connecting Content	These questions ask you about the relationships among ideas in a lecture or conversation or to make inferences based on important points that were discussed.

Most questions are multiple choice with one correct answer. Some questions require more than one answer. You may also encounter questions that ask you to place the steps of a process in order, place check marks in a grid, or listen again to a portion of a conversation or lecture.

Speaking Section

This section measures your ability to speak in English about a variety of topics.

For each question, you will be given a short time to prepare your response. When the preparation time is up, answer the question as completely as possible in the time indicated for that question. For the tests in this book, you should record your responses on a recording device. That way, you can review them later and compare them with the notes in the Answers section and rubrics.

For the first question, Paired Choice, you will give your opinion about a familiar topic. You will need to explain what your opinion is and explain the reasons you have for holding that opinion.

For the second question, Fit and Explain, you will first read a short passage and then listen to or read a transcript of a conversation on the same topic. You will then be asked a question about both. You will need to combine appropriate information from the passage and the conversation to provide a complete answer to the question. Your response is scored on your ability to speak clearly and coherently and on your ability to accurately convey information about the passage and the conversation.

For the third question, General/Specific, you will first read a short passage on an academic subject and then listen to or read a transcript of a talk on the same subject. You will then be asked a question about both. Your response is scored on your ability to speak clearly and coherently and on your ability to integrate and convey key information from the passage and the talk.

For the last question, Summary, you will listen to or read a transcript of part of a lecture. You will then be asked a question about it. Your response is scored on your ability to speak clearly and coherently and on your ability to accurately convey information from the lecture.

Speaking responses are scored in terms of three important dimensions: delivery, language use, and topic development. When raters evaluate responses, they consider all three dimensions equally. No single dimension is weighted more heavily than another.

Writing Section

This section measures your ability to write in English to communicate in an academic environment.

For Writing question 1, you will read a passage and listen to or read a transcript of a lecture. Then you will respond to a question that asks you about the relationship between the reading passage and the lecture. You will have 20 minutes to plan and write your response. Try to answer as completely as possible using information from both the reading passage and the lecture. The question does *not* ask you to express your personal opinion. You may consult the reading passage again when it is time for you to write. Typically, an effective response will contain a minimum of 150 words. Your response is evaluated on the quality of your writing and on the completeness and accuracy of the content.

For Writing question 2, Writing for an Academic Discussion, you will read a question from a professor and responses from other students in an online discussion. You will then be asked to state and support an opinion that contributes to the topic under discussion. You will have 10 minutes to read the posts and write your response. An effective response typically contains at least 100 words. Your response is evaluated on how relevant and clearly expressed your contribution to the online discussion is, and on whether it demonstrates consistent facility in the use of language.

How to Use This Book/Digital Resources

Official TOEFL iBT® Tests, Volume 1 can help you prepare for the test. It contains five TOEFL iBT tests. All the test questions are authentic TOEFL iBT questions, but some are presented differently than on the real test. (Please note that you should use a recording device for the Speaking section.) You can take each test in two ways:

- **In the book**, using a pen or pencil to mark your answers or to write your responses. Whenever you need to listen to an audio track, you will see the headphones icon 🎧 printed on the page. The audio tracks are provided with the digital download. Open the Audio folder, and you will see the tracks listed by number. Select each one when you are instructed to do so in the book.
- **On your computer**, using the interactive versions of the tests provided on the digital download. Follow the instructions provided on the first page of this book, titled "Using the Digital Resources." Select your answers and enter your written responses as instructed. The audio tracks will play automatically as the test questions are presented to you on screen.

Written transcripts of the audio tracks are located in Appendix B. If you do not have access to the audio tracks but do have access to people with good English pronunciation, ask them to read the transcripts aloud to you. Listening to the transcripts is better practice than reading them to yourself. If someone reads the transcripts to you, make sure you see the pictures.

If you are using the print versions of the tests, listen to each audio track only one time. As in the real test, you may take notes while you listen and use your notes to help you answer the questions.

Answers

An Answers section for each test in this book is provided at the end of the test.

For the Reading and Listening sections, answer keys are provided.

For the Speaking and Writing sections, there is no single correct answer for each question. The Answers section has descriptions of what you need to do to get a high score. You can also evaluate your responses using the scoring rubrics provided in Appendix A.

In the Speaking section, if you have recorded your responses on a recording device, you can compare them with the descriptions in the Answers section and with the rubrics.

If you are using the computerized tests, follow the on-screen instructions to see the Reading and Listening answers and the answer descriptions for Speaking and Writing.

Rubrics

Rubrics are scoring guides used by raters to evaluate Speaking and Writing responses. All TOEFL iBT test rubrics can be found in Appendix A.

Speaking scores represent an overall judgment of how well a response communicates its intended message. **Delivery** and **language use** are two key categories that raters consider when scoring responses to all four of the Speaking questions. **Topic development** is a third key category.

For the Independent Speaking question, topic development is characterized by the *fullness* of the content provided in the response as well as its overall *coherence*. Using memorized responses or examples is strongly discouraged and could lower your score. It is very easy for ETS raters to distinguish memorized responses from those that are natural and spontaneous. For Integrated Speaking questions, topic development is characterized by the *accuracy* and *completeness* of the content provided in the response as well as its overall *coherence*.

Writing scores also represent an overall judgment of how well a response communicates its intended message. The **quality of the writing** is a key characteristic that raters consider when scoring responses to the Integrated Writing question (question 1) and the Writing for an Academic Discussion question (question 2). For the Integrated Writing question, high-quality writing is characterized by appropriate and precise use of grammar and vocabulary. For the Writing for an Academic Discussion question, you should also make sure that your ideas are well-supported by reasons and examples and are expressed clearly. Since your response represents an online post, it does not need to be organized into separate paragraphs. However, your ideas need to be **well-connected, coherent, and clear.** If you use a lot of words and sentences that are not well connected and do not support each other, you'll receive a low score. Do not try to add words to your response by using long memorized introductory or concluding phrases and sentences. They represent neither authentic writing nor the type of writing used in online discussions.

The **completeness and accuracy of the content** is a key characteristic of responses that raters consider when scoring responses to an Integrated Writing question. A complete and accurate response presents the relevant main points from both the lecture and the reading, demonstrates the relationship between each of these main points, and includes all the important supporting details from the lecture. It does not include information from sources other than the lecture and the reading. For a Writing for an Academic Discussion question, **contribution to the discussion** is a very important criterion used to evaluate your response. The discussion includes a professor's question as well as posts by other students. Contributing to a discussion does not necessarily mean coming up with a lot of new ideas. One can also contribute to a discussion by agreeing or disagreeing with what someone else has already written and then explaining why in your own words. Make sure that you don't just repeat what someone else has written—use your own words, and your own voice, and elaborate on the ideas in your own way.

More Official Resources

ETS has many official resources to help you prepare for the TOEFL iBT test, including:

- *The Official Guide to the TOEFL® Test*
- *TOEFL® Practice Online*
- *"Inside the TOEFL® Test"* Video Series
- *TOEFL® Test Preparation: The Insider's Guide (MOOC)*
- *Official TOEFL iBT® Prep Course*

For information about these resources and more, and to register for the test, visit **www.ets.org/toefl.**

TOEFL iBT® Test 1

READING

In this section, you will be able to demonstrate your ability to understand academic passages in English. You will read and answer questions about **two passages**.

In the actual test, you will have 36 minutes total to read both passages and answer the questions. A clock will indicate how much time remains.

Some passages may include one or more notes explaining words or phrases. The words or phrases are marked with footnote numbers, and the notes explaining them appear at the end of the passage.

Most questions are worth 1 point, but the last question for each passage is worth 2 points.

You may review and revise your answers in this section as long as time remains.

At the end of this practice test, you will find an answer key.

Directions: Read the passage. Then answer the questions. Give yourself about 18 minutes to answer the questions.

DEER POPULATIONS OF THE PUGET SOUND

Two species of deer have been prevalent in the Puget Sound area of Washington State in the Pacific Northwest of the United States. The black-tailed deer, a lowland, west-side cousin of the mule deer of eastern Washington, is now the most common. The other species, the Columbian white-tailed deer, in earlier times was common in the open prairie country; it is now restricted to the low, marshy islands and floodplains along the lower Columbia River.

Nearly any kind of plant of the forest understory can be part of a deer's diet. Where the forest inhibits the growth of grass and other meadow plants, the black-tailed deer browses on huckleberry, salal, dogwood, and almost any other shrub or herb. But this is fair-weather feeding. What keeps the black-tailed deer alive in the harsher seasons of plant decay and dormancy? One compensation for not hibernating is the built-in urge to migrate. Deer may move from high-elevation browse areas in summer down to the lowland areas in late fall. Even with snow on the ground, the high bushy understory is exposed; also snow and wind bring down leafy branches of cedar, hemlock, red alder, and other arboreal fodder.

The numbers of deer have fluctuated markedly since the entry of Europeans into Puget Sound country. The early explorers and settlers told of abundant deer in the early 1800s and yet almost in the same breath bemoaned the lack of this succulent game animal. Famous explorers of the North American frontier, Lewis and Clark arrived at the mouth of the Columbia River on November 14, 1805, in nearly starved circumstances. They had experienced great difficulty finding game west of the Rockies, and not until the second of December did they kill their first elk. To keep 40 people alive that winter, they consumed approximately 150 elk and 20 deer. And when game moved out of the lowlands in early spring, the expedition decided to return east rather than face possible starvation. Later on in the early years of the nineteenth century, when Fort Vancouver became the headquarters for the Hudson's Bay Company, deer populations continued to fluctuate. David Douglas, Scottish botanical explorer of the 1830s, found a disturbing change in the animal life around the fort during the period between his first visit in 1825 and his final contact with the fort in 1832. A recent Douglas biographer states: "The deer which once picturesquely dotted the meadows around the fort were gone [in 1832], hunted to extermination in order to protect the crops."

Reduction in numbers of game should have boded ill for their survival in later times. A worsening of the plight of deer was to be expected as settlers encroached on the land, logging, burning, and clearing, eventually replacing a wilderness landscape with roads, cities, towns, and factories. No doubt the numbers of deer declined still further. Recall the fate of the Columbian white-tailed deer, now in a protected status. But for the black-tailed deer, human pressure has had just the opposite effect. Wildlife zoologist Helmut Buechner (1953), in reviewing the nature of biotic changes in Washington through recorded time, says that "since the early 1940s, the state has had more deer than at any other time in its history, the winter population fluctuating around approximately 320,000 deer (mule and black-tailed deer), which will yield about 65,000 of either sex and any age annually for an indefinite period."

The causes of this population rebound are consequences of other human actions. First, the major predators of deer—wolves, cougar, and lynx—have been greatly reduced in numbers. Second, conservation has been insured by limiting times for and types of hunting. But the most profound reason for the restoration of high population numbers has been the fate of the forests. Great tracts of lowland country deforested by logging, fire, or both have become ideal feeding grounds for deer. In addition to finding an increase of suitable browse, like huckleberry and vine maple, Arthur Einarsen, longtime game biologist in the Pacific Northwest, found quality of browse in the open areas to be substantially more nutritive. The protein content of shade-grown vegetation, for example, was much lower than that for plants grown in clearings.

Directions: Now answer the questions.

PARAGRAPH 1

Two species of deer have been prevalent in the Puget Sound area of Washington State in the Pacific Northwest of the United States. The black-tailed deer, a lowland, west-side cousin of the mule deer of eastern Washington, is now the most common. The other species, the Columbian white-tailed deer, in earlier times was common in the open prairie country; it is now restricted to the low, marshy islands and floodplains along the lower Columbia River.

1. According to paragraph 1, which of the following is true of the white-tailed deer of Puget Sound?
   - (A) It is native to lowlands and marshes.
   - (B) It is more closely related to the mule deer of eastern Washington than to other types of deer.
   - (C) It has replaced the black-tailed deer in the open prairie.
   - (D) It no longer lives in a particular type of habitat that it once occupied.

PARAGRAPH 2

Nearly any kind of plant of the forest understory can be part of a deer's diet. Where the forest inhibits the growth of grass and other meadow plants, the black-tailed deer browses on huckleberry, salal, dogwood, and almost any other shrub or herb. But this is fair-weather feeding. What keeps the black-tailed deer alive in the harsher seasons of plant decay and dormancy? One compensation for not hibernating is the built-in urge to migrate. Deer may move from high-elevation browse areas in summer down to the lowland areas in late fall. Even with snow on the ground, the high bushy understory is exposed; also snow and wind bring down leafy branches of cedar, hemlock, red alder, and other arboreal fodder.

2. It can be inferred from the discussion in paragraph 2 that winter conditions
   - (A) cause some deer to hibernate
   - (B) make food unavailable in the highlands for deer
   - (C) make it easier for deer to locate understory plants
   - (D) prevent deer from migrating during the winter

PARAGRAPH 3

The numbers of deer have fluctuated markedly since the entry of Europeans into Puget Sound country. The early explorers and settlers told of abundant deer in the early 1800s and yet almost in the same breath bemoaned the lack of this succulent game animal. Famous explorers of the North American frontier, Lewis and Clark arrived at the mouth of the Columbia River on November 14, 1805, in nearly starved circumstances. They had experienced great difficulty finding game west of the Rockies, and not until the second of December did they kill their first elk. To keep 40 people alive that winter, they consumed approximately 150 elk and 20 deer. And when game moved out of the lowlands in early spring, the expedition decided to return east rather than face possible starvation. Later on in the early years of the nineteenth century, when Fort Vancouver became the headquarters for the Hudson's Bay Company, deer populations continued to fluctuate. David Douglas, Scottish botanical explorer of the 1830s, found a disturbing change in the animal life around the fort during the period between his first visit in 1825 and his final contact with the fort in 1832. A recent Douglas biographer states: "The deer which once picturesquely dotted the meadows around the fort were gone [in 1832], hunted to extermination in order to protect the crops."

3. The author tells the story of the explorers Lewis and Clark in paragraph 3 in order to illustrate which of the following points?

   (A) The number of deer within the Puget Sound region has varied over time.
   (B) Most of the explorers who came to the Puget Sound area were primarily interested in hunting game.
   (C) There was more game for hunting in the East of the United States than in the West.
   (D) Individual explorers were not as successful at locating game as were the trading companies.

4. According to paragraph 3, how had Fort Vancouver changed by the time David Douglas returned in 1832?

   (A) The fort had become the headquarters for the Hudson's Bay Company.
   (B) Deer had begun populating the meadows around the fort.
   (C) Deer populations near the fort had been destroyed.
   (D) Crop yields in the area around the fort had decreased.

Reduction in numbers of game should have boded ill for their survival in later times. A worsening of the plight of deer was to be expected as settlers encroached on the land, logging, burning, and clearing, eventually replacing a wilderness landscape with roads, cities, towns, and factories. No doubt the numbers of deer declined still further. Recall **the fate of the Columbian white-tailed deer**, now in a protected status. But for the black-tailed deer, human pressure has had just the opposite effect. Wildlife zoologist Helmut Buechner (1953), in reviewing the nature of biotic changes in Washington through recorded time, says that "since the early 1940s, the state has had more deer than at any other time in its history, the winter population fluctuating around approximately 320,000 deer (mule and black-tailed deer), which will yield about 65,000 of either sex and any age annually for an **indefinite period**."

5. Why does the author ask readers to recall "**the fate of the Columbian white-tailed deer**" in the discussion of changes in the wilderness landscape?

    Ⓐ To provide support for the idea that habitat destruction would lead to population decline
    Ⓑ To compare how two species of deer caused biotic changes in the wilderness environment
    Ⓒ To provide an example of a species of deer that has successfully adapted to human settlement
    Ⓓ To argue that some deer species must be given a protected status

6. The phrase "**indefinite period**" in the passage is closest in meaning to a period

    Ⓐ whose end has not been determined
    Ⓑ that does not begin when expected
    Ⓒ that lasts only briefly
    Ⓓ whose importance remains unknown

7. Which of the following statements about deer populations is supported by the information in paragraph 4 ?

    Ⓐ Deer populations reached their highest point during the 1940s and then began to decline.
    Ⓑ The activities of settlers contributed in unexpected ways to the growth of some deer populations in later times.
    Ⓒ The clearing of wilderness land for construction caused biotic changes from which the black-tailed deer population has never recovered.
    Ⓓ Since the 1940s the winter populations of deer have fluctuated more than the summer populations have.

PARAGRAPH 5

The causes of this population rebound are consequences of other human actions. First, the major predators of deer—wolves, cougar, and lynx—have been greatly reduced in numbers. Second, conservation has been ensured by limiting times for and types of hunting. But the most profound reason for the restoration of high population numbers has been the fate of the forests. Great tracts of lowland country deforested by logging, fire, or both have become ideal feeding grounds for deer. **In addition to finding an increase of suitable browse, like huckleberry and vine maple, Arthur Einarsen, longtime game biologist in the Pacific Northwest, found quality of browse in the open areas to be substantially more nutritive.** The protein content of shade-grown vegetation, for example, was much lower than that for plants grown in clearings.

8. Which of the sentences below best expresses the essential information in the highlighted sentence in paragraph 5 ? Incorrect choices change the meaning in important ways or leave out essential information.

   Ⓐ Arthur Einarsen's longtime familiarity with the Pacific Northwest helped him discover areas where deer had an increase in suitable browse.
   Ⓑ Arthur Einarsen found that deforested feeding grounds provided deer with more and better food.
   Ⓒ Biologists like Einarsen believe it is important to find additional open areas with suitable browse for deer to inhabit.
   Ⓓ According to Einarsen, huckleberry and vine maple are examples of vegetation that may someday improve the nutrition of deer in the open areas of the Pacific Northwest.

PARAGRAPHS 2 & 3

What keeps the black-tailed deer alive in the harsher seasons of plant decay and dormancy? One compensation for not hibernating is the built-in urge to migrate. **(A)** Deer may move from high-elevation browse areas in summer down to the lowland areas in late fall. **(B)** Even with snow on the ground, the high bushy understory is exposed; also snow and wind bring down leafy branches of cedar, hemlock, red alder, and other arboreal fodder. **(C)**

The numbers of deer have fluctuated markedly since the entry of Europeans into Puget Sound country. **(D)** The early explorers and settlers told of abundant deer in the early 1800s and yet almost in the same breath bemoaned the lack of this succulent game animal.

9. Look at the part of the passage that is displayed above. The letters **(A)**, **(B)**, **(C)**, and **(D)** indicate where the following sentence could be added.

   There food is available and accessible throughout the winter.

   Where would the sentence best fit?
   Ⓐ Choice A
   Ⓑ Choice B
   Ⓒ Choice C
   Ⓓ Choice D

10. **Directions**: An introductory sentence for a brief summary of the passage is provided below. Complete the summary by selecting the THREE answer choices that express the most important ideas in the passage. Some sentences do not belong in the summary because they express ideas that are not presented in the passage or are minor ideas in the passage. **This question is worth 2 points.**

Write your answer choices in the spaces where they belong. You can either write the letter of your answer choice or you can copy the sentence.

> **Deer in the Puget Sound area eat a wide variety of foods and migrate seasonally to find food.**
>
> ●
>
> ●
>
> ●

Answer Choices

A The balance of deer species in the Puget Sound region has changed over time, with the Columbian white-tailed deer now outnumbering other types of deer.

B Because Puget Sound deer migrate, it was and still remains difficult to determine accurately how many deer are living at any one time in the western United States.

C Deer populations naturally fluctuate, but early settlers in the Puget Sound environment caused an overall decline in the deer populations of the area at that time.

D Although it was believed that human settlement of the American West would cause the total number of deer to decrease permanently, the opposite has actually occurred for certain types of deer.

E In the long term, black-tailed deer in the Puget Sound area have benefitted from human activities through the elimination of their natural predators and more and better food in deforested areas.

F Wildlife biologists have long been concerned that the loss of forests may create nutritional deficiencies for deer.

Directions: Read the passage. Then answer the questions. Give yourself about 18 minutes to answer the questions.

CAVE ART IN EUROPE

The earliest discovered traces of art are beads and carvings, and then paintings, from sites dating back to the Upper Paleolithic period. We might expect that early artistic efforts would be crude, but the cave paintings of Spain and southern France show a marked degree of skill. So do the naturalistic paintings on slabs of stone excavated in southern Africa. Some of those slabs appear to have been painted as much as 28,000 years ago, which suggests that painting in Africa is as old as painting in Europe. But painting may be even older than that. The early Australians may have painted on the walls of rock shelters and cliff faces at least 30,000 years ago and maybe as much as 60,000 years ago.

The researchers Peter Ucko and Andrée Rosenfeld identified three principal locations of paintings in the caves of western Europe: (1) in obviously inhabited rock shelters and cave entrances; (2) in galleries immediately off the inhabited areas of caves; and (3) in the inner reaches of caves, whose difficulty of access has been interpreted by some as a sign that magical-religious activities were performed there.

The subjects of the paintings are mostly animals. The paintings rest on bare walls, with no backdrops or environmental trappings. Perhaps, like many contemporary peoples, Upper Paleolithic men and women believed that the drawing of a human image could cause death or injury, and if that were indeed their belief, it might explain why human figures are rarely depicted in cave art. Another explanation for the focus on animals might be that these people sought to improve their luck at hunting. This theory is suggested by evidence of chips in the painted figures, perhaps made by spears thrown at the drawings. But if improving their hunting luck was the chief motivation for the paintings, it is difficult to explain why only a few show signs of having been speared. Perhaps the paintings were inspired by the need to increase the supply of animals. Cave art seems to have reached a peak toward the end of the Upper Paleolithic period, when the herds of game were decreasing.

The particular symbolic significance of the cave paintings in southwestern France is more explicitly revealed, perhaps, by the results of a study conducted by researchers Patricia Rice and Ann Paterson. The data they present suggest that the animals portrayed in the cave paintings were mostly the ones that the painters preferred for meat and for materials such as hides. For example, wild cattle (bovines) and horses are portrayed more often than we would expect by chance, probably because they were larger and heavier (meatier) than other animals in the environment. In addition, the paintings mostly portray animals that the painters may have feared the most because of their size, speed, natural weapons such as tusks and horns, and the unpredictability of their behavior. That is, mammoths, bovines, and horses are portrayed more often than deer and reindeer. Thus, the paintings are consistent with the idea that the art is related to the importance of hunting in the economy of Upper Paleolithic people. Consistent with this idea, according to the investigators, is the fact that the art of the cultural period that followed the Upper Paleolithic also seems to reflect how people got their food. But in that period, when getting food no longer depended on hunting large game animals (because they were becoming extinct), the art ceased to focus on portrayals of animals.

Upper Paleolithic art was not confined to cave paintings. Many shafts of spears and similar objects were decorated with figures of animals. The anthropologist Alexander Marshack has an interesting interpretation of some of the engravings made during the Upper Paleolithic. He believes that as far back as 30,000 B.C.E., hunters may have used a system of notation, engraved on bone and stone, to mark phases of the Moon. If this is true, it would mean that Upper Paleolithic people were capable of complex thought and were consciously aware of their environment. In addition to other artworks, figurines representing the human female in exaggerated form have also been found at Upper Paleolithic sites. It has been suggested that these figurines were an ideal type or an expression of a desire for fertility.

Directions: Now answer the questions.

PARAGRAPH 1

The earliest discovered traces of art are beads and carvings, and then paintings, from sites dating back to the Upper Paleolithic period. We might expect that early artistic efforts would be crude, but the cave paintings of Spain and southern France show a **marked** degree of skill. So do the naturalistic paintings on slabs of stone excavated in southern Africa. Some of those slabs appear to have been painted as much as 28,000 years ago, which suggests that painting in Africa is as old as painting in Europe. But painting may be even older than that. The early Australians may have painted on the walls of rock shelters and cliff faces at least 30,000 years ago and maybe as much as 60,000 years ago.

11. The word "**marked**" in the passage is closest in meaning to
    (A) considerable
    (B) surprising
    (C) limited
    (D) adequate

12. Paragraph 1 supports which of the following statements about painting in Europe?
    (A) It is much older than painting in Australia.
    (B) It is as much as 28,000 years old.
    (C) It is not as old as painting in southern Africa.
    (D) It is much more than 30,000 years old.

P
A
R
A
G
R
A
P
H

2

The researchers Peter Ucko and Andrée Rosenfeld identified three principal locations of paintings in the caves of western Europe: (1) in obviously inhabited rock shelters and cave entrances; (2) in galleries immediately off the inhabited areas of caves; and (3) in the inner reaches of caves, whose difficulty of access has been interpreted by some as a sign that magical-religious activities were performed there.

13. According to paragraph 2, what makes some researchers think that certain cave paintings were connected with magical-religious activities?

    Ⓐ The paintings were located where many people could easily see them, allowing groups of people to participate in the magical-religious activities.

    Ⓑ Upper Paleolithic people shared similar beliefs with contemporary peoples who use paintings of animals in their magical-religious rituals.

    Ⓒ Evidence of magical-religious activities has been found in galleries immediately off the inhabited areas of caves.

    Ⓓ The paintings were found in hard-to-reach places away from the inhabited parts of the cave.

P
A
R
A
G
R
A
P
H

3

The subjects of the paintings are mostly animals. The paintings rest on bare walls, with no backdrops or environmental trappings. Perhaps, like many contemporary peoples, Upper Paleolithic men and women believed that the drawing of a human image could cause death or injury, and if that were indeed their belief, it might explain why human figures are rarely depicted in cave art. Another explanation for the focus on animals might be that these people sought to improve their luck at hunting. This theory is suggested by evidence of chips in the painted figures, perhaps made by spears thrown at the drawings. But if improving their hunting luck was the chief motivation for the paintings, it is difficult to explain why only a few show signs of having been speared. Perhaps the paintings were inspired by the need to increase the supply of animals. Cave art seems to have **reached a peak toward the end of the Upper Paleolithic period, when the herds of game were decreasing**.

14. According to paragraph 3, scholars explained chips in the painted figures of animals by proposing that

    Ⓐ Upper Paleolithic artists used marks to record the animals they had seen

    Ⓑ the paintings were inspired by the need to increase the supply of animals for hunting

    Ⓒ the artists had removed rough spots on the cave walls

    Ⓓ Upper Paleolithic people used the paintings to increase their luck at hunting

15. Why does the author mention that Upper Paleolithic cave art seemed to have "**reached a peak toward the end of the Upper Paleolithic period, when the herds of game were decreasing**"?

    Ⓐ To argue that Upper Paleolithic art ceased to include animals when herds of game became scarce

    Ⓑ To provide support for the idea that the aim of the paintings was to increase the supply of animals for hunting

    Ⓒ To emphasize the continued improvement in the quality of cave art throughout the Upper Paleolithic period

    Ⓓ To show the direct connection between the decrease in herds of game and the end of the Upper Paleolithic period

The particular symbolic significance of the cave paintings in southwestern France is more explicitly revealed, perhaps, by the results of a study conducted by researchers Patricia Rice and Ann Paterson. The data they present suggest that the animals portrayed in the cave paintings were mostly the ones that the painters preferred for meat and for materials such as hides. For example, wild cattle (bovines) and horses are portrayed more often than we would expect by chance, probably because they were larger and heavier (meatier) than other animals in the environment. In addition, the paintings mostly portray animals that the painters may have feared the most because of their size, speed, natural weapons such as tusks and horns, and the unpredictability of their behavior. That is, mammoths, bovines, and horses are portrayed more often than deer and reindeer. Thus, the paintings are consistent with the idea that the art is related to the importance of hunting in the economy of Upper Paleolithic people. Consistent with this idea, according to the investigators, is the fact that the art of the cultural period that followed the Upper Paleolithic also seems to reflect how people got their food. But in that period, when getting food no longer depended on hunting large game animals (because they were becoming extinct), the art ceased to focus on portrayals of animals.

16. According to paragraph 4, which of the following may best represent the attitude of hunters toward deer and reindeer in the Upper Paleolithic period?

   Ⓐ Hunters did not fear deer and reindeer as much as they did large game animals such as horses and mammoths.
   Ⓑ Hunters were not interested in hunting deer and reindeer because of their size and speed.
   Ⓒ Hunters preferred the meat and hides of deer and reindeer to those of other animals.
   Ⓓ Hunters avoided deer and reindeer because of their natural weapons, such as horns.

17. According to paragraph 4, what change is evident in the art of the period following the Upper Paleolithic?

   Ⓐ This new art starts to depict small animals rather than large ones.
   Ⓑ This new art ceases to reflect the ways in which people obtained their food.
   Ⓒ This new art no longer consists mostly of representations of animals.
   Ⓓ This new art begins to show the importance of hunting to the economy.

P
A
R
A
G
R
A
P
H

5

Upper Paleolithic art was not confined to cave paintings. Many shafts of spears and similar objects were decorated with figures of animals. The anthropologist Alexander Marshack has an interesting interpretation of some of the engravings made during the Upper Paleolithic. He believes that as far back as 30,000 B.C.E., hunters may have used a system of notation, engraved on bone and stone, to mark phases of the Moon. If this is true, it would mean that Upper Paleolithic people were capable of complex thought and were consciously aware of their environment. In addition to other artworks, figurines representing the human female in exaggerated form have also been found at Upper Paleolithic sites. It has been suggested that these figurines were an ideal type or an expression of a desire for fertility.

18. According to paragraph 5, which of the following has been used as evidence to suggest that Upper Paleolithic people were capable of complex thought and conscious awareness of their environment?

Ⓐ They engraved animal figures on the shafts of spears and other objects.
Ⓑ They may have used engraved signs to record the phases of the Moon.
Ⓒ Their figurines represented the human female in exaggerated form.
Ⓓ They may have used figurines to portray an ideal type or to express a desire for fertility.

P
A
R
A
G
R
A
P
H

3

The subjects of the paintings are mostly animals. The paintings rest on bare walls, with no backdrops or environmental trappings. Perhaps, like many contemporary peoples, Upper Paleolithic men and women believed that the drawing of a human image could cause death or injury, and if that were indeed their belief, it might explain why human figures are rarely depicted in cave art. Another explanation for the focus on animals might be that these people sought to improve their luck at hunting. **(A)** This theory is suggested by evidence of chips in the painted figures, perhaps made by spears thrown at the drawings. **(B)** But if improving their hunting luck was the chief motivation for the paintings, it is difficult to explain why only a few show signs of having been speared. **(C)** Perhaps the paintings were inspired by the need to increase the supply of animals. Cave art seems to have reached a peak toward the end of the Upper Paleolithic period, when the herds of game were decreasing. **(D)**

19. Look at the part of the passage that is displayed above. The letters **(A)**, **(B)**, **(C)**, and **(D)** indicate where the following sentence could be added.

Therefore, if the paintings were connected with hunting, some other explanation is needed.

Where would the sentence best fit?

Ⓐ Choice A
Ⓑ Choice B
Ⓒ Choice C
Ⓓ Choice D

20. **Directions**: An introductory sentence for a brief summary of the passage is provided below. Complete the summary by selecting the THREE answer choices that express the most important ideas in the passage. Some sentences do not belong in the summary because they express ideas that are not presented in the passage or are minor ideas in the passage. **This question is worth 2 points.**

Write your answer choices in the spaces where they belong. You can either write the letter of your answer choice or you can copy the sentence.

> **Upper Paleolithic cave paintings in western Europe are among humanity's earliest artistic efforts.**
>
> ●
>
> ●
>
> ●

Answer Choices

A   Researchers have proposed several different explanations for the fact that animals were the most common subjects in the cave paintings.

B   The cave paintings focus on portraying animals without also depicting the natural environments in which these animals are typically found.

C   The art of the cultural period that followed the Upper Paleolithic ceased to portray large game animals and focused instead on the kinds of animals that people of that period preferred to hunt.

D   Some researchers have argued that the cave paintings mostly portrayed large animals that provided Upper Paleolithic people with meat and materials.

E   Some researchers believe that the paintings found in France provide more explicit evidence of their symbolic significance than those found in Spain, southern Africa, and Australia.

F   Besides cave paintings, Upper Paleolithic people produced several other kinds of artwork, one of which has been thought to provide evidence of complex thought.

LISTENING

In this section, you will be able to demonstrate your ability to understand conversations and lectures in English.

In the actual test, the section is divided into two separately timed parts. You will hear each conversation or lecture only one time. A clock will indicate how much time remains. The clock will count down only while you are answering questions, not while you are listening. You may take up to 16.5 minutes to answer the questions.

In this practice test, there is no time limit for answering questions.

You may take notes while you listen. You may use your notes to help you answer the questions. Your notes will not be scored.

Answer the questions based on what is stated or implied by the speakers.

In some questions, you will see this icon: 🎧 . This means that you will hear, but not see, part of the question.

In the actual test, you must answer each question. You cannot return to previous questions.

At the end of this practice test, you will find an answer key.

Directions: Listen to Track 1.

Directions: Now answer the questions.

1. Why does the man need the woman's assistance? *Select 2 answers.*

   [A] He does not know the publication date of some reviews he needs.
   [B] He does not know the location of the library's video collection of plays.
   [C] He does not know how to find out where the play is currently being performed.
   [D] He does not know how to determine which newspapers he should look at.

2. What does the woman imply about critical reaction to the play *Happy Strangers*?

   (A) Negative critical reaction led to its content being revised after it premiered.
   (B) The play has always been quite popular among university students.
   (C) Reactions to the play are more positive nowadays than they were in the past.
   (D) The play is rarely performed nowadays because critics have never liked it.

3. What does the woman say about her experience seeing a performance of *Happy Strangers* when she was younger? *Select 2 answers.*

   [A] It was the first play she had seen performed professionally.
   [B] She saw it against the wishes of her parents.
   [C] She was surprised at how traditional the performance was.
   [D] She had a variety of emotional reactions to the play.

4. What is the man's attitude toward his current assignment?

   (A) He is not confident that he will find the materials he needs.
   (B) He feels that performing in a play is less boring than reading one.
   (C) He thinks his review of the play will be more objective than the contemporary reviews were.
   (D) He is optimistic that he will learn to appreciate the play he is researching.

5. *Listen again to part of the conversation by playing Track 2.* *Then answer the question.*

Why does the woman say this?

- Ⓐ To ask the man to clarify his request
- Ⓑ To state the man's request more precisely
- Ⓒ To make sure that she heard the man correctly
- Ⓓ To correct a mistake the man has made

Biology

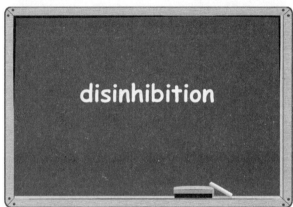

Directions: Now answer the questions.

6. What is the lecture mainly about?

    Ⓐ Methods of observing unusual animal behavior
    Ⓑ A theory about ways birds attract mates
    Ⓒ Ways animals behave when they have conflicting drives
    Ⓓ Criteria for classifying animal behaviors

7. Indicate whether each of the activities below describes a displacement activity. *Put a check (✓) in the correct boxes.*

	Yes	No
An animal attacks the ground instead of its enemy.		
An animal falls asleep in the middle of a mating ritual.		
An animal eats some food when confronted by its enemy.		
An animal takes a drink of water after grooming itself.		

8. What does the professor say about disinhibition?

    Ⓐ It can prevent displacement activities from occurring.
    Ⓑ It can cause animals to act on more than one drive at a time.
    Ⓒ It is not useful for explaining many types of displacement activities.
    Ⓓ It is responsible for the appearance of seemingly irrelevant behavior.

9. According to the lecture, what is one possible reason that displacement activities are often grooming behaviors?

    Ⓐ Grooming may cause an enemy or predator to be confused.
    Ⓑ Grooming is a convenient and accessible behavior.
    Ⓒ Grooming often occurs before eating and drinking.
    Ⓓ Grooming is a common social activity.

10. Why does the professor mention the wood thrush?

    Ⓐ To contrast its displacement activities with those of other animal species
    Ⓑ To explain that some animals display displacement activities other than grooming
    Ⓒ To point out how displacement activities are influenced by the environment
    Ⓓ To give an example of an animal that does not display displacement activities

11. *Listen again to part of the lecture by playing Track 4.* *Then answer the question.*

    What does the professor mean when she says this?

    Ⓐ She is impressed by how much the student knows about redirecting.
    Ⓑ She thinks it is time to move on to the next part of this lecture.
    Ⓒ The student's answer is not an example of a displacement activity.
    Ⓓ The student should suggest a different animal behavior to discuss next.

Directions: Listen to Track 5.

Directions: Now answer the questions.

12. What is the main purpose of the lecture?

   (A) To point out similarities in Emerson's essays and poems
   (B) To prepare the students to read an essay by Emerson
   (C) To compare Emerson's concept of universal truth to that of other authors
   (D) To show the influence of early United States society on Emerson's writing

13. On what basis did Emerson criticize the people of his time?

   (A) They refused to recognize universal truths.
   (B) They did not recognize the genius of certain authors.
   (C) Their convictions were not well-defined.
   (D) They were too interested in conformity.

14. What does Emerson say about the past?

   Ⓐ It should guide a person's present actions.
   Ⓑ It must be examined closely.
   Ⓒ It is less important than the future.
   Ⓓ It lacks both clarity and universal truth.

15. What point does the professor make when he mentions a ship's path?

   Ⓐ It is easy for people to lose sight of their true path.
   Ⓑ Most people are not capable of deciding which path is best for them.
   Ⓒ The path a person takes can only be seen clearly after the destination has been reached.
   Ⓓ A person should establish a goal before deciding which path to take.

16. What does the professor imply about himself when he recounts some life experiences he had before becoming a literature professor? *Select 2 answers.*

   Ⓐ He did not consider the consequences of his decisions.
   Ⓑ He did not plan to become a literature professor.
   Ⓒ He has always tried to act consistently.
   Ⓓ He has trusted in himself and his decisions.

17. *Listen again to part of the lecture by playing Track 6.* *Then answer the question.*

   Why does the professor say this?

   Ⓐ To suggest that United States citizens have not changed much over time
   Ⓑ To encourage the class to find more information about this time period
   Ⓒ To explain why Emerson's essay has lost some relevance
   Ⓓ To provide background for the concept he is explaining

Directions: Listen to Track 7.

Directions: Now answer the questions.

18. What is the conversation mainly about?

   Ⓐ Methods for finding appropriate sources for a project
   Ⓑ Reasons the woman is having difficulties with a project
   Ⓒ Criteria the professor uses to evaluate group projects
   Ⓓ Ways to develop the skills needed to work in groups

19. Why does the professor mention the "free-rider" problem?

   Ⓐ To review a concept he explained in class
   Ⓑ To give the student a plan to solve her problem
   Ⓒ To clarify the problem the student is facing
   Ⓓ To explain a benefit of working in groups

20. What is the professor's opinion of the other students in the woman's group?

   Ⓐ They try to take credit for work they did not do.
   Ⓑ They did not perform well in previous courses with him.
   Ⓒ They are more motivated when they are working in a group.
   Ⓓ They do good work when they are interested in the subject.

21. Why did the woman choose property rights as a topic?

   Ⓐ The professor recommended the topic.
   Ⓑ She already had a lot of reference materials on the subject.
   Ⓒ She wanted to learn something new.
   Ⓓ It was easy to research at the school library.

22. What mistakes does the professor imply the woman has made while working on a project?
Select 2 answers.

   A Finding sources for her group partners
   B Writing the weekly progress reports for her group
   C Forgetting to pay attention to the project's deadlines
   D Failing to involve the group members in the selection of a topic

Directions: Listen to Track 8.

United States Government

National Endowment for the Arts (NEA)

Directions: Now answer the questions.

23. What is the discussion mainly about?
    - (A) Reasons the United States government should not support the arts
    - (B) The history of government support for the arts in the United States
    - (C) Strengths and weaknesses of different government-sponsored arts programs
    - (D) Different ways in which governments can help support artists

24. According to the discussion, in what two ways was the Federal Art Project successful? *Choose 2 answers.*
    - A It established standards for art schools.
    - B It provided jobs for many artists.
    - C It produced many excellent artists.
    - D It gave many people greater access to the arts.

25. The class discusses some important events related to government support for the arts in the United States. Put the events in order from earliest to latest.

    Write your answer choices in the spaces where they belong. You can either write the letter of your answer choice or you can copy the sentence. The first one is done for you.

1. The government provided no official support for the arts.
2.
3.
4.
5.

Answer Choices

- A Arts councils were established in all 50 states of the country.
- B The federal budget supporting the arts was reduced by half.
- C The Federal Art Project helped reduce unemployment.
- D The National Endowment for the Arts was established.

26. Why does the professor mention the Kennedy Center and Lincoln Center?

    Ⓐ To give examples of institutions that benefit from corporate support
    Ⓑ To illustrate why some artists oppose the building of cultural centers
    Ⓒ To show how two centers were named after presidents who supported the arts
    Ⓓ To name two art centers built by the government during the Depression

27. What does the professor say about artists' opinions of government support for the arts?

    Ⓐ Most artists believe that the government should provide more funding for the arts.
    Ⓑ Most artists approve of the ways in which the government supports the arts.
    Ⓒ Even artists do not agree on whether the government should support the arts.
    Ⓓ Even artists have a low opinion of government support for the arts.

28. *Listen again to part of the discussion by playing Track 9.* *Then answer the question.*

    What does the professor imply when she says this?

    Ⓐ Other students should comment on the man's remark.
    Ⓑ Most people would agree with the man's opinion.
    Ⓒ Artwork funded by the government is usually of excellent quality.
    Ⓓ The government project was not a waste of money.

SPEAKING

In this section, you will be able to demonstrate your ability to speak about a variety of topics.

In the actual test, the Speaking section will last approximately 16 minutes. You will answer four questions by speaking into the microphone. You may take notes while you listen. You may use your notes to help you answer the questions. Your notes will not be scored. For each question, you will have time to prepare before giving your response. You should answer the questions as completely as possible in the time allowed.

For this practice test, you may want to use a personal recording device to record and play back your responses.

For each question, play the audio track listed and follow the directions to complete the task.

At the end of this practice test, you will find important points about each question.

1.   You will now give your opinion about a familiar topic. After you hear the question, you should give yourself 15 seconds to prepare and 45 seconds to speak.

Listen to Track 10.

> Many universities now offer academic courses over the Internet. However, some people still prefer learning in traditional classrooms. Which do you think is better? Explain why.
>
> | **Preparation Time: 15 seconds** |
> |---|
> | **Response Time: 45 seconds** |

2.   Now you will read a passage about a campus situation and then listen to a conversation about the same topic. You will then answer a question, using information from both the reading passage and the conversation. You should give yourself 30 seconds to prepare and 60 seconds to speak.

Listen to Track 11.

Reading Time: 45 seconds

> ### Evening Computer Science Classes May Be Added
>
> The computer science department is considering offering evening classes in the fall. The proposal to add the classes is a response to student complaints that daytime computer science classes have become increasingly overcrowded and there are no longer enough computers available. The department has decided that despite some added expense, the most cost-effective way of addressing this problem is by adding computer science classes in the evening. It is hoped that this change will decrease the number of students enrolled in day classes and thus guarantee individual access to computers for all students in computer science classes.

Listen to Track 12.

The man expresses his opinion about the proposal described in the article. Briefly summarize the proposal. Then state his opinion about the proposal and explain the reasons he gives for holding that opinion.

Preparation Time: 30 seconds
Response Time: 60 seconds

3. Now you will read a passage about an academic subject and then listen to a lecture on the same topic. You will then answer a question, using information from both the reading passage and the lecture. You should give yourself 30 seconds to prepare and 60 seconds to speak.

Listen to Track 13.

Reading Time: 45 seconds

Verbal and Nonverbal Communication

When we speak with other people face-to-face, the nonverbal signals we give—our facial expressions, hand gestures, body movements, and tone of voice—often communicate as much as, or more than, the words we utter. When our nonverbal signals, which we often produce unconsciously, agree with our verbal message, the verbal message is enhanced and supported, made more convincing. But when they conflict with the verbal message, we may be communicating an entirely different and more accurate message than what we intend.

Listen to Track 14.

Explain how the examples from the professor's lecture illustrate the relationship between verbal and nonverbal communication.

| Preparation Time: 30 seconds |
| Response Time: 60 seconds |

4. Now you will listen to a lecture. You will then be asked to summarize the lecture. You should give yourself 20 seconds to prepare and 60 seconds to speak.

Listen to Track 15.

Using points and examples from the lecture, explain the importance of visual elements in painting.

| Preparation Time: 20 seconds |
| Response Time: 60 seconds |

WRITING

In this section, you will be able to demonstrate your ability to use writing to communicate in an academic environment. There will be two writing tasks.

At the end of this practice test, you will find topic notes for each question.

Turn the page to see the directions for the first writing task.

Writing Based on Reading and Listening

For this task, you will read a passage about an academic topic. Then you will listen to a lecture about the same topic. You may take notes while you listen.

In your response, provide a detailed summary of the lecture and explain how the lecture relates to the reading passage.

In the actual test, you will have 3 minutes to read the passage and 20 minutes to write your response. While you write, you will be able to see the reading passage. If you finish your response before time is up, you may go on to the second writing task.

Reading Time: 3 minutes

Endotherms are animals such as modern birds and mammals that keep their body temperatures constant. For instance, humans are endotherms and maintain an internal temperature of 37°C, no matter whether the environment is warm or cold. Because dinosaurs were reptiles, and modern reptiles are not endotherms, it was long assumed that dinosaurs were not endotherms. However, dinosaurs differ in many ways from modern reptiles, and there is now considerable evidence that dinosaurs were, in fact, endotherms.

Polar dinosaurs

One reason for believing that dinosaurs were endotherms is that dinosaur fossils have been discovered in polar regions. Only animals that can maintain a temperature well above that of the surrounding environment could be active in such cold climates.

Leg position and movement

There is a connection between endothermy and the position and movement of the legs. The physiology of endothermy allows sustained physical activity, such as running. But running is efficient only if an animal's legs are positioned underneath its body, not at the body's side, as they are for crocodiles and many lizards. The legs of all modern endotherms are underneath the body, and so were the legs of dinosaurs. This strongly suggests that dinosaurs were endotherms.

Haversian canals

There is also a connection between endothermy and bone structure. The bones of endotherms usually include structures called Haversian canals. These canals house nerves and blood vessels that allow the living animal to grow quickly, and rapid body growth is in fact a characteristic of endothermy. The presence of Haversian canals in bone is a strong indicator that the animal is an endotherm, and fossilized bones of dinosaurs are usually dense with Haversian canals.

Listen to Track 16.

Directions: You have 20 minutes to plan and write your response. Your response will be judged on the basis of the quality of your writing and on how well your response presents the points in the lecture and their relationship to the reading passage. Typically, an effective response will contain a minimum of 150 words.

Listen to Track 17.

Response Time: 20 minutes

Question 1

Summarize the points made in the lecture, being sure to explain how they challenge the specific points made in the reading passage.

_____

_____

_____

_____

_____

_____

_____

_____

_____

Writing for an Academic Discussion

For this task, you will read an online discussion. A professor has posted a question about a topic, and some classmates have responded with their ideas.

In the actual test, you will have 10 minutes to write a response that contributes to the discussion.

Question 2

Your professor is teaching a class on sociology. Write a post responding to the professor's question.

In your response, you should do the following.

- Express and support your opinion.
- Make a contribution to the discussion in your own words.

An effective response will contain at least 100 words.

Dr. Achebe

Recently economic and technological changes have made it possible for some people to give up the idea of a "home" as a city or town where one resides for many years, thus becoming more nomadic—living and working from place to place, without ever "settling down" in one location. For those with the means to accomplish it, this lifestyle might be very fulfilling or liberating, but there must be disadvantages as well. What do you think those disadvantages are?

Claire

I think this is a romantic idea that is only realistic for younger people. As people age, they need more and more support. For example, it is helpful for them to have a regular doctor who knows their medical history. That sort of support can't happen if you're always moving.

Kelly

Being a modern nomad seems appealing, but how empowering is it? The disadvantage to this lifestyle is that you will likely feel like a foreigner in the places you spend your time, and that can be an obstacle to your success. Only at "home," where you feel culturally connected to other people within familiar surroundings, can you really thrive.

Response Time: 10 minutes

ANSWERS

Reading Section

1. D
2. B
3. A
4. C
5. A
6. A
7. B
8. B
9. B
10. C, D, E

11. A
12. B
13. D
14. D
15. B
16. A
17. C
18. B
19. C
20. A, D, F

Listening Section

1. A, D
2. C
3. A, D
4. D
5. B
6. C

7.

	Yes	No
An animal attacks the ground instead of its enemy.		✓
An animal falls asleep in the middle of a mating ritual.	✓	
An animal eats some food when confronted by its enemy.	✓	
An animal takes a drink of water after grooming itself.		✓

8. D
9. B
10. C

11. C
12. B
13. D
14. C
15. C
16. B, D
17. D
18. B
19. C
20. D
21. C
22. A, D
23. B
24. B, D
25. C, D, A, B
26. A
27. C
28. D

Speaking Section

1. To respond to this particular question, you should clearly state what your opinion is: Do you think it is better to learn in traditional classrooms or take classes over the Internet? Then you should give reasons to support your opinion. If you take the position that you believe Internet or online courses are more effective, you might give the reason that they are more effective because a student can study at any time from anywhere. You might further support that reason by using an example from your own experience. You might say that you learn best in the evenings and so online courses allow you to learn when you are best able to concentrate, whereas in a traditional classroom, you have to concentrate at a particular time.

If you believe that online courses are not better than learning in a traditional classroom, you might give an example of something that happens in the classroom that makes learning effective. You might say that direct contact with a teacher is important. You could continue to develop your response by giving examples of how direct contact is beneficial to learning.

Keep in mind that there is no "correct" answer to this question. Whether you prefer courses over the Internet or in traditional classrooms, your answer can be supported with your own examples and details. It is important to make sure that you state your opinion and develop your response with good examples and relevant details.

Your response should be intelligible, should demonstrate effective use of grammar and vocabulary, and should be well-developed and coherent. Your response is scored using the Independent Speaking Rubric (see Appendix A).

2. First, as the question states, you should provide a brief summary of the proposal, which is for the computer science department to add evening classes in the fall. You can also provide a brief summary of the reason that they are doing this (overcrowded conditions in the daytime computer classes). You should not spend too much time on this summary; if you attempt to provide many details from the reading, you may not have enough time to discuss both of the man's reasons for disagreeing with the proposal. For this item type, a brief summary is all that is necessary. You should make sure that your summary is clear enough for the listener to understand the proposal without having access to additional information.

After the summary, you should state the man's opinion of the university's proposal to add computer science courses in the evening. In this case, the man disagrees with the university's proposal.

You should then convey the two main reasons he gives for holding that opinion. You will need to connect information from the conversation to the reading in order for your response to be complete. First, the man says that the idea to add evening classes will not solve the problem of overcrowding because most students are too busy to take classes at night. You could also provide one of the examples why students are busy, such as jobs or family.

Your response should also convey the man's second reason for not agreeing with the university's proposal. You should say that the man thinks that offering evening classes won't save money because it will be expensive to add the new classes and it will be more expensive than buying new computers. You could add that hiring new teachers and keeping the building open late is expensive or that the rooms are big enough for more computers and that computers are now less expensive than they used to be. You do not, however, have to describe every detail

from the conversation as long as you make it clear why the man disagrees with the proposal.

Your response should be intelligible, should demonstrate effective use of grammar and vocabulary, and should be well-developed and coherent. Your response is scored using the Integrated Speaking Rubric (see Appendix A).

3. To respond to this particular question, you should discuss how verbal and nonverbal communication are related and explain how the examples that the professor gives support the reading text. You should include relevant points and examples from the lecture (and not from any other source).

To begin your response, you could give a brief summary of the reading, such as a definition of what verbal and nonverbal communication is; that is, that gestures and body movements often provide as much information to another person as spoken language does. You could also say that nonverbal signals can agree or conflict with a verbal message.

Then you should explain how the professor's examples illustrate these general ideas. In the first example, the professor's happy nonverbal behaviors on seeing his uncle, such as his big smile and his jumping up and down, agreed with his verbal message, so the verbal message was supported. You could also say that his uncle knew he was very happy.

You should then discuss the second example. In this example, when the professor hit himself with the hammer, he did not want to upset his daughter and told her not to worry. These words, however, conflicted with his nonverbal behavior, such as his shaking his hand in pain and his trembling voice, so his daughter did not believe the verbal message. In this case, the nonverbal message was more accurate.

You will not have time to repeat all of the details from the lecture and reading, and you should not try to do that. You should integrate points from both to answer the question completely. You need to give only sufficient details to explain how the two examples relate to the overall idea of how nonverbal communication contributes to verbal messages.

Your response should be intelligible, should demonstrate effective use of grammar and vocabulary, and should be well-developed and coherent. Your response is scored using the Integrated Speaking Rubric (see Appendix A).

4.   To respond to this particular question, you should talk about some of the visual elements of painting and explain why they are important. You should include relevant points and examples from the lecture (and not from any other source).

To begin your response, you should briefly state the main idea: that visual elements convey meaning and express emotion in paintings. You would then talk about the different points the professor gives to support this. You would say, for example, that colors can evoke strong emotions, and give the example that red can evoke anger or blue can make somebody feel calm. Then you could talk about texture. You could say that texture can be physical or visual or that texture can also evoke emotions; for example, a smooth texture can be calming. You could then talk about how artists combine these elements to create meaning; for example, strong colors, such as reds, plus wide sweeping brushstrokes suggest chaos and stronger emotions.

As the goal of this item is to provide a summary of the professor's lecture, you do not need to repeat all of the details from the lecture. You need to give only sufficient details to explain why visual details are important in a painting.

Your response should be intelligible, should demonstrate effective use of grammar and vocabulary, and should be well-developed and coherent. Your response is scored using the Integrated Speaking Rubric (see Appendix A).

Writing Section

1.   What is important to understand from the lecture is that the professor disagrees with the arguments presented in the reading to support the idea that dinosaurs were endotherms—namely that dinosaurs inhabited polar regions, that their legs were positioned underneath their bodies, and that their bones included structures called Haversian canals.

In your response, you should convey the reasons presented by the professor for why the information presented in the reading does not prove that dinosaurs were endotherms. A high-scoring response will include the following points made by the professor that cast doubt on the points made in the reading.

Point made in the reading	Counterpoint made in the lecture
The presence of dinosaur fossils in the polar regions indicates that dinosaurs were able to survive in very cold climates and therefore must have been endotherms.	When dinosaurs lived, the polar regions were much warmer than they are today, so even animals that were not endotherms could have survived there for at least part of the year. Furthermore, polar dinosaurs could have migrated or hibernated during the months when the temperatures were the coldest.
Dinosaurs' legs were positioned underneath their bodies. Such leg positioning allows for running and similar physical activities typical of endotherms.	The positioning of dinosaurs' legs underneath their bodies may have served a function unrelated to running and similar activities. The positioning of legs underneath the body may have evolved to support the great body weight of many dinosaurs.
Dinosaurs' bones contained Haversian canals, structures that allow for fast bone growth and, again, are typical of endotherms.	Despite containing Haversian canals, dinosaur bones also had features one would expect to see in animals that are not endotherms. In particular, dinosaur bones contained growth rings, which indicate periods of slow growth alternating with periods of fast growth. Such an uneven pattern of growth is typical of animals that are not endotherms.

Your response is scored using the Integrated Writing Rubric (see Appendix A). A response that receives a score of 5 clearly conveys all three of the main points in the table using accurate sentence structure and vocabulary.

2. To earn a top score, you should develop a response that contributes to the discussion about the potential disadvantages of a modern nomadic lifestyle. An effective response will contain at least 100 words.

One discussion participant argues that moving around might be fulfilling for people of younger ages, whereas older people would find such a lifestyle problematic since older people cherish the stability and support that would not be present in a modern nomadic lifestyle. Another discussion participant argues that a major disadvantage of such a lifestyle is the absence of a sense of belonging as a result of frequent moving. In your response, you might seize on the ideas already stated and develop them in greater detail or introduce entirely new ideas. You may argue, for example, that a potential disadvantage could be the cost of moving from one place to another or the difficulty of having long-lasting friends with constant moving.

You should make sure that your ideas are well-supported by reasons and examples and are expressed clearly. Since your response represents an online post, it does not need to be organized into separate paragraphs. However, your ideas need to be well-connected, coherent, and clear. Your response is scored using the Writing for an Academic Discussion Rubric (see Appendix A).

TOEFL iBT® Test 2

READING

In this section, you will be able to demonstrate your ability to understand academic passages in English. You will read and answer questions about **two passages**.

In the actual test, you will have 36 minutes total to read both passages and answer the questions. A clock will indicate how much time remains.

Some passages may include one or more notes explaining words or phrases. The words or phrases are marked with footnote numbers, and the notes explaining them appear at the end of the passage.

Most questions are worth 1 point, but the last question for each passage is worth 2 points.

You may review and revise your answers in this section as long as time remains.

At the end of this practice test, you will find an answer key.

Directions: Read the passage. Then answer the questions. You have 18 minutes on average to answer the questions.

MINERALS AND PLANTS

Research has shown that certain minerals are required by plants for normal growth and development. The soil is the source of these minerals, which are absorbed by the plant with the water from the soil. Even nitrogen, which is a gas in its elemental state, is normally absorbed from the soil as nitrate ions. Some soils are notoriously deficient in micronutrients and are therefore unable to support most plant life. So-called serpentine soils, for example, are deficient in calcium, and only plants able to tolerate low levels of this mineral can survive. In modern agriculture, mineral depletion of soils is a major concern, since harvesting crops interrupts the recycling of nutrients back to the soil.

Mineral deficiencies can often be detected by specific symptoms such as chlorosis (loss of chlorophyll resulting in yellow or white leaf tissue), necrosis (isolated dead patches), anthocyanin formation (development of deep red pigmentation of leaves or stem), stunted growth, and development of woody tissue in an herbaceous plant. Soils are most commonly deficient in nitrogen and phosphorus. Nitrogen-deficient plants exhibit many of the symptoms just described. Leaves develop chlorosis; stems are short and slender; and anthocyanin discoloration occurs on stems, petioles, and lower leaf surfaces. Phosphorus-deficient plants are often stunted, with leaves turning a characteristic dark green, often with the accumulation of anthocyanin. Typically, older leaves are affected first as the phosphorus is mobilized to young growing tissue. Iron deficiency is characterized by chlorosis between veins in young leaves.

Much of the research on nutrient deficiencies is based on growing plants hydroponically, that is, in soilless liquid nutrient solutions. This technique allows researchers to create solutions that selectively omit certain nutrients and then observe the resulting effects on the plants. Hydroponics has applications beyond basic research, since it facilitates the growing of greenhouse vegetables during winter. Aeroponics, a technique in which plants are suspended and the roots misted with a nutrient solution, is another method for growing plants without soil.

While mineral deficiencies can limit the growth of plants, an overabundance of certain minerals can be toxic and can also limit growth. Saline soils, which have high concentrations of sodium chloride and other salts, limit plant growth, and research continues to focus on developing salt-tolerant varieties of agricultural crops. Research has focused on the toxic effects of heavy metals such as lead, cadmium, mercury, and aluminum; however, even copper and zinc, which are essential elements, can become toxic in high concentrations. Although most plants cannot survive in these soils, certain plants have the ability to tolerate high levels of these minerals.

Scientists have known for some time that certain plants, called hyperaccumulators, can concentrate minerals at levels a hundredfold or greater than normal. A survey of known hyperaccumulators identified that 75 percent of them amassed nickel; cobalt, copper, zinc, manganese, lead, and cadmium are other minerals of choice. Hyperaccumulators run the entire range of the plant world. They may be herbs, shrubs, or trees. Many members of the mustard family, spurge family, legume family, and grass family are top hyperaccumulators. Many are found in tropical and subtropical areas of the world, where accumulation of high concentrations of metals may afford some protection against plant-eating insects and microbial pathogens.

Only recently have investigators considered using these plants to clean up soil and waste sites that have been contaminated by toxic levels of heavy metals—an environmentally friendly approach known as phytoremediation. This scenario begins with the planting of hyperaccumulating species in the target area, such as an abandoned mine or an irrigation pond contaminated by runoff. Toxic minerals would first be absorbed by roots but later relocated to the stem and leaves. A harvest of the shoots would remove the toxic compounds off-site to be burned or composted to recover the metal for industrial uses. After several years of cultivation and harvest, the site would be restored at a cost much lower than the price of excavation and reburial, the standard practice for remediation of contaminated soils. For example, in field trials, the plant alpine pennycress removed zinc and cadmium from soils near a zinc smelter, and Indian mustard, native to Pakistan and India, has been effective in reducing levels of selenium salts by 50 percent in contaminated soils.

Directions: Now answer the questions.

PARAGRAPH 1

Research has shown that certain minerals are required by plants for normal growth and development. The soil is the source of these minerals, which are absorbed by the plant with the water from the soil. Even nitrogen, which is a gas in its elemental state, is normally absorbed from the soil as nitrate ions. Some soils are notoriously deficient in micronutrients and are therefore unable to support most plant life. So-called serpentine soils, for example, are deficient in calcium, and only plants able to tolerate low levels of this mineral can survive. In modern agriculture, mineral depletion of soils is a major concern, since harvesting crops interrupts the recycling of nutrients back to the soil.

1. According to paragraph 1, what is true of plants that can grow in serpentine soils?

    (A) They absorb micronutrients unusually well.
    (B) They require far less calcium than most plants do.
    (C) They are able to absorb nitrogen in its elemental state.
    (D) They are typically crops raised for food.

PARAGRAPH 2

Mineral deficiencies can often be detected by specific symptoms such as chlorosis (loss of chlorophyll resulting in yellow or white leaf tissue), necrosis (isolated dead patches), anthocyanin formation (development of deep red pigmentation of leaves or stem), stunted growth, and development of woody tissue in an herbaceous plant. Soils are most commonly deficient in nitrogen and phosphorus. Nitrogen-deficient plants exhibit many of the symptoms just described. Leaves develop chlorosis; stems are short and slender; and anthocyanin discoloration occurs on stems, petioles, and lower leaf surfaces. Phosphorus-deficient plants are often stunted, with leaves turning a characteristic dark green, often with the accumulation of anthocyanin. Typically, older leaves are affected first as the phosphorus is mobilized to young growing tissue. Iron deficiency is characterized by chlorosis between veins in young leaves.

2. According to paragraph 2, which of the following symptoms occurs in phosphorus-deficient plants but not in plants deficient in nitrogen or iron?

    (A) Chlorosis on leaves
    (B) Change in leaf pigmentation to a dark shade of green
    (C) Short, stunted appearance of stems
    (D) Reddish pigmentation on the leaves or stem

3. According to paragraph 2, a symptom of iron deficiency is the presence in young leaves of

(A) deep red discoloration between the veins
(B) white or yellow tissue between the veins
(C) dead spots between the veins
(D) characteristic dark green veins

PARAGRAPH 3

Much of the research on nutrient deficiencies is based on growing plants hydroponically, that is, in soilless liquid nutrient solutions. This technique allows researchers to create solutions that selectively omit certain nutrients and then observe the resulting effects on the plants. Hydroponics has applications beyond basic research, since it **facilitates** the growing of greenhouse vegetables during winter. Aeroponics, a technique in which plants are suspended and the roots misted with a nutrient solution, is another method for growing plants without soil.

4. The word "**facilitates**" in the passage is closest in meaning to

(A) slows down
(B) affects
(C) makes easier
(D) focuses on

5. According to paragraph 3, what is the advantage of hydroponics for research on nutrient deficiencies in plants?

(A) It allows researchers to control what nutrients a plant receives.
(B) It allows researchers to observe the growth of a large number of plants simultaneously.
(C) It is possible to directly observe the roots of plants.
(D) It is unnecessary to keep misting plants with nutrient solutions.

PARAGRAPH 5

Scientists have known for some time that certain plants, called hyperaccumulators, can concentrate minerals at levels a hundredfold or greater than normal. A survey of known hyperaccumulators identified that 75 percent of them amassed nickel; cobalt, copper, zinc, manganese, lead, and cadmium are other minerals of choice. Hyperaccumulators run the entire range of the plant world. They may be **herbs**, **shrubs**, or **trees**. Many members of the mustard family, spurge family, legume family, and grass family are top hyperaccumulators. Many are found in tropical and subtropical areas of the world, where accumulation of high concentrations of metals may afford some protection against plant-eating insects and microbial pathogens.

6. Why does the author mention "**herbs**," "**shrubs**," and "**trees**"?

(A) To provide examples of plant types that cannot tolerate high levels of harmful minerals
(B) To show why so many plants are hyperaccumulators
(C) To help explain why hyperaccumulators can be found in so many different places
(D) To emphasize that hyperaccumulators occur in a wide range of plant types

Only recently have investigators considered using these plants to clean up soil and waste sites that have been contaminated by toxic levels of heavy metals—an environmentally friendly approach known as phytoremediation. **This scenario begins with the planting of hyperaccumulating species in the target area, such as an abandoned mine or an irrigation pond contaminated by runoff.** Toxic minerals would first be absorbed by roots but later relocated to the stem and leaves. A harvest of the shoots would remove the toxic compounds off site to be burned or composted to recover the metal for industrial uses. After several years of cultivation and harvest, the site would be restored at a cost much lower than the price of excavation and reburial, the standard practice for remediation of contaminated soils. For example, in field trials, the plant alpine pennycress removed zinc and cadmium from soils near a zinc smelter, and Indian mustard, native to Pakistan and India, has been effective in reducing levels of selenium salts by 50 percent in contaminated soils.

PARAGRAPH 6

7.   Which of the sentences below best expresses the essential information in the highlighted sentence in paragraph 6 ? Incorrect choices change the meaning in important ways or leave out essential information.

   Ⓐ Before considering phytoremediation, hyperaccumulating species of plants local to the target area must be identified.
   Ⓑ The investigation begins with an evaluation of toxic sites in the target area to determine the extent of contamination.
   Ⓒ The first step in phytoremediation is the planting of hyperaccumulating plants in the area to be cleaned up.
   Ⓓ Mines and irrigation ponds can be kept from becoming contaminated by planting hyperaccumulating species in targeted areas.

8.   It can be inferred from paragraph 6 that compared with standard practices for remediation of contaminated soils, phytoremediation

   Ⓐ does not allow for the use of the removed minerals for industrial purposes
   Ⓑ can be faster to implement
   Ⓒ is equally friendly to the environment
   Ⓓ is less suitable for soils that need to be used within a short period of time

PARAGRAPH 5

Scientists have known for some time that certain plants, called hyperaccumulators, can concentrate minerals at levels a hundredfold or greater than normal. **(A)** A survey of known hyperaccumulators identified that 75 percent of them amassed nickel; cobalt, copper, zinc, manganese, lead, and cadmium are other minerals of choice. **(B)** Hyperaccumulators run the entire range of the plant world. **(C)** They may be herbs, shrubs, or trees. **(D)** Many members of the mustard family, spurge family, legume family, and grass family are top hyperaccumulators. Many are found in tropical and subtropical areas of the world, where accumulation of high concentrations of metals may afford some protection against plant-eating insects and microbial pathogens.

9. Look at the part of the passage that is displayed above. The letters **(A)**, **(B)**, **(C)**, and **(D)** indicate where the following sentence could be added.

    Certain minerals are more likely to be accumulated in large quantities than others.

    Where would the sentence best fit?
    Ⓐ Choice A
    Ⓑ Choice B
    Ⓒ Choice C
    Ⓓ Choice D

10. **Directions:** An introductory sentence for a brief summary of the passage is provided below. Complete the summary by selecting the THREE answer choices that express the most important ideas in the passage. Some sentences do not belong in the summary because they express ideas that are not presented in the passage or are minor ideas in the passage. **This question is worth 2 points.**

Write your answer choices in the spaces where they belong. You can either write the letter of your answer choice or you can copy the sentence.

> **Plants need to absorb certain minerals from the soil in adequate quantities for normal growth and development.**

- ●

- ●

- ●

Answer Choices

A Some plants can tolerate comparatively low levels of certain minerals, but such plants are of little use for recycling nutrients back into depleted soils.

B When plants do not absorb sufficient amounts of essential minerals, characteristic abnormalities result.

C Mineral deficiencies in many plants can be cured by misting their roots with a nutrient solution or by transferring the plants to a soilless nutrient solution.

D Though beneficial in lower levels, high levels of salts, other minerals, and heavy metals can be harmful to plants.

E Because high concentrations of sodium chloride and other salts limit growth in most plants, much research has been done in an effort to develop salt-tolerant agricultural crops.

F Some plants are able to accumulate extremely high levels of certain minerals and thus can be used to clean up soils contaminated with toxic levels of these minerals.

Directions: Read the passage. Then answer the questions. You have 18 minutes on average to answer the questions.

THE ORIGIN OF THE PACIFIC ISLAND PEOPLE

The greater Pacific region, traditionally called Oceania, consists of three cultural areas: Melanesia, Micronesia, and Polynesia. Melanesia, in the southwest Pacific, contains the large islands of New Guinea, the Solomons, Vanuatu, and New Caledonia. Micronesia, the area north of Melanesia, consists primarily of small scattered islands. Polynesia is the central Pacific area in the great triangle defined by Hawaii, Easter Island, and New Zealand. Before the arrival of Europeans, the islands in the two largest cultural areas, Polynesia and Micronesia, together contained a population estimated at 700,000.

Speculation on the origin of these Pacific Islanders began as soon as outsiders encountered them; in the absence of solid linguistic, archaeological, and biological data, many fanciful and mutually exclusive theories were devised. Pacific Islanders were variously thought to have come from North America, South America, Egypt, Israel, and India, as well as Southeast Asia. Many older theories implicitly deprecated the navigational abilities and overall cultural creativity of the Pacific Islanders. For example, British anthropologists G. Elliot Smith and W. J. Perry assumed that only Egyptians would have been skilled enough to navigate and colonize the Pacific. They speculated that the Egyptians even crossed the Pacific to found the great civilizations of the New World (North and South America). In 1947 Norwegian adventurer Thor Heyerdahl drifted on a balsa-log raft westward with the winds and currents across the Pacific from South America to prove his theory that Pacific Islanders were Native Americans (also called American Indians). Later Heyerdahl suggested that the Pacific was peopled by three migrations: by Native Americans from the Pacific Northwest of North America drifting to Hawaii, by Peruvians drifting to Easter Island, and by Melanesians. In 1969 he crossed the Atlantic in an Egyptian-style reed boat to prove Egyptian influences in the Americas. Contrary to these theorists, the overwhelming evidence of physical anthropology, linguistics, and archaeology shows that the Pacific Islanders came from Southeast Asia and were skilled enough as navigators to sail against the prevailing winds and currents.

The basic cultural requirements for the successful colonization of the Pacific Islands include the appropriate boat-building, sailing, and navigation skills to get to the islands in the first place; domesticated plants and gardening skills suited to often marginal conditions; and a varied inventory of fishing implements and techniques. It is now generally believed that these prerequisites originated with peoples speaking Austronesian languages (a group of several hundred related languages) and began to emerge in Southeast Asia by about 5000 B.C.E. The culture of that time, based on archaeology and linguistic reconstruction, is assumed to have had a broad inventory of cultivated plants including taro, yams, banana, sugarcane, breadfruit, coconut, sago, and rice. Just as important, the culture also possessed the basic foundation for an effective maritime adaptation, including outrigger canoes and a variety of fishing techniques that could be effective for overseas voyaging.

Contrary to the arguments of some that much of the Pacific was settled by Polynesians accidentally marooned after being lost and adrift, it seems reasonable that this feat was accomplished by deliberate colonization expeditions that set out fully stocked with food and domesticated plants and animals. Detailed studies of the winds and currents using computer simulations suggest that drifting canoes would have been a most unlikely means of colonizing the

Pacific. These expeditions were likely driven by population growth and political dynamics on the home islands, as well as the challenge and excitement of exploring unknown waters. Because all Polynesians, Micronesians, and many Melanesians speak Austronesian languages and grow crops derived from Southeast Asia, all these peoples most certainly derived from that region and not the New World or elsewhere. The undisputed pre-Columbian presence in Oceania of the sweet potato, which is a New World domesticate, has sometimes been used to support Heyerdahl's "American Indians in the Pacific" theories. However, this is one plant out of a long list of Southeast Asian domesticates. As Patrick Kirch, an American anthropologist, points out, rather than being brought by rafting South Americans, sweet potatoes might just have easily been brought back by returning Polynesian navigators who could have reached the west coast of South America.

Directions: Now answer the questions.

P
A
R
A
G
R
A
P
H

2

Speculation on the origin of these Pacific Islanders began as soon as outsiders encountered them; in the absence of solid linguistic, archaeological, and biological data, many fanciful and **mutually exclusive** theories were devised. Pacific Islanders were variously thought to have come from North America, South America, Egypt, Israel, and India, as well as Southeast Asia. Many older theories implicitly deprecated the navigational abilities and overall cultural creativity of the Pacific Islanders. For example, British anthropologists G. Elliot Smith and W. J. Perry assumed that only Egyptians would have been skilled enough to navigate and colonize the Pacific. They speculated that the Egyptians even crossed the Pacific to found the great civilizations of the New World (North and South America). In 1947 Norwegian adventurer Thor Heyerdahl drifted on a balsa-log raft westward with the winds and currents across the Pacific from South America to prove his theory that Pacific Islanders were Native Americans (also called American Indians). Later Heyerdahl suggested that the Pacific was peopled by three migrations: by Native Americans from the Pacific Northwest of North America drifting to Hawaii, by Peruvians drifting to Easter Island, and by Melanesians. In 1969 he crossed the Atlantic in an Egyptian-style reed boat to prove Egyptian influences in the Americas. Contrary to these theorists, the overwhelming evidence of physical anthropology, linguistics, and archaeology shows that the Pacific Islanders came from Southeast Asia and were skilled enough as navigators to sail against the prevailing winds and currents.

11. By stating that the theories are "**mutually exclusive**" the author means that

    (A) if one of the theories is true, then all the others must be false
    (B) the differences between the theories are unimportant
    (C) taken together, the theories cover all possibilities
    (D) the theories support each other

12. According to paragraph 2, which of the following led some early researchers to believe that the Pacific Islanders originally came from Egypt?

    (A) Egyptians were known to have founded other great civilizations.
    (B) Sailors from other parts of the world were believed to lack the skills needed to travel across the ocean.
    (C) Linguistic, archaeological, and biological data connected the islands to Egypt.
    (D) Egyptian accounts claimed responsibility for colonizing the Pacific as well as the Americas.

PARAGRAPH 3

The basic cultural requirements for the successful colonization of the Pacific Islands include the appropriate boat-building, sailing, and navigation skills to get to the islands in the first place; domesticated plants and gardening skills suited to often marginal conditions; and a varied inventory of fishing **implements** and techniques. It is now generally believed that these prerequisites originated with peoples speaking Austronesian languages (a group of several hundred related languages) and began to emerge in Southeast Asia by about 5000 B.C.E. The culture of that time, based on archaeology and linguistic reconstruction, is assumed to have had a broad inventory of cultivated plants including taro, yams, banana, sugarcane, breadfruit, coconut, sago, and rice. Just as important, the culture also possessed the basic foundation for an effective maritime adaptation, including outrigger canoes and a variety of fishing techniques that could be effective for overseas voyaging.

13. The word "**implements**" in the passage is closest in meaning to

    Ⓐ skills
    Ⓑ tools
    Ⓒ opportunities
    Ⓓ practices

14. All of the following are mentioned in paragraph 3 as required for successful colonization of the Pacific islands EXCEPT

    Ⓐ knowledge of various Austronesian languages
    Ⓑ a variety of fishing techniques
    Ⓒ navigational skills
    Ⓓ knowledge of plant cultivation

15. In paragraph 3, why does the author provide information about the types of crops grown and boats used in Southeast Asia during the period around 5000 B.C.E.?

    Ⓐ To evaluate the relative importance of agriculture and fishing to early Austronesian peoples
    Ⓑ To illustrate the effectiveness of archaeological and linguistic methods in discovering details about life in ancient times
    Ⓒ To contrast living conditions on the continent of Asia with living conditions on the Pacific Islands
    Ⓓ To demonstrate that people from this region had the skills and resources necessary to travel to and survive on the Pacific Islands

**P
A
R
A
G
R
A
P
H

4**

Contrary to the arguments of some that much of the Pacific was settled by Polynesians accidentally marooned after being lost and adrift, it seems reasonable that this feat was accomplished by deliberate colonization expeditions that set out fully stocked with food and domesticated plants and animals. Detailed studies of the winds and currents using computer simulations suggest that drifting canoes would have been a most unlikely means of colonizing the Pacific. These expeditions were likely driven by population growth and political dynamics on the home islands, as well as the challenge and excitement of exploring unknown waters. Because all Polynesians, Micronesians, and many Melanesians speak Austronesian languages and grow crops derived from Southeast Asia, all these peoples most certainly derived from that region and not the New World or elsewhere. The undisputed pre-Columbian presence in Oceania of the sweet potato, which is a New World domesticate, has sometimes been used to support Heyerdahl's "American Indians in the Pacific" theories. However, this is one plant out of a long list of Southeast Asian domesticates. As **Patrick Kirch**, an American anthropologist, points out, rather than being brought by rafting South Americans, sweet potatoes might just have easily been brought back by returning Polynesian navigators who could have reached the west coast of South America.

16. Which of the sentences below best expresses the essential information in the highlighted sentence in paragraph 4 ? Incorrect choices change the meaning in important ways or leave out essential information.

    (A) Some people have argued that the Pacific was settled by traders who became lost while transporting domesticated plants and animals.
    (B) The original Polynesian settlers were probably marooned on the islands, but they may have been joined later by carefully prepared colonization expeditions.
    (C) Although it seems reasonable to believe that colonization expeditions would set out fully stocked, this is contradicted by much of the evidence.
    (D) The settlement of the Pacific Islands was probably intentional and well planned rather than accidental as some people have proposed.

17. According to paragraph 4, which of the following is NOT an explanation for why a group of people might have wanted to colonize the Pacific Islands?

    (A) As their numbers increased, they needed additional territory.
    (B) The winds and currents made the islands easy to reach.
    (C) The political situation at home made emigration desirable.
    (D) They found exploration challenging and exciting.

18. Why does the author mention the views of "**Patrick Kirch**"?

    (A) To present evidence in favor of Heyerdahl's idea about American Indians reaching Oceania
    (B) To emphasize the familiarity of Pacific Islanders with crops from many different regions of the world
    (C) To indicate that a supposed proof for Heyerdahl's theory has an alternative explanation
    (D) To demonstrate that some of the same crops were cultivated in both South America and Oceania

P A R A G R A P H 2

Speculation on the origin of these Pacific Islanders began as soon as outsiders encountered them; in the absence of solid linguistic, archaeological, and biological data, many fanciful and mutually exclusive theories were devised. Pacific Islanders were variously thought to have come from North America, South America, Egypt, Israel, and India, as well as Southeast Asia. **(A)** Many older theories implicitly deprecated the navigational abilities and overall cultural creativity of the Pacific Islanders. **(B)** For example, British anthropologists G. Elliot Smith and W. J. Perry assumed that only Egyptians would have been skilled enough to navigate and colonize the Pacific. **(C)** They speculated that the Egyptians even crossed the Pacific to found the great civilizations of the New World (North and South America). **(D)** In 1947 Norwegian adventurer Thor Heyerdahl drifted on a balsa-log raft westward with the winds and currents across the Pacific from South America to prove his theory that Pacific Islanders were Native Americans (also called American Indians). Later Heyerdahl suggested that the Pacific was peopled by three migrations: by Native Americans from the Pacific Northwest of North America drifting to Hawaii, by Peruvians drifting to Easter Island, and by Melanesians. In 1969 he crossed the Atlantic in an Egyptian-style reed boat to prove Egyptian influences in the Americas. Contrary to these theorists, the overwhelming evidence of physical anthropology, linguistics, and archaeology shows that the Pacific Islanders came from Southeast Asia and were skilled enough as navigators to sail against the prevailing winds and currents.

19. Look at the part of the passage that is displayed above. The letters **(A)**, **(B)**, **(C)**, and **(D)** indicate where the following sentence could be added.

   Later theories concentrated on journeys in the other direction.

   Where would the sentence best fit?

   Ⓐ Choice A
   Ⓑ Choice B
   Ⓒ Choice C
   Ⓓ Choice D

20. **Directions:** An introductory sentence for a brief summary of the passage is provided below. Complete the summary by selecting the THREE answer choices that express the most important ideas in the passage. Some sentences do not belong in the summary because they express ideas that are not presented in the passage or are minor ideas in the passage. **This question is worth 2 points.**

Write your answer choices in the spaces where they belong. You can either write the letter of your answer choice or you can copy the sentence.

Together, Melanesia, Micronesia, and Polynesia make up the region described as the Pacific Islands, or Oceania.

- ●

- ●

- ●

Answer Choices

A Many theories about how inhabitants first came to the islands have been proposed, including the idea that North and South Americans simply drifted across the ocean.

B Although early colonizers of the islands probably came from agriculture-based societies, they were obliged to adopt an economy based on fishing.

C New evidence suggests that, rather than being isolated, Pacific Islanders engaged in trade and social interaction with peoples living in Southeast Asia.

D Computer simulations of the winds and currents in the Pacific have shown that reaching the Pacific Islands was probably much easier than previously thought.

E It is now believed that the process of colonization required a great deal of skill, determination, and planning and could not have happened by chance.

F Using linguistic and archaeological evidence, anthropologists have determined that the first Pacific Islanders were Austronesian people from Southeast Asia.

LISTENING

In this section, you will be able to demonstrate your ability to understand conversations and lectures in English.

In the actual test, the section is divided into two separately timed parts. You will hear each conversation or lecture only one time. A clock will indicate how much time remains. The clock will count down only while you are answering questions, not while you are listening. You may take up to 16.5 minutes to answer the questions.

In this practice test, there is no time limit for answering questions.

You may take notes while you listen. You may use your notes to help you answer the questions. Your notes will not be scored.

Answer the questions based on what is stated or implied by the speakers.

In some questions, you will see this icon: 🎧. This means that you will hear, but not see, part of the question.

In the actual test, you must answer each question. You cannot return to previous questions.

At the end of this practice test, you will find an answer key.

Directions: Listen to Track 18.

Directions: Now answer the questions.

1. What do the speakers mainly discuss?

 Ⓐ Why the woman has little in common with her roommates
 Ⓑ How the woman can keep up in her academic studies
 Ⓒ The woman's adjustment to life at the university
 Ⓓ The woman's decision to transfer to another university

2. Why does the woman mention her hometown?

 Ⓐ To draw a contrast to her current situation
 Ⓑ To acknowledge that she is accustomed to living in big cities
 Ⓒ To indicate that she has known some people on campus for a long time
 Ⓓ To emphasize her previous success in academic studies

3. What does the woman imply about the incident that occurred in her sociology class?

 Ⓐ She was embarrassed because she gave an incorrect answer.
 Ⓑ She was upset because the professor seemed to ignore her.
 Ⓒ She was confused by the organization of the professor's lecture.
 Ⓓ She was surprised by the comments of the other students.

4. According to the counselor, why should the woman visit her professor's office?
 Select 2 answers.

 Ⓐ To offer a compliment
 Ⓑ To offer to help other students
 Ⓒ To introduce herself
 Ⓓ To suggest ways of making the class more personal

5. What does the woman imply about joining the string quartet?

    Ⓐ It would enable her to continue a hobby she gave up when she was ten.

    Ⓑ It would allow her to spend more time in her major area of study.

    Ⓒ It would help her stop worrying about her academic studies.

    Ⓓ It would be a way to meet students with similar interests.

Directions: Listen to Track 19.

Directions: Now answer the questions.

6. What is the main purpose of the lecture?

   Ⓐ To introduce a method that can help students remember new information

   Ⓑ To introduce a way to study how information passes from one person to another

   Ⓒ To explain the differences between biological information and cultural information

   Ⓓ To explain the differences between stories, songs, and other pieces of information

7. Why does the professor tell the story about alligators?

   Ⓐ To explain the difference between true and false stories

   Ⓑ To draw an analogy between alligator reproduction and cultural transmission

   Ⓒ To give an example of a piece of information that functions as a meme

   Ⓓ To show how a story can gradually change into a song

8. According to the professor, which of the following are examples of meme transfer? *Select 2 answers.*

    A Telling familiar stories
    B Sharing feelings
    C Composing original music
    D Learning a scientific theory

9. What example does the professor give of a meme's longevity?

    Ⓐ A story has been changing since it first appeared in the 1930s.
    Ⓑ A person remembers a story for many years.
    Ⓒ A gene is passed on through many generations without changing.
    Ⓓ A song quickly becomes popular all over the world.

10. What does the professor compare to a housefly laying many eggs?

    Ⓐ A child learning many different ideas from his or her parents
    Ⓑ Alligators reproducing in New York sewers
    Ⓒ Different people remembering different versions of a story
    Ⓓ A person singing the "Twinkle, Twinkle" song many times

11. *Listen to Track 20 to answer the question.*

    Why does the professor say this?

    Ⓐ To explain why some memes do not change much
    Ⓑ To ask the students for their opinion about songs as memes
    Ⓒ To acknowledge a problem with the meme theory
    Ⓓ To ask the students to test an idea about memes

Directions: Listen to Track 21.

12. What do the speakers mainly discuss?

   Ⓐ Stories told by desert travelers throughout history
   Ⓑ Efforts to locate unique sand formations in deserts around the world
   Ⓒ An effect caused by sand sliding down the slopes of some dunes
   Ⓓ Evidence that sound travels farthest in the driest regions of the world

13. What can be inferred from the students' reactions when the professor begins to discuss sand dunes?

   Ⓐ They appreciate the professor's unusual way of summarizing the previous discussion.
   Ⓑ They suspect that the professor is not completely serious.
   Ⓒ They would prefer to learn more about beach sand before beginning a new topic.
   Ⓓ They look forward to asking the professor about a topic they have wondered about for a long time.

14. Why does the professor mention an airplane?

   Ⓐ To describe a sound that is sometimes heard in the desert
   Ⓑ To emphasize the wide geographic distribution of sand dunes
   Ⓒ To introduce an anecdote about doing research in the desert
   Ⓓ To illustrate the power of a desert sandstorm

15. According to the professor's description of the unusual dunes, how does the sand in the outer layer typically differ from the sand underneath? *Select two answers.*

   Ⓐ The sand in the outer layer is extremely dry.
   Ⓑ The sand in the outer layer is packed less tightly.
   Ⓒ The grains of sand in the outer layer are smaller.
   Ⓓ The grains of sand in the outer layer are less uniform in size.

16. Why does one of the students refer to dormitory stairways?

    (A) To estimate the steepness of the slope on the side of a sand dune
    (B) To emphasize that scientific proof is a step-by-step process
    (C) To suggest that the human voice may be compared to a musical instrument
    (D) To demonstrate her understanding of the professor's explanation

17. *Listen to Track 22 to answer the question.*

    What does the professor imply when he says this?

    (A) Most experts would agree that the comparison is correct.
    (B) The comparison seems reasonable but is not actually true.
    (C) The student has not explained his point clearly.
    (D) The student has used an unusual approach to reach the same conclusion that the professor does.

Directions: Listen to Track 23.

Directions: Now answer the questions.

18. What is the conversation mainly about?

    Ⓐ An assignment about which the student would like advice

    Ⓑ Concerns as to whether the student should be in the professor's course

    Ⓒ The selection of films to be viewed by students in a film theory course

    Ⓓ The structure and sequence of courses in the Film Department

19. What is the professor's attitude toward the student's high school film course?

    Ⓐ He does not consider it satisfactory preparation for the class he teaches.

    Ⓑ He does not think that literary works should be discussed in film classes.

    Ⓒ He believes that this type of course often confuses inexperienced students.

    Ⓓ He feels that the approach taken in this course is the best way to learn about film.

20. Why was the student permitted to sign up for the professor's film theory course?

    Ⓐ Her high school course fulfilled the requirement for previous coursework.

    Ⓑ The computer system that usually blocks students was not working properly.

    Ⓒ An employee in the department did not follow instructions.

    Ⓓ The professor made an exception in her case.

21. Why does the professor decide to allow the student to remain in his class? *Select 2 answers.*

    Ⓐ She needs to take the course in order to graduate.

    Ⓑ He is impressed with her eagerness to continue.

    Ⓒ She convinces him that she does have adequate preparation for the course.

    Ⓓ He learns that she is not studying film as her main course of study.

22. What does the professor advise the student to do in order to keep up with the class she is in?
    - (A) Take the introductory course
    - (B) Watch some video recordings
    - (C) Do extra reading
    - (D) Drop out of her marketing class

Directions: Listen to Track 24.

Literature

folktales
fairy tales

Directions: Now answer the questions.

23. What is the lecture mainly about?

    Ⓐ Oral traditions in folktales and fairy tales
    Ⓑ Common characters and plots in folktales and fairy tales
    Ⓒ Differences between folktales and fairy tales
    Ⓓ Hidden meanings in folktales and fairy tales

24. What does the professor mean when he says that folktales are communal?

    Ⓐ They vary little from one community to another.
    Ⓑ They serve to strengthen ties among individuals within a community.
    Ⓒ They relate important events in the history of a community.
    Ⓓ They can be adapted to meet the needs of a community.

25. Why does the professor clarify the concept of a "fairy"?

    Ⓐ To explain the origins of the term "fairy tale"
    Ⓑ To eliminate a possible definition of the term "fairy tale"
    Ⓒ To support a claim about the function of fairy tales
    Ⓓ To indicate that fairies are a major element in fairy tales

26. What does the professor say about the setting of fairy tales?

    Ⓐ The tales are usually set in a nonspecific location.
    Ⓑ The location is determined by the country of origin of a tale.
    Ⓒ The tales are set in a location familiar to the author.
    Ⓓ A storyteller varies the location of a tale depending on the audience.

27. In the lecture, the professor discusses characteristics of folktales and fairy tales. Indicate the characteristics of each type of tale. *Put a check in the correct boxes.*

	Folktales	Fairy Tales
Their appeal is now mainly to children.		
The plot is the only stable element.		
The tales are transmitted orally.		
There is one accepted version.		
Characters are well-developed.		
The language is relatively formal.		

28. *Listen again to part of the lecture by playing Track 25.* *Then answer the question.*

    Why does the professor say this?

    Ⓐ To support the student's statement
    Ⓑ To ask the student to clarify her statement
    Ⓒ To find out if the students know what story the line comes from
    Ⓓ To clarify the relationship between time and space in fairy tales

SPEAKING

In this section, you will be able to demonstrate your ability to speak about a variety of topics.

In the actual test, the Speaking section will last approximately 16 minutes. You will answer four questions by speaking into the microphone. You may take notes while you listen. You may use your notes to help you answer the questions. Your notes will not be scored. For each question, you will have time to prepare before giving your response. You should answer the questions as completely as possible in the time allowed.

For this practice test, you may want to use a personal recording device to record and play back your responses.

For each question, play the audio track listed and follow the directions to complete the task.

At the end of this practice test, you will find important points about each question.

1. You will now give your opinion about a familiar topic. After you hear the question, you should give yourself 15 seconds to prepare and 45 seconds to speak.

   Listen to Track 26.

   > Do you agree or disagree with the following statement? Why or why not? Use details and examples to explain your answer.
   >
   > **It is more important to study math or science than it is to study art or literature.**
   >
   > | Preparation Time: 15 seconds |
   > | :---: |
   > | Response Time: 45 seconds |

2. Now you will read a passage about a campus situation and then listen to a conversation about the same topic. You will then answer a question, using information from both the reading passage and the conversation. You should give yourself 30 seconds to prepare and 60 seconds to speak.

   Listen to Track 27.

Reading Time: 50 seconds

   > ### Campus Dining Club Announced
   >
   > Starting this year, the university dining hall will be transformed into the Campus Dining Club for one week at the end of each semester. During the last week of each semester, the dining hall will feature special meals prepared by the university's culinary arts students. The school feels that this will give students who are studying cooking and food preparation valuable experience that will help them later, when they pursue careers. The university has announced that it will charge a small additional fee for these dinners in order to pay for the special gourmet food ingredients that will be required.

Listen to Track 28.

The man expresses his opinion about the plan described in the article. Briefly summarize the plan. Then state his opinion about the plan and explain the reasons he gives for holding that opinion.

Preparation Time: 30 seconds
Response Time: 60 seconds

3. Now you will read a passage about an academic subject and then listen to a lecture on the same topic. You will then answer a question, using information from both the reading passage and the lecture. You should give yourself 30 seconds to prepare and 60 seconds to speak.

Listen to Track 29.

Reading Time: 45 seconds

Target Marketing

Advertisers in the past have used radio and television in an attempt to provide information about their products to large, general audiences; it was once thought that the best way to sell a product was to advertise it to as many people as possible. However, more recent trends in advertising have turned toward target marketing. Target marketing is the strategy of advertising to smaller, very specific audiences—audiences that have been determined to have the greatest need or desire for the product being marketed. Target marketing has proved to be very effective in reaching potential customers.

Listen to Track 30.

Using the professor's examples, explain the advertising technique of target marketing.

Preparation Time: 30 seconds
Response Time: 60 seconds

4. Now you will listen to a lecture. You will then be asked to summarize the lecture. You should give yourself 20 seconds to prepare and 60 seconds to speak.

Listen to Track 31.

Using points and examples from the talk, explain the two types of motivation.

Preparation Time: 20 seconds
Response Time: 60 seconds

WRITING

In this section, you will be able to demonstrate your ability to use writing to communicate in an academic environment. There will be two writing tasks.

At the end of this practice test, you will find topic notes for each question.

Turn the page to see the directions for the first writing task.

Writing Based on Reading and Listening

For this task, you will read a passage about an academic topic. Then you will listen to a lecture about the same topic. You may take notes while you listen.

In your response, provide a detailed summary of the lecture and explain how the lecture relates to the reading passage.

In the actual test, you will have 3 minutes to read the passage and 20 minutes to write your response. While you write, you will be able to see the reading passage. If you finish your response before time is up, you may go on to the second writing task.

Reading Time: 3 minutes

As early as the twelfth century A.D., the settlements of Chaco Canyon in New Mexico in the American Southwest were notable for their "great houses," massive stone buildings that contain hundreds of rooms and often stand three or four stories high. Archaeologists have been trying to determine how the buildings were used. While there is still no universally agreed upon explanation, there are three competing theories.

One theory holds that the Chaco structures were purely residential, with each housing hundreds of people. Supporters of this theory have interpreted Chaco great houses as earlier versions of the architecture seen in more recent Southwest societies. In particular, the Chaco houses appear strikingly similar to the large, well-known "apartment buildings" at Taos, New Mexico, in which many people have been living for centuries.

A second theory contends that the Chaco structures were used to store food supplies. One of the main crops of the Chaco people was grain maize, which could be stored for long periods of time without spoiling and could serve as a long-lasting supply of food. The supplies of maize had to be stored somewhere, and the size of the great houses would make them very suitable for the purpose.

A third theory proposes that houses were used as ceremonial centers. Close to one house, called Pueblo Alto, archaeologists identified an enormous mound formed by a pile of old material. Excavations of the mound revealed deposits containing a surprisingly large number of broken pots. This finding has been interpreted as evidence that people gathered at Pueblo Alto for special ceremonies. At the ceremonies, they ate festive meals and then discarded the pots in which the meals had been prepared or served. Such ceremonies have been documented for other Native American cultures.

Listen to Track 32.

Directions: You have 20 minutes to plan and write your response. Your response will be judged on the basis of the quality of your writing and on how well your response presents the points in the lecture and their relationship to the reading passage. Typically, an effective response will contain a minimum of 150 words.

Listen to Track 33.

Response Time: 20 minutes

Question 1

Summarize the points made in the lecture, being sure to explain how they cast doubt on the specific theories discussed in the reading passage.

_____

_____

_____

_____

_____

_____

_____

_____

_____

Writing for an Academic Discussion

For this task, you will read an online discussion. A professor has posted a question about a topic, and some classmates have responded with their ideas.

In the actual test, you will have 10 minutes to write a response that contributes to the discussion.

Question 2

Your professor is teaching a class on public policy. Write a post responding to the professor's question.

In your response, you should do the following.

- Express and support your opinion.
- Make a contribution to the discussion in your own words.

An effective response will contain at least 100 words.

Dr. Diaz

Next week we are scheduled to discuss the economic impacts of tourism. Tourism is a source of income for many cities and regions around the world. On the other hand, tourism can also bring with it a number of well-known disadvantages. In general, do you think governments should continue to develop and encourage a tourism industry in their countries? Why or why not?

Kelly

Even considering the economic argument, I think it's time for governments to stop encouraging tourism. That's because the tourist economy is unstable. Tourists may visit a region for a while, but then people's preferences change, and tourists stop coming. It's economically better for a country to promote other industries that are more stable.

Paul

I see your point, Kelly, but I believe tourism is almost always helpful for a country—and not just for economic reasons. If a city is made more attractive for tourists, it will also become more livable for the residents. To lure tourists, cities are often made safer and cleaner, for example, and they add attractions such as museums.

Response Time: 10 minutes

ANSWERS

Reading Section

1. B
2. B
3. B
4. C
5. A
6. D
7. C
8. D
9. A
10. B, D, F

11. A
12. B
13. B
14. A
15. D
16. D
17. B
18. C
19. D
20. A, E, F

Listening Section

1. C
2. A
3. B
4. A, C
5. D
6. B
7. C
8. A, D
9. B
10. D
11. A
12. C
13. B

14. A
15. A, B
16. D
17. B
18. B
19. A
20. C
21. B, D
22. B
23. C
24. D
25. B
26. A

27.

	Folktales	Fairy Tales
Their appeal is now mainly to children.		✓
The plot is the only stable element.	✓	
The tales are transmitted orally.	✓	
There is one accepted version.		✓
Characters are well-developed.		✓
The language is relatively formal.		✓

28. A

Speaking Section

1.   To respond to this particular question, you should clearly state what your opinion is regarding the statement. Be sure to read the statement carefully to make sure you understand it. In this case, you would either agree or disagree that studying math or science is more important than studying art or literature. You should then give reasons to support your opinion. If you agree that studying math or science is more important, you might say that math and science are used in many important areas, such as engineering, and are necessary to make calculations when building structures, for example. You could also provide a personal example and say that you prefer math because it has helped you in certain situations, such as planning your personal finances. You may also want to make a statement about how art has not helped you as much.

If you disagree with the statement, you would also need to support this with specific information. One possibility is to say that math and science are not actually important because not many people need to know math very well. Most people need to know only a little math or science to do their jobs. Then you should provide an example of why art or literature is more important. There are many possibilities, and the specific example you choose is not important as long as it contributes to your argument. Your goal is for your listener to understand why you agree or disagree with the statement.

Your response should be intelligible, should demonstrate effective use of grammar and vocabulary, and should be well-developed and coherent. Your response is scored using the Independent Speaking Rubric (see Appendix A).

2.   First, as the question states, you should provide a brief summary of the university's plan from the reading, which is to offer meals prepared by culinary arts students at the dining hall. You can also provide a brief summary of the reason that they are doing this, which is to provide culinary arts students with some experience. You should not, however, spend too much time on this summary. Your summary should be clear enough for the listener to understand the plan without having access to additional information.

After the summary, you should state the man's opinion of the university's plan. In this case, the man agrees with the university's proposal.

You should then convey the two main reasons he gives for holding that opinion. You will need to connect information from the conversation to the reading in order for the response to be complete. The man says that he agrees that a dining club will be good experience for culinary arts students because cooking for many people under pressure is different from cooking for classmates. You should go beyond simply saying that the man agrees that it will be good experience. You need to give the explanation for why he believes that.

Your response should also convey the man's second reason for agreeing with the university's plan. The man agrees that the extra cost students will pay for these dinners will be worth it. He believes this because the culinary arts students will cook meals that are as good as those served in nice restaurants in the area.

You should manage your time so that you are able to discuss the summary and give a full description of both reasons that the man provides.

Your response should be intelligible, should demonstrate effective use of grammar and vocabulary, and should be well-developed and coherent. Your response is scored using the Integrated Speaking Rubric (see Appendix A).

3.   To respond to this particular question, you should first explain the technique of target marketing as it was presented in the reading. Target marketing is designing or creating advertising so that it appeals to a specific group of people.

You should then use the example given by the professor to explain the technique. The professor discusses how a telephone company may produce two very different advertisements to be shown during different television programs, even though the phone is basically the same. A commercial shown during young people's programming, such as a music show, would appeal to their interests, and would show how the phone is fun. On the other hand, a commercial shown during a business program would emphasize factors important to businesspeople, such as efficiency. This example by the professor illustrates the concept of target marketing.

You do not need to repeat all of the details from the reading and the lecture, but instead integrate points from both to answer the question completely.

Your response should be intelligible, should demonstrate effective use of grammar and vocabulary, and should be well-developed and coherent. Your response is scored using the Integrated Speaking Rubric (see Appendix A).

4.   This particular question requires you to summarize the contents of a lecture you hear. In your response, you should talk about the two different kinds of motivation, which are extrinsic (or external) motivation and intrinsic (or internal) motivation. You should include relevant points and examples from the lecture (and not from any other source).

To begin your response, you should briefly state the main idea, that there are two types of motivation, and name the two types. You would then talk about the first type, extrinsic motivation. You would explain that when we are externally motivated, we do something for an external reward. You would then talk about the professor's example of a child doing household chores for an allowance. The money that the child receives is motivation.

You would next talk about the second type, extrinsic motivation. You would explain that when we are internally motivated, we do something because it makes us feel good. You should then discuss the professor's example. The professor goes to the gym several times a week because it's good for her health and she enjoys it. You could then say that she has gone for several years, which shows that intrinsic motivation is long-lasting. You do not, however, need to repeat all of the details from the lecture. You need to give only sufficient details to explain the types of motivation. You should plan your time so that you have enough time to cover both types of motivation and their examples.

Your response should be intelligible, should demonstrate effective use of grammar and vocabulary, and should be well-developed and coherent. Your response is scored using the Integrated Speaking Rubric (see Appendix A).

Writing Section

1. What is important to understand from the lecture is that the professor disagrees with each of the theories presented in the reading about the function of the massive stone buildings, or "great houses," of Chaco Canyon, namely that the great houses served a residential purpose; that they were used to store food supplies; and that they were used to hold ceremonies.

In your response, you should convey the reasons presented by the professor for why the theories about the function of the Chaco great houses are not convincing. A high-scoring response will include the following points made by the professor that cast doubt on the points made in the reading.

Point made in the reading	Counterpoint made in the lecture
The Chaco houses may have been used for residential purposes, because they are similar to residential buildings built by other societies in the American Southwest.	It is unlikely that the Chaco houses were residential, because they contain very few fireplaces, many fewer than the families living in the houses would need for cooking.
The Chaco houses may have been used to store food. The Chaco people needed a place to store their grain maize, and the Chaco houses, thanks to their large capacity, could serve that purpose.	The theory that the function of the Chaco houses was to store grain maize is undermined by the fact that very few traces of maize or maize containers have been found during excavations of the Chaco houses.
The Chaco houses may have served as ceremonial centers. The large quantity of broken pottery in a mound located near the "Pueblo Alto" house suggests that the houses hosted ceremonial feasts after which people discarded the pots in which the food was prepared and served.	The mound near the "Pueblo Alto" house also contains construction materials and tools, which suggests that such mounds were just construction trash heaps and had nothing to do with ceremonies. The pots found in the mounds were probably used by construction workers building the houses.

Your response is scored using the Integrated Writing Rubric (see Appendix A). A response that receives a score of 5 clearly conveys all three of the main points in the table using accurate sentence structure and vocabulary.

2. To earn a top score, you should develop a response that contributes to the discussion about whether, in general, governments should continue to develop and promote tourism. An effective response will contain at least 100 words.

One discussion participant argues that governments should stop encouraging tourism because tourist economies are unstable, while another discussion participant thinks governments should continue promoting tourism because tourism improves living conditions for the residents. You may seize on the ideas already stated and develop them in greater detail or may introduce entirely new ideas. You may agree with the first discussion participant and add, for example, that many other factors, including weather and current events, can stop tourists from visiting a country, so governments' focus should be on the development of stable industries. You may agree with the second discussion participant and cite examples from a city that created improvements for all residents as a result of efforts to encourage tourism. You may add new arguments by stating, for example, that tourism should be discouraged because tourists use too many precious resources, make cities more crowded and polluted, or do not respect the local culture.

You should make sure that your ideas are well-supported by reasons and examples and are expressed clearly. Since your response represents an online post, it does not need to be organized into separate paragraphs. However, your ideas need to be well-connected, coherent, and clear. Your response is scored using the Writing for an Academic Discussion Rubric (see Appendix A).

TOEFL iBT® Test 3

READING

In this section, you will be able to demonstrate your ability to understand academic passages in English. You will read and answer questions about **two passages**.

In the actual test, you will have 36 minutes total to read both passages and answer the questions. A clock will indicate how much time remains.

Some passages may include one or more notes explaining words or phrases. The words or phrases are marked with footnote numbers, and the notes explaining them appear at the end of the passage.

Most questions are worth 1 point, but the last question for each passage is worth 2 points.

You may review and revise your answers in this section as long as time remains.

At the end of this practice test, you will find an answer key.

Directions: Read the passage. Then answer the questions. You have 18 minutes on average to answer the questions.

POWERING THE INDUSTRIAL REVOLUTION

In Britain one of the most dramatic changes of the Industrial Revolution was the harnessing of power. Until the reign of George III (1760–1820), available sources of power for work and travel had not increased since the Middle Ages. There were three sources of power: animal or human muscles; the wind, operating on sail or windmill; and running water. Only the last of these was suited at all to the continuous operating of machines, and although waterpower abounded in Lancashire and Scotland and ran grain mills as well as textile mills, it had one great disadvantage: streams flowed where nature intended them to, and water-driven factories had to be located on their banks, whether or not the location was desirable for other reasons. Furthermore, even the most reliable waterpower varied with the seasons and disappeared in a drought. The new age of machinery, in short, could not have been born without a new source of both movable and constant power.

The source had long been known but not exploited. Early in the century, a pump had come into use in which expanding steam raised a piston in a cylinder, and atmospheric pressure brought it down again when the steam condensed inside the cylinder to form a vacuum. This "atmospheric engine," invented by Thomas Savery and vastly improved by his partner, Thomas Newcomen, embodied revolutionary principles, but it was so slow and wasteful of fuel that it could not be employed outside the coal mines for which it had been designed. In the 1760s, James Watt perfected a separate condenser for the steam, so that the cylinder did not have to be cooled at every stroke; then he devised a way to make the piston turn a wheel and thus convert reciprocating (back and forth) motion into rotary motion. He thereby transformed an inefficient pump of limited use into a steam engine of a thousand uses. The final step came when steam was introduced into the cylinder to drive the piston backward as well as forward, thereby increasing the speed of the engine and cutting its fuel consumption.

Watt's steam engine soon showed what it could do. It liberated industry from dependence on running water. The engine eliminated water in the mines by driving efficient pumps, which made possible deeper and deeper mining. The ready availability of coal inspired William Murdoch during the 1790s to develop the first new form of nighttime illumination to be discovered in a millennium and a half. Coal gas rivaled smoky oil lamps and flickering candles, and early in the new century, well-to-do Londoners grew accustomed to gaslit houses and even streets. Iron manufacturers, which had starved for fuel while depending on charcoal, also benefited from ever-increasing supplies of coal; blast furnaces with steam-powered bellows turned out more iron and steel for the new machinery. Steam became the motive force of the Industrial Revolution, as coal and iron ore were the raw materials.

By 1800 more than a thousand steam engines were in use in the British Isles, and Britain retained a virtual monopoly on steam engine production until the 1830s. Steam power did not merely spin cotton and roll iron; early in the new century, it also multiplied ten times over the amount of paper that a single worker could produce in a day. At the same time, operators of the first printing presses run by steam rather than by hand found it possible to produce a thousand pages in an hour rather than thirty. Steam also promised to eliminate a transportation problem not fully solved by either canal boats or turnpikes. Boats could carry heavy weights, but canals could not cross hilly terrain; turnpikes could cross the hills, but the roadbeds could not stand up under great weights. These problems needed still another solution, and the ingredients for it lay close at hand. In some industrial regions, heavily laden wagons, with flanged wheels, were being hauled by horses along metal rails;

and the stationary steam engine was puffing in the factory and mine. Another generation passed before inventors succeeded in combining these ingredients, by putting the engine on wheels and the wheels on the rails, so as to provide a machine to take the place of the horse. Thus the railroad age sprang from what had already happened in the eighteenth century.

Directions: Now answer the questions.

PARAGRAPHS 1 & 2

In Britain one of the most dramatic changes of the Industrial Revolution was the harnessing of power. Until the reign of George III (1760–1820), available sources of power for work and travel had not increased since the Middle Ages. There were three sources of power: animal or human muscles; the wind, operating on sail or windmill; and running water. **Only the last of these was suited at all to the continuous operating of machines, and although waterpower abounded in Lancashire and Scotland and ran grain mills as well as textile mills, it had one great disadvantage: streams flowed where nature intended them to, and water-driven factories had to be located on their banks, whether or not the location was desirable for other reasons.** Furthermore, even the most reliable waterpower varied with the seasons and disappeared in a drought. The new age of machinery, in short, could not have been born without a new source of both movable and constant power.

The source had long been known but not exploited. Early in the century, a pump had come into use in which expanding steam raised a piston in a cylinder, and atmospheric pressure brought it down again when the steam condensed inside the cylinder to form a vacuum. This "atmospheric engine," invented by Thomas Savery and vastly improved by his partner, Thomas Newcomen, embodied revolutionary principles, but it was so slow and wasteful of fuel that it could not be employed outside the coal mines for which it had been designed. In the 1760s, James Watt perfected a separate condenser for the steam, so that the cylinder did not have to be cooled at every stroke; then he devised a way to make the piston turn a wheel and thus convert reciprocating (back and forth) motion into rotary motion. He thereby transformed an inefficient pump of limited use into a steam engine of a thousand uses. The final step came when steam was introduced into the cylinder to drive the piston backward as well as forward, thereby increasing the speed of the engine and cutting its fuel consumption.

1. Which of the sentences below best expresses the essential information in the highlighted sentence in paragraph 1 ? Incorrect choices change the meaning in important ways or leave out essential information.

    Ⓐ Running water was the best power source for factories since it could keep machines operating continuously, but since it was abundant only in Lancashire and Scotland, most mills and factories that were located elsewhere could not be water driven.

    Ⓑ The disadvantage of using waterpower is that streams do not necessarily flow in places that are the most suitable for factories, which explains why so many water-powered grain and textile mills were located in undesirable places.

    Ⓒ Since machines could be operated continuously only where running water was abundant, grain and textile mills, as well as other factories, tended to be located only in Lancashire and Scotland.

    Ⓓ Running water was the only source of power that was suitable for the continuous operation of machines, but to make use of it, factories had to be located where the water was, regardless of whether such locations made sense otherwise.

2. Which of the following best describes the relationship of paragraph 2 to paragraph 1 ?

  Ⓐ Paragraph 2 shows how the problem discussed in paragraph 1 arose.
  Ⓑ Paragraph 2 explains how the problem presented in paragraph 1 came to be solved.
  Ⓒ Paragraph 2 provides a more technical discussion of the problem introduced in paragraph 1.
  Ⓓ Paragraph 2 shows why the problem discussed in paragraph 1 was especially important to solve.

3. According to paragraph 2, the "atmospheric engine" was slow because

  Ⓐ it had been designed to be used in coal mines
  Ⓑ the cylinder had to cool between each stroke
  Ⓒ it made use of expanding steam to raise the piston in its cylinder
  Ⓓ it could be operated only when a large supply of fuel was available

4. According to paragraph 2, Watt's steam engine differed from earlier steam engines in each of the following ways EXCEPT:

  Ⓐ It used steam to move a piston in a cylinder.
  Ⓑ It worked with greater speed.
  Ⓒ It was more efficient in its use of fuel.
  Ⓓ It could be used in many different ways.

Watt's steam engine soon showed what it could do. It liberated industry from dependence on running water. The engine eliminated water in the mines by driving efficient pumps, which made possible deeper and deeper mining. The ready availability of coal inspired William Murdoch during the 1790s to develop the first new form of nighttime illumination to be discovered in a millennium and a half. Coal gas rivaled smoky oil lamps and flickering candles, and early in the new century, well-to-do Londoners **grew accustomed to** gaslit houses and even streets. Iron manufacturers, which had starved for fuel while depending on charcoal, also benefited from ever-increasing supplies of coal; blast furnaces with steam-powered bellows turned out more iron and steel for the new machinery. Steam became the motive force of the Industrial Revolution, as coal and iron ore were the raw materials.

5. In paragraph 3, the author mentions William Murdoch's invention of a new form of nighttime illumination in order to

  Ⓐ indicate one of the important developments made possible by the introduction of Watt's steam engine
  Ⓑ make the point that Watt's steam engine was not the only invention of importance to the Industrial Revolution
  Ⓒ illustrate how important coal was as a raw material for the Industrial Revolution
  Ⓓ provide an example of another eighteenth-century invention that used steam as a power source

6. The phrase "**grew accustomed to**" in the passage is closest in meaning to

    (A) began to prefer
    (B) wanted to have
    (C) became used to
    (D) insisted on

PARAGRAPH 4

By 1800 more than a thousand steam engines were in use in the British Isles, and Britain retained a virtual monopoly on steam engine production until the 1830s. Steam power did not merely spin cotton and roll iron; early in the new century, it also multiplied ten times over the amount of paper that a single worker could produce in a day. At the same time, operators of the first printing presses run by steam rather than by hand found it possible to produce a thousand pages in an hour rather than thirty. Steam also promised to eliminate a transportation problem not fully solved by either canal boats or turnpikes. Boats could carry heavy weights, but canals could not cross hilly terrain; turnpikes could cross the hills, but the roadbeds could not stand up under great weights. These problems needed still another solution, and the ingredients for it lay close at hand. In some industrial regions, heavily laden wagons, with flanged wheels, were being hauled by horses along metal rails; and the stationary steam engine was puffing in the factory and mine. Another generation passed before inventors succeeded in combining these ingredients, by putting the engine on wheels and the wheels on the rails, so as to provide a machine to take the place of the horse. Thus the railroad age sprang from what had already happened in the eighteenth century.

7. According to paragraph 4, which of the following statements about steam engines is true?

    (A) They were used for the production of paper but not for printing.
    (B) By 1800, significant numbers of them were produced outside of Britain.
    (C) They were used in factories before they were used to power trains.
    (D) They were used in the construction of canals and turnpikes.

8. According to paragraph 4, providing a machine to take the place of the horse involved combining which two previously separate ingredients?

    (A) Turnpikes and canals
    (B) Stationary steam engines and wagons with flanged wheels
    (C) Metal rails in roadbeds and wagons capable of carrying heavy loads
    (D) Canal boats and heavily laden wagons

**P
A
R
A
G
R
A
P
H
3**

(A) Watt's steam engine soon showed what it could do. **(B)** It liberated industry from dependence on running water. **(C)** The engine eliminated water in the mines by driving efficient pumps, which made possible deeper and deeper mining. **(D)** The ready availability of coal inspired William Murdoch during the 1790s to develop the first new form of nighttime illumination to be discovered in a millennium and a half. Coal gas rivaled smoky oil lamps and flickering candles, and early in the new century, well-to-do Londoners grew accustomed to gaslit houses and even streets. Iron manufacturers, which had starved for fuel while depending on charcoal, also benefited from ever-increasing supplies of coal; blast furnaces with steam-powered bellows turned out more iron and steel for the new machinery. Steam became the motive force of the Industrial Revolution, as coal and iron ore were the raw materials.

9. Look at the part of the passage that is displayed above. The letters **(A)**, **(B)**, **(C)**, and **(D)** indicate where the following sentence could be added.

The factories did not have to go to the streams when power could come to the factories.

Where would the sentence best fit?

Ⓐ Choice A
Ⓑ Choice B
Ⓒ Choice C
Ⓓ Choice D

10. **Directions**: An introductory sentence for a brief summary of the passage is provided below. Complete the summary by selecting the THREE answer choices that express the most important ideas in the passage. Some sentences do not belong in the summary because they express ideas that are not presented in the passage or are minor ideas in the passage. **This question is worth 2 points.**

Write your answer choices in the spaces where they belong. You can either write the letter of your answer choice or you can copy the sentence.

> **The Industrial Revolution would not have been possible without a new source of power that was efficient, movable, and continuously available.**
>
> ●
>
> ●
>
> ●

Answer Choices

A In the early eighteenth century, Savery and Newcomen discovered that expanding steam could be used to raise a piston in a cylinder.

B In the mid-1700s, James Watt transformed an inefficient steam pump into a fast, flexible, fuel-efficient engine.

C Watt's steam engine played a leading role in greatly increasing industrial production of all kinds.

D In the 1790s, William Murdoch developed a new way of lighting houses and streets using coal gas.

E Until the 1830s, Britain was the world's major producer of steam engines.

F The availability of steam engines was a major factor in the development of railroads, which solved a major transportation problem.

Directions: Read the passage. Then answer the questions. You have 18 minutes on average to answer the questions.

PEST CONTROL

Many pest species that are native to North America, such as white-footed mice and ground moles, are more nuisance pests and are usually regulated by native predators and parasites. This situation is not true for nonindigenous pests in North America, such as brown rats and cockroaches. After centuries, it is evident that these pests cannot be eradicated. The best that can be done is to introduce pest control measures that will control their numbers.

An ancient and popular means of pest control is chemical. For example, the Sumerians used sulfur to combat crop pests, and by the early 1800s such chemicals as arsenic were used to combat insect and fungal pests.

However, chemical control has its dark side. Chemical pesticides have many unintended consequences through their effects not just on the target species but on a wide array of nontarget species as well, often eliminating them and thereby upsetting the existing food webs, especially through the suppression of native predator species. The surviving pests then rebound in greater numbers than ever.

Perhaps more insidious is that a pesticide loses its effectiveness because the target species evolves resistance to it. As one pesticide replaces another, the pests acquire a resistance to them all. Some species, notably certain mosquitoes, have overcome the toxic effects of every pesticide to which they have been exposed. Insect pests need only about five years to evolve pesticide resistance; their predators do so much more slowly. So after the pest develops resistance, pest outbreaks become even more disastrous.

Farmers long ago observed that enemies of pests act as controls. As early as 300 C.E., the Chinese were introducing predatory ants into their citrus orchards to control leaf-eating caterpillars. Insect pests have their own array of enemies in their native habitats. When an animal or plant is introduced, intentionally or unintentionally, into a new habitat outside of its natural range, it may adapt to the new environment and leave its enemies behind. Freed from predation and finding an abundance of resources, the species quickly becomes a pest or a weed. This fact has led to the search for natural enemies to introduce into populations of pests to reduce their populations.

Because the serious pest is usually a nonnative species, biological control involves the introduction of a nonindigenous predator or parasite to control the pest. The introduction of the cactus-eating moth, a native of Argentina, into Australia effectively reduced and controlled the rapidly spreading prickly pear, which had been introduced into Australia in 1901.

But biological control, like chemical control, can backfire. The success of the cactus-feeding moth in controlling prickly pear in Australia encouraged its introduction to several West Indies islands to control prickly pear there. In time the moth made its way to Florida, where it now threatens the existence of several native prickly pear species. The moral is that although using nonindigenous predators as biological controls can be effective, these species possess their own inherent dangers that must be assessed before they are released. They, too, can become alien invaders.

Because chemical, biological, and other methods used individually are obviously not the solution to pest control, entomologists have developed a holistic approach to pest control, called integrated pest management (IPM). IPM considers the biological, ecological, economic, social, and even aesthetic aspects of pest control and employs a variety of techniques. The objective of IPM is to control the pest not at the time of a major outbreak but at an earlier time, when the size of the population is easier to control. The approach is to rely first on natural mortality caused by weather and natural enemies, with as little disruption of the natural system as possible, and to use other methods only if they are needed to hold the pest below the economic injury level.

Successful IPM requires the knowledge of the population ecology of each pest and its associated species and the dynamics of the host species. It involves considerable fieldwork monitoring the pest species and its natural enemies by such techniques as egg counts and the trapping of adults to acquire information to determine the necessity, timing, and intensity of control measures. These control measures must be adjusted to the situation, which may vary from one location to another. The intensity of control or no control is based on the degree of pest damage that can be tolerated, the costs of control, and the benefits to be derived.

Directions: Now answer the questions.

PARAGRAPH 1

Many pest species that are native to North America, such as white-footed mice and ground moles, are more nuisance pests and are usually regulated by native predators and parasites. This situation is not true for nonindigenous pests in North America, such as brown rats and cockroaches. After centuries, it is evident that these pests cannot be eradicated. The best that can be done is to introduce pest control measures that will control their numbers.

11. What can be inferred from paragraph 1 about nonindigenous pests such as brown rats and cockroaches?

(A) Attempts to limit the size of their populations have been unsuccessful.

(B) They have inhabited North America longer than white-footed mice and ground moles.

(C) Their numbers cannot usually be controlled by native predators and parasites.

(D) They do not pose as many problems for humans as do white-footed mice and ground moles.

PARAGRAPH 3

However, chemical control has its dark side. **Chemical pesticides have many unintended consequences through their effects not just on the target species but on a wide array of nontarget species as well, often eliminating them and thereby upsetting the existing food webs, especially through the suppression of native predator species.** The surviving pests then rebound in greater numbers than ever.

12. Which of the sentences below best expresses the essential information in the highlighted sentence in the passage? Incorrect choices change the meaning in important ways or leave out essential information.

(A) Chemical pesticides often eliminate species other than the intended target and thereby upset food webs, especially by suppressing native predator species.

(B) Native predator species are often eliminated by chemical pesticides that are intended to have consequences for other pests.

(C) Chemical pesticides upset existing food webs by eliminating native species and by increasing the number of nonnative predators.

(D) The effects of chemical pesticides on a wide array of food webs and native predators are often unintended.

Farmers long ago observed that enemies of pests act as controls. As early as 300 C.E., the Chinese were introducing predatory ants into their citrus orchards to control leaf-eating caterpillars. Insect pests have their own array of enemies in their native habitats. When an animal or plant is introduced, intentionally or unintentionally, into a new habitat outside of its natural range, it may adapt to the new environment and leave its enemies behind. Freed from predation and finding an abundance of resources, the species quickly becomes a pest or a weed. This fact has led to the search for natural enemies to introduce into populations of pests to reduce their populations.

13. According to paragraph 5, why is a species likely to become a pest when it is introduced into a new habitat?

Ⓐ The species becomes more effective at escaping from its enemies.
Ⓑ The species has no natural predators in its new habitat.
Ⓒ The species adapts to habitats outside its natural range.
Ⓓ The species does not have to compete for resources with other plants and animals.

Because the serious pest is usually a nonnative species, biological control involves the introduction of a nonindigenous predator or parasite to control the pest. The introduction of the cactus-eating moth, a native of Argentina, into Australia effectively reduced and controlled the rapidly spreading prickly pear, which had been introduced into Australia in 1901.

14. In paragraph 6, the discussion of the cactus-eating moth and the prickly pear in Australia illustrates which of the following about biological control?

Ⓐ Nonnative pests cannot be controlled through biological means once they have begun to spread rapidly.
Ⓑ A nonnative pest can sometimes be controlled by the introduction of a nonnative predator.
Ⓒ A nonindigenous pest can be controlled only by a predator that comes from the same original habitat as the pest.
Ⓓ A native pest can be controlled by either a native or a nonnative predator.

But biological control, like chemical control, can backfire. The success of the cactus-feeding moth in controlling prickly pear in Australia encouraged its introduction to several West Indies islands to control prickly pear there. In time the moth made its way to **Florida**, where it now threatens the existence of several native prickly pear species. The moral is that although using nonindigenous predators as biological controls can be effective, these species possess their own inherent dangers that must be **assessed** before they are released. They, too, can become alien invaders.

15. The word "**assessed**" in the passage is closest in meaning to

Ⓐ minimized
Ⓑ identified
Ⓒ evaluated
Ⓓ dealt with

16. The author discusses the cactus-feeding moth in "**Florida**" in order to

  (A) explain why the prickly pear species that are native to Florida have no indigenous predators

  (B) show how a predator spreads more rapidly in alien environments than it does in its native environment

  (C) indicate that a single nonindigenous predator species can be effective against a wide array of nonindigenous pest species

  (D) argue that controlling pests with nonindigenous predators can have unintended consequences

Because chemical, biological, and other methods used individually are obviously not the solution to pest control, entomologists have developed a holistic approach to pest control, called integrated pest management (IPM). IPM considers the biological, ecological, economic, social, and even aesthetic aspects of pest control and employs a variety of techniques. The objective of IPM is to control the pest not at the time of a major outbreak but at an earlier time, when the size of the population is easier to control. The approach is to rely first on natural mortality caused by weather and natural enemies, with as little disruption of the natural system as possible, and to use other methods only if they are needed to hold the pest below the economic injury level.

17. According to paragraph 8, each of the following is a principle of integrated pest management EXCEPT

  (A) to control pest populations before a major outbreak occurs

  (B) to first determine if weather and natural enemies are able to control a pest

  (C) to increase the populations of the pest's natural enemies during certain seasons of the year

  (D) to use artificial methods of pest control only when pests begin to cause economic injury

Successful IPM requires the knowledge of the population ecology of each pest and its associated species and the dynamics of the host species. It involves considerable fieldwork monitoring the pest species and its natural enemies by such techniques as egg counts and the trapping of adults to acquire information to determine the necessity, timing, and intensity of control measures. These control measures must be adjusted to the situation, which may vary from one location to another. The intensity of control or no control is based on the degree of pest damage that can be tolerated, the costs of control, and the benefits to be derived.

18. According to paragraph 9, each of the following helps to determine how intensely to apply pest control measures EXCEPT

  (A) how much pest damage can be tolerated

  (B) the cost of pest control measures

  (C) what can be gained through pest control measures

  (D) whether pest control measures have been used before

Perhaps more insidious is that a pesticide loses its effectiveness because the target species evolves resistance to it. As one pesticide replaces another, the pests acquire a resistance to them all. **(A)** Some species, notably certain mosquitoes, have overcome the toxic effects of every pesticide to which they have been exposed. **(B)** Insect pests need only about five years to evolve pesticide resistance; their predators do so much more slowly. **(C)** So after the pest develops resistance, pest outbreaks become even more disastrous. **(D)**

Farmers long ago observed that enemies of pests act as controls. As early as 300 C.E, the Chinese were introducing predatory ants into their citrus orchards to control leaf-eating caterpillars. Insect pests have their own array of enemies in their native habitats. When an animal or plant is introduced, intentionally or unintentionally, into a new habitat outside of its natural range, it may adapt to the new environment and leave its enemies behind. Freed from predation and finding an abundance of resources, the species quickly becomes a pest or a weed. This fact has led to the search for natural enemies to introduce into populations of pests to reduce their populations.

19. Look at the part of the passage that is displayed above. The letters **(A)**, **(B)**, **(C)**, an **(D)** indicate where the following sentence could be added.

   These flare-ups continue to occur until a new pesticide is developed, at which time the cycle begins anew.

   Where would the sentence best fit?

   (A) Choice A
   (B) Choice B
   (C) Choice C
   (D) Choice D

20. **Directions:** An introductory sentence for a brief summary of the passage is provided below. Complete the summary by selecting the THREE answer choices that express the most important ideas in the passage. Some sentences do not belong in the summary because they express ideas that are not presented in the passage or are minor ideas in the passage. **This question is worth 2 points.**

Write your answer choices in the spaces where they belong. You can either write the letter of your answer choice or you can copy the sentence.

Pest control measures vary in their approach and overall degree of success.

-
-
-

Answer Choices

A Biological methods of pest control were introduced by the ancient Sumerians, and chemical control was first used in ancient China.

B Pesticides are limited in their usefulness because pests quickly become resistant to them, and because they can harm species for which they were not intended.

C Biological control, for example, the use of natural enemies of pests, has been effective at regulating nonnative pests, though it can also threaten the existence of native species.

D The success of biological and chemical approaches to pest control has been difficult to measure because situations vary significantly from one location to another.

E Integrated pest management is a holistic approach that has been successful at controlling major pest outbreaks in locations where chemical and biological control have already failed.

F Integrated pest management, an approach that considers biological, ecological, economic, and aesthetic aspects of pest control, uses a variety of techniques adjusted to specific situations.

LISTENING

In this section, you will be able to demonstrate your ability to understand conversations and lectures in English.

In the actual test, the section is divided into two separately timed parts. You will hear each conversation or lecture only one time. A clock will indicate how much time remains. The clock will count down only while you are answering questions, not while you are listening. You may take up to 16.5 minutes to answer the questions.

In this practice test, there is no time limit for answering questions.

You may take notes while you listen. You may use your notes to help you answer the questions. Your notes will not be scored.

Answer the questions based on what is stated or implied by the speakers.

In some questions, you will see this icon: 🎧 . This means that you will hear, but not see, part of the question.

In the actual test, you must answer each question. You cannot return to previous questions.

At the end of this practice test, you will find an answer key.

Directions: Listen to Track 34.

Directions: Now answer the questions.

1. Why does the student go to the career services office?

   (A) To confirm the date and time of the career fair
   (B) To learn the location of the career fair
   (C) To find out if he is allowed to attend the career fair
   (D) To get advice about interviewing at the career fair

2. Why does the student think that companies' representatives would not be interested in talking to him?

   (A) He will not be graduating this year.
   (B) He is not currently taking business classes.
   (C) He has not declared a major yet.
   (D) He does not have a current résumé.

3. What does the woman imply about the small print on the career fair posters and flyers?

   (A) The information in the small print was incomplete.
   (B) The print was smaller than she expected it to be.
   (C) The information the small print contains will be updated.
   (D) The information in the small print will be presented in a more noticeable way.

4. What does the woman say is a good way for the student to prepare for speaking to companies' representatives? *Select 2 answers.*

   [A] Take some business classes
   [B] Familiarize himself with certain businesses beforehand
   [C] Have questions ready to ask the representatives
   [D] Talk to people who work for accounting firms

5. *Listen to Track 35 to answer the question.*

    Why does the student say this?

    (A) To acknowledge that he cannot go to this year's career fair
    (B) To acknowledge the amount of preparation he will have
    (C) To indicate that he has schoolwork he must complete before the career fair
    (D) To indicate that he needs to go to his job now

Directions: Listen to Track 36.

Biology

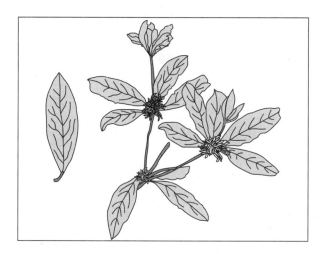

Directions: Now answer the questions.

6. What topics related to the Nightcap Oak does the professor mainly discuss? *Select 2 answers.*

   A Factors that relate to the size of the area in which it grows
   B The size of its population over the last few centuries
   C Whether anything can be done to ensure its survival
   D Why it did not change much over the last one hundred million years

7. According to the professor, what led scientists to characterize the Nightcap Oak as primitive?

   Ⓐ It has no evolutionary connection to other trees growing in Australia today.
   Ⓑ It has an inefficient reproductive system.
   Ⓒ Its flowers are located at the bases of the leaves.
   Ⓓ It is similar to some ancient fossils.

8. What point does the professor make about the Nightcap Oak's habitat?

   (A) It is stable despite its limited size.
   (B) Unlike the habitats of many plants, it is expanding.
   (C) Its recent changes have left the Nightcap Oak struggling to adapt.
   (D) Its size is much larger than the area where the Nightcap Oak grows.

9. According to the professor, what are two factors that prevent the Nightcap Oak population from spreading? *Choose 2 answers.*

   [A] The complex conditions required for the trees to produce fruit
   [B] The fact that the seed cannot germinate while locked inside the shell
   [C] The limited time the seed retains the ability to germinate
   [D] Competition with tree species that evolved more recently

10. Why does the professor mention the size of the Nightcap Oak population over the last few hundred years?

    (A) To explain why it is likely that the Nightcap Oak population will increase in the future
    (B) To point out that the Nightcap Oak's limited reproductive success has not led to a decrease in its population
    (C) To present evidence that the Nightcap Oak is able to tolerate major changes in its environment
    (D) To point out that the Nightcap Oak is able to resist diseases that have destroyed other tree species

11. *Listen again to part of the lecture by playing Track 37.* 🎧 *Then answer the question.*

    Why does the professor say this?

    (A) She wants the students to think about a possible connection.
    (B) She wants to know if the students have any questions.
    (C) She is implying that researchers have been asking the wrong questions.
    (D) She is implying that there may be no connection between the questions.

Directions: Listen to Track 38.

Directions: Now answer the questions.

12. Why does the student go to see the professor?

    Ⓐ She is having trouble finding a topic for her term paper.

    Ⓑ She needs his help to find resource materials.

    Ⓒ She wants to ask him for an extension on a term paper.

    Ⓓ She wants him to approve her plans for a term paper.

13. Why is the student interested in learning more about dialects?

    Ⓐ She often has trouble understanding what other students are saying.

    Ⓑ She is trying to change the way she speaks.

    Ⓒ She is aware that her own dialect differs from those of her roommates.

    Ⓓ She spent her childhood in various places where different dialects are spoken.

14. Based on the conversation, what can be concluded about "dialect accommodation"?
Select 2 answers.

    Ⓐ It is a largely subconscious process.

    Ⓑ It is a process that applies only to some dialects.

    Ⓒ It is a very common phenomenon.

    Ⓓ It is a topic that has not been explored extensively.

15. What does the professor want the student to do next?

    Ⓐ Read some articles he has recommended

    Ⓑ Present her proposal before the entire class

    Ⓒ Submit a design plan for the project

    Ⓓ Listen to recordings of different dialects

16. *Listen again to part of the conversation by playing Track 39.* *Then answer the question.*

What can be inferred about the professor when he says this?

Ⓐ He thinks the topic goes beyond his expertise.
Ⓑ He thinks the topic is too broad for the student to manage.
Ⓒ He thinks the topic is not relevant for a linguistics class.
Ⓓ He thinks other students may have chosen the same topic.

Directions: Listen to Track 40.

Directions: Now answer the questions.

17. What aspect of creative writing does the professor mainly discuss?

    Ⓐ How to keep a reader's interest
    Ⓑ How to create believable characters
    Ⓒ Key differences between major and minor characters
    Ⓓ Techniques for developing short-story plots

18. Why does the professor recommend that students pay attention to the people they see every day?

    Ⓐ The behavior and characteristics of these people can be used in character sketches.
    Ⓑ Observing people in real-life situations can provide ideas for story plots.
    Ⓒ It is easier to observe the behavior of familiar people than of new people.
    Ⓓ Students can gather accurate physical descriptions for their characters.

19. The professor discusses an example of three friends who run out of gas. What point does he use the example to illustrate?

    Ⓐ Writers should know their characters as well as they know their friends.
    Ⓑ Writers should create characters that interact in complex ways.
    Ⓒ Friends do not always behave the way we expect them to behave.
    Ⓓ Friends' behavior is often more predictable than fictional characters' behavior.

20. What warning does the professor give when he talks about the man who lives on the mountain?

    Ⓐ Avoid placing characters in remote settings.
    Ⓑ Avoid having more than one major character.
    Ⓒ Avoid using people as models whose lives are unusual.
    Ⓓ Avoid making characters into stereotypes.

21. What does the professor imply is the importance of flat characters?

    Ⓐ They act more predictably than other characters.
    Ⓑ They are difficult for readers to understand.
    Ⓒ They help reveal the main character's personality.
    Ⓓ They are the only characters able to experience defeat.

22. *Listen again to part of the lecture by playing Track 41.* *Then answer the question.*

    Why does the professor say this?

    Ⓐ To indicate that he is about to explain what type of drawing he wants
    Ⓑ To help students understand a term that may be confusing
    Ⓒ To indicate that he used the wrong word earlier
    Ⓓ To motivate the students to do better work

Directions: Listen to Track 42.

Earth Science

Sahara Desert

Directions: Now answer the questions.

23. What is the lecture mainly about?

    Ⓐ An example of rapid climate change

    Ⓑ A comparison of two mechanisms of climate change

    Ⓒ The weather conditions in the present-day Sahara

    Ⓓ Recent geological findings made in the Sahara

24. Not long ago, the Sahara had a different climate. What evidence does the professor mention to support this? *Select 3 answers.*

    ☐A Ancient pollen

    ☐B Bones from large animals

    ☐C Rock paintings

    ☐D Agriculture in ancient Egypt

    ☐E Underground water

25. In the lecture, what do the Ice Age and the creation of the Sahara Desert both illustrate about past climate changes? *Select 2 answers.*

    ☐A That some climate changes benefitted the development of civilization

    ☐B That some climate changes were not caused by human activity

    ☐C That some climate changes were caused by a decrease of moisture in the atmosphere

    ☐D That some climate changes were caused by changes in Earth's motion and position

26. What started the runaway effect that led to the Sahara area of North Africa becoming a desert?

    Ⓐ The prevailing winds became stronger.

    Ⓑ The seasonal rains moved to a different area.

    Ⓒ The vegetation started to die off in large areas.

    Ⓓ The soil lost its ability to retain rainwater.

27. The professor mentions a theory that people migrating from the Sahara were important to the development of the Egyptian civilization. Which sentence best describes the professor's attitude toward this theory?

    (A) It is exciting because it perfectly explains recent archaeological discoveries.
    (B) It is problematic because it goes too far beyond the generally available data.
    (C) It raises an interesting possibility and he hopes to see more evidence for it.
    (D) It cannot be taken seriously until it explains how the migrants got to Egypt.

28. *Listen again to part of the lecture by playing Track 43.* *Then answer the question.*

    Why does the professor say this?

    (A) To correct a misstatement he made about the Sahara's climate
    (B) To suggest that the current dryness of the Sahara is exaggerated
    (C) To indicate that scientists are not in agreement about the Sahara's past climate
    (D) To emphasize the difference between the current and past climates of the Sahara

SPEAKING

In the actual test, the Speaking section will last approximately 16 minutes. You will answer four questions by speaking into the microphone. You may take notes while you listen. You may use your notes to help you answer the questions. Your notes will not be scored. For each question, you will have time to prepare before giving your response. You should answer the questions as completely as possible in the time allowed.

For this practice test, you may want to use a personal recording device to record and play back your responses.

For each question, play the audio track listed and follow the directions to complete the task.

At the end of this practice test, you will find important points about each question.

1. You will now give your opinion about a familiar topic. After you hear the question, you should give yourself 15 seconds to prepare and 45 seconds to speak.

   Listen to Track 44.

   > Some people have one career throughout their lives. Other people do different kinds of work at different points in their lives. Which do you think is better? Explain why.
   >
   > | **Preparation Time: 15 seconds** |
   > | --- |
   > | **Response Time: 45 seconds** |

2. Now you will read a passage about a campus situation and then listen to a conversation about the same topic. You will then answer a question, using information from both the reading passage and the conversation. You should give yourself 30 seconds to prepare and 60 seconds to speak.

   Listen to Track 45.

Reading Time: 50 seconds

   > ### History Seminars Should Be Shorter
   >
   > Currently, all of the seminar classes in the history department are three hours long. I would like to propose that history seminars be shortened to two hours. I make this proposal for two reasons. First, most students just cannot concentrate for three hours straight. I myself have taken these three-hour seminars and found them tiring and sometimes boring. Also, when a seminar lasts that long, people stop concentrating and stop learning, so the third hour of a three-hour seminar is a waste of everyone's time. Two-hour seminars would be much more efficient.
   >
   > Sincerely,
   >
   > Tim Lawson

Listen to Track 46.

> The woman expresses her opinion about the proposal described in the letter. Briefly summarize the proposal. Then state her opinion about the proposal and explain the reasons she gives for holding that opinion.
>
> **Preparation Time: 30 seconds**
> **Response Time: 60 seconds**

3. Now you will read a passage about an academic subject and then listen to a lecture on the same topic. Answer the question, using information from both the reading passage and the lecture. Give yourself 30 seconds to prepare and 60 seconds to speak.

Listen to Track 47.

Reading Time: 45 seconds

> ### Explicit Memories and Implicit Memories
>
> In everyday life, when people speak of memory, they are almost always speaking about what psychologists would call explicit memories. An explicit memory is a conscious or intentional recollection, usually of facts, names, events, or other things that a person can state or declare. There is another kind of memory that is not conscious. Memories of this kind are called implicit memories. An individual can have an experience that he or she cannot consciously recall yet still display reactions that indicate the experience has been somehow recorded in his or her brain.

Listen to Track 48.

> Using the example of the car advertisement, explain what is meant by implicit memory.
>
> | Preparation Time: 30 seconds |
> |---|
> | Response Time: 60 seconds |

4. Now you will listen to a lecture. You will then be asked to summarize the lecture. You should give yourself 20 seconds to prepare and 60 seconds to speak.

Listen to Track 49.

> Using points and examples from the talk, explain the difference between active and passive attention.
>
> | Preparation Time: 20 seconds |
> |---|
> | Response Time: 60 seconds |

WRITING

In this section, you will be able to demonstrate your ability to use writing to communicate in an academic environment. There will be two writing tasks.

At the end of this practice test, you will find topic notes for each question.

Turn the page to see the directions for the first writing task.

Writing Based on Reading and Listening

For this task, you will read a passage about an academic topic. Then you will listen to a lecture about the same topic. You may take notes while you listen.

In your response, provide a detailed summary of the lecture and explain how the lecture relates to the reading passage.

In the actual test, you will have 3 minutes to read the passage and 20 minutes to write your response. While you write, you will be able to see the reading passage. If you finish your response before time is up, you may go on to the second writing task.

Reading Time: 3 minutes

Communal online encyclopedias represent one of the most widely used resources to be found on the Internet. They are in many respects like traditional encyclopedias: collections of articles on various subjects. What is specific to these communal online encyclopedias, however, is that any Internet user can contribute a new article or make an editorial change in an existing one. As a result, the encyclopedia is authored by the whole community of Internet users. The idea might sound attractive, but the communal online encyclopedias have several important problems that make them much less valuable than traditional encyclopedias.

First, contributors to a communal online encyclopedia often lack academic credentials, thereby making their contributions partially informed at best and downright inaccurate in many cases. Traditional encyclopedias are written by trained experts who adhere to standards of academic rigor that nonspecialists cannot really achieve.

Second, even if the original entry in the online encyclopedia is correct, the communal nature of these online encyclopedias gives unscrupulous users and vandals or hackers the opportunity to fabricate, delete, and corrupt information in the encyclopedia. Once changes have been made to the original text, an unsuspecting user cannot tell the entry has been tampered with. None of this is possible with a traditional encyclopedia.

Third, the communal encyclopedias focus too frequently, and in too great a depth, on trivial and popular topics, which creates a false impression of what is important and what is not. A child doing research for a school project may discover that a major historical event receives as much attention in an online encyclopedia as, say, a single long-running television program. The traditional encyclopedia provides a considered view of what topics to include or exclude and contains a sense of proportion that online "democratic" communal encyclopedias do not.

Listen to Track 50.

Directions: You have 20 minutes to plan and write your response. Your response will be judged on the basis of the quality of your writing and on how well your response presents the points in the lecture and their relationship to the reading passage. Typically, an effective response will contain a minimum of 150 words.

Listen to Track 51.

Response Time: 20 minutes

Question 1

Summarize the points made in the lecture, being sure to explain how they oppose the specific points made in the reading passage.

_____

_____

_____

_____

_____

_____

_____

_____

Writing for an Academic Discussion

For this task, you will read an online discussion. A professor has posted a question about a topic, and some classmates have responded with their ideas.

In the actual test, you will have 10 minutes to write a response that contributes to the discussion.

Question 2

Your professor is teaching a class on advertising. Write a post responding to the professor's question.

In your response, you should do the following.

- Express and support your opinion.
- Make a contribution to the discussion in your own words.

An effective response will contain at least 100 words.

Dr. Achebe

Let's discuss advertising for organizations that do charitable work. Many of these organizations use images, particularly photographs, in their advertisements to motivate people to donate money or goods to support their charity. Some use sad images, for example, photographs of people who are in difficult situations and need help. Others use happy or inspirational images, for example, of people already receiving help. In your view, which strategy is more effective to bring in donations—using sad or happy images? Why?

Claire

I think you've got to show the problem if you want people to understand that it's serious and help is truly needed. Consider a charity that builds schools and provides school supplies. If their advertisements only show happy children attending nice schools, why is my donation necessary?

Paul

Let's not forget that people often see lots of advertisements from many different charities—too many to even keep track of. Honestly, many potential donors may not want to look at advertisements containing unpleasant or sad images. In my opinion, inspirational images of all the good a charity does will get more attention and ultimately bring in more donations.

Response Time: 10 minutes

ANSWERS

Reading Section

1. D
2. B
3. B
4. A
5. A
6. C
7. C
8. B
9. C
10. B, C, F

11. C
12. A
13. B
14. B
15. C
16. D
17. C
18. D
19. D
20. B, C, F

Listening Section

1. C
2. A
3. D
4. B, C
5. B
6. A, B
7. D
8. D
9. B, C
10. B
11. A
12. D
13. C
14. A, C

15. C
16. B
17. B
18. A
19. A
20. D
21. C
22. B
23. A
24. A, C, E
25. B, D
26. B
27. C
28. D

Speaking Section

1. To respond to this particular question, you should clearly state what your opinion is: do you think it is better to have one career or do different kinds of work? You should then give reasons to support your opinion. If you think that it is better to have one career, you could say that if you have a career that you love, there is no reason to change. Many people enjoy doing one thing that they are very good at. You may then talk about other advantages, such as money or the possibility to advance over time. You may give a more specific example to help you explain. For example, you could say that a doctor has gone to school for a long time and it takes a long time to learn to be a good doctor, so in this case changing careers would not make sense.

    If you think it is better to do different kinds of work, you would develop your opinion in a similar way. You could say that doing one job for your whole life would not be interesting, and that as technology progresses, many new fields to work in become available. You might then provide specific information about new fields, such as those connected to new computer technology.

    It is important to understand that that there is no "correct" answer to this question. Whichever option you prefer, your answer should be supported with examples. It is important to make sure that you state your opinion and develop your response with good examples and relevant details.

    Your response should be intelligible, should demonstrate effective use of grammar and vocabulary, and should be well-developed and coherent. Your response is scored using the Independent Speaking Rubric (see Appendix A).

2. To respond to this particular question, you should state the woman's opinion of the letter writer's proposal to shorten history seminars to two hours. In this case, the woman disagrees with the letter writer's proposal.

    After stating that the woman disagrees with the proposal, you should convey the two main reasons she gives for holding that opinion. You will need to connect information from the conversation to the reading in order for the response to be complete. The woman says that the first reason given for shortening history seminars—that students cannot concentrate for three hours—isn't valid. She says that Tim, the letter writer, is not a typical student and that he stays up late at night and sometimes even sleeps in class.

    Your response should also convey the woman's second reason for not agreeing with the letter writer's proposal. The letter writer thinks that the third hour of the seminar is a waste of time because people don't learn anything. The woman thinks, however, that the last hour is when the discussions are the most interesting and that it is the most important part of the seminar.

    Your response should be intelligible, should demonstrate effective use of grammar and vocabulary, and should be well-developed and coherent. Your response is scored using the Integrated Speaking Rubric (see Appendix A).

3. To respond to this particular question, you should first explain the idea of implicit memory as it was presented in the reading. An implicit memory is not conscious and cannot be recalled, but it is recorded in our brains. You may choose to contrast this with explicit memory, which is consciously recalled. However, do not spend too much time at this stage. You must give yourself enough time to discuss the professor's example.

    You should then use the example given by the professor to explain implicit memory. In the example, implicit memory is demonstrated when a person drives by a billboard and sees an advertisement for a car called "Panther" but has no recollection of the billboard. Then later, the same person recalls the word "Panther" when asked to name an animal that starts with the letter "P," even though "pig" is a more common animal that begins with "p." This shows that the billboard has had an effect on the person's memory; this is an illustration of implicit memory.

You do not need to repeat all of the details from the reading and the lecture, but instead integrate points from both to answer the question completely.

Your response should be intelligible, should demonstrate effective use of grammar and vocabulary, and should be well-developed and coherent. Your response is scored using the Integrated Speaking Rubric (see Appendix A).

4. This particular question requires you to summarize the contents of a lecture you hear. In your response, you should talk about the two different kinds of attention that the professor describes.

The order in which you discuss the two types of attention is not important as long as you discuss both types fully and make clear what is different about them. The professor says that active attention is voluntary; it occurs when people force themselves to pay attention to something. A boring lecture about frogs will require students to pay active attention, but they will not be able to maintain their attention for long.

You would then talk about passive attention. Passive attention is involuntary and requires no effort to maintain, unlike active attention, which does require effort; it occurs

when people are naturally interested in the material. If a teacher pulls out a live frog, the students become more interested and passive attention is maintained.

You should budget your time so that you are able to include a good summary of both types of attention and talk about both examples in the lecture.

Your response should be intelligible, should demonstrate effective use of grammar and vocabulary, and should be well-developed and coherent. Your response is scored using the Integrated Speaking Rubric (see Appendix A).

Writing Section

1. What is important to understand from the lecture is that the professor disagrees with the criticisms of communal online encyclopedias presented in the reading—namely that the encyclopedias contain inaccurate information, that unscrupulous users can tamper with the information in the encyclopedias, and that the encyclopedias do not distinguish important topics from unimportant ones.

In your response, you should convey the reasons presented by the professor for why the criticisms of communal online encyclopedias are not convincing. A high-scoring response will include the following points made by the professor that cast doubt on the points made in the reading.

Point made in the reading	Counterpoint made in the lecture
Since entries in communal online encyclopedias are not always written by experts, they can be inaccurate and unreliable.	No encyclopedia is perfectly accurate. What really matters is how easily and quickly the mistakes can be corrected. In this regard, online encyclopedias are better than the traditional ones, because inaccurate content in online encyclopedias can be revised much faster.
Because anyone can make revisions to the content of online encyclopedias, unscrupulous users, vandals, and hackers can intentionally corrupt the content of articles in the encyclopedias.	Online encyclopedias have taken steps to protect their content from unscrupulous users, vandals, and hackers. Some important content is presented in a "read-only" format that cannot be revised. Also, special editors now monitor changes made to articles and eliminate revisions that are malicious.
Communal online encyclopedias often give equal space to articles on trivial topics and articles on serious topics. This creates a false impression about which information is important and which is not.	The fact that online encyclopedias contain information on all kinds of subjects is not a weakness but a strength. Diversity of topics covered by online encyclopedias is a true reflection of the diversity of people's interests. In contrast, traditional encyclopedias have limited space, and editors who choose which entries to include do not always take diverse interests into account.

Your response is scored using the Integrated Writing Rubric (see Appendix A). A response that receives a score of 5 clearly conveys all three of the main points in the table using accurate sentence structure and vocabulary.

2. To earn a top score, you should develop a response that contributes to the discussion about the issue of whether happy or sad (pleasant or unpleasant) images make better advertisements for charities. An effective response will contain at least 100 words.

One discussion participant argues that sad images are necessary to show the seriousness of a problem and contrasts this with the limited effects of happy images; the other discussion participant argues that, in general, people are more attracted to happy images and that these will inspire support for charities. You might expand on the ideas already stated by the discussion participants or introduce entirely new ideas. You may choose between happy or sad images, or you might describe conditions under which one or the other type of image would be more effective. You may explain the emotional or psychological effects of either type of image and how these effects relate to supporting a charity. You may also describe the use of certain images related to specific real-world events, problems, or charitable organizations; you might relate their own experiences with charities and how advertising images affected them personally.

You should make sure that your ideas are well-supported by reasons and examples and are expressed clearly. Since your response represents an online post, it does not need to be organized into separate paragraphs. However, your ideas need to be well-connected, coherent, and clear. Your response is scored using the Writing for an Academic Discussion Rubric (see Appendix A).

TOEFL iBT® Test 4

READING

In this section, you will be able to demonstrate your ability to understand academic passages in English. You will read and answer questions about **two passages**.

In the actual test, you will have 36 minutes total to read both passages and answer the questions. A clock will indicate how much time remains.

Some passages may include one or more notes explaining words or phrases. The words or phrases are marked with footnote numbers, and the notes explaining them appear at the end of the passage.

Most questions are worth 1 point, but the last question for each passage is worth 2 points.

You may review and revise your answers in this section as long as time remains.

At the end of this practice test, you will find an answer key.

Directions: Read the passage. Then answer the questions. You have 18 minutes on average to answer the questions.

UNDERSTANDING ANCIENT MESOAMERICAN ART

Starting at the end of the eighteenth century and continuing up to the present, explorers have searched for the ruins of ancient Mesoamerica, a region that includes Central America and central and southern Mexico. With the progress of time, archaeologists have unearthed civilizations increasingly remote in age. It is as if with each new century in the modern era an earlier stratum of antiquity has been revealed. Nineteenth-century explorers, particularly John Lloyd Stephens and Frederick Catherwood, came upon Maya cities in the jungle, as well as evidence of other Classic cultures. Twentieth-century research revealed a much earlier high civilization, the Olmec. It now scarcely seems possible that the frontiers of early Mesoamerican civilization can be pushed back any further, although new work—such as in Oaxaca, southern Mexico—will continue to fill in details of the picture.

The process of discovery often shapes what we know about the history of Mesoamerican art. New finds are just as often made accidentally as intentionally. In 1971 workers installing sound and light equipment under the Pyramid of the Sun at Teotihuacán stumbled upon a remarkable cave that has since been interpreted by some scholars as a royal burial chamber. Archaeology has its own fashions too: the isolation of new sites may be the prime goal in one decade and the excavation of pyramids the focus in the next. In a third decade, outlying structures rather than principal buildings may absorb archaeologists' energies. Nor should one forget that excavators are vulnerable to local interests. At one point, reconstruction of pyramids to attract tourism may be desired; at another, archaeologists may be precluded from working at what has already become a tourist attraction. Also, modern construction often determines which ancient sites can be excavated. In Mexico City, for example, the building of the subway initiated the excavations there and renewed interest in the old Aztec capital.

But the study of Mesoamerican art is not based exclusively on archaeology. Much useful information about the native populations was written down in the sixteenth century, particularly in central Mexico, and it can help us unravel the pre-Columbian past (the time prior to the arrival of Columbus in the Americas in 1492). Although many sources exist, the single most important one to the art historian is Bernardino de Sahagún's *General History of the Things of New Spain*. A Franciscan friar (member of the Roman Catholic religious order), Sahagún recorded for posterity many aspects of pre-Hispanic life in his encyclopedia of twelve books, including history, ideology, and cosmogony (theories of the origin of the universe), as well as detailed information on the materials and methods of the skilled native craft workers. Furthermore, traditional ways of life survive among the native peoples of Mesoamerica, and scholars have increasingly found that modern practice and belief can decode the past. Remarkably, some scholars have even turned this process around, teaching ancient writing to modern peoples who may use it to articulate their identity in the twenty-first century.

During the past 40 years, scholars also have made great progress in deciphering and interpreting ancient Mesoamerican writing systems, a breakthrough that has transformed our understanding of the pre-Columbian mind. Classic Maya inscriptions, for example—long thought to record only calendrical information and astrological incantations—can now be read, and we find that most of them glorify family and ancestry by displaying the right of individual sovereigns to rule. The carvings can thus be seen as portraits or public records of dynastic power. Although scholars long believed that Mesoamerican artists did not sign their works, Mayanist scholar David Stuart's 1986 deciphering of the Maya glyphs (written symbols) for "scribe" and "to write" opened a window on Maya practice; now we know at least one painter of ceramic vessels was the son of a king. Knowledge of the minor arts has also come in large part through an active art market. Thousands more small-scale objects are known now than in the twentieth century, although at a terrible cost to the ancient ruins from which they have been plundered.

Directions: Now answer the questions.

PARAGRAPH 1

Starting at the end of the eighteenth century and continuing up to the present, explorers have searched for the ruins of ancient Mesoamerica, a region that includes Central America and central and southern Mexico. With the progress of time, archaeologists have unearthed civilizations increasingly remote in age. It is as if with each new century in the modern era an earlier stratum of antiquity has been revealed. Nineteenth-century explorers, particularly John Lloyd Stephens and Frederick Catherwood, came upon Maya cities in the jungle, as well as evidence of other Classic cultures. Twentieth-century research revealed a much earlier high civilization, the Olmec. It now scarcely seems possible that the frontiers of early Mesoamerican civilization can be pushed back any further, although new work—such as in Oaxaca, southern Mexico—will continue to fill in details of the picture.

1. Paragraph 1 supports which of the following statements about the revealing of early Mesoamerican civilization?

   (A) The Maya and Olmec civilizations were discovered by explorers at approximately the same time.
   (B) Most of our understanding of Mesoamerican civilization comes from discoveries made in the twentieth century.
   (C) The discoveries made at Oaxaca in southern Mexico show that the Olmec civilization had its origins there.
   (D) Evidence still to be found in Oaxaca, Mexico, is likely to provide additional information about the high civilization of early Mesoamerica.

The process of discovery often shapes what we know about the history of Mesoamerican art. New finds are just as often made accidentally as intentionally. In 1971 workers installing sound and light equipment under the Pyramid of the Sun at Teotihuacán stumbled upon a remarkable cave that has since been interpreted by some scholars as a royal burial chamber. Archaeology has its own fashions too: the isolation of new sites may be the prime goal in one decade and the excavation of pyramids the focus in the next. In a third decade, **outlying** structures rather than principal buildings may absorb archaeologists' energies. Nor should one forget that excavators are vulnerable to local interests. At one point, reconstruction of pyramids to attract tourism may be desired; at another, archaeologists may be precluded from working at what has already become a tourist attraction. Also, modern construction often determines which ancient sites can be excavated. In Mexico City, for example, the building of the subway initiated the excavations there and renewed interest in the old Aztec capital.

2.   The word "**outlying**" in the passage is closest in meaning to

    (A) ceremonial

    (B) temporary

    (C) far from the center

    (D) simple

3.   In paragraph 2, why does the author discuss the Pyramid of the Sun at Teotihuacán?

    (A) To introduce the discussion of a specific style of Mesoamerican art

    (B) To illustrate the importance of an accidental discovery

    (C) To emphasize the necessity of systematic study

    (D) To argue against the use of modern equipment in archaeology

4.   Which of the following is NOT mentioned in paragraph 2 as a factor affecting the process of discovery in archaeology?

    (A) Fashions that change over time

    (B) The popularity of archaeology as a field of study

    (C) The interests of local inhabitants

    (D) The building of modern structures

But the study of Mesoamerican art is not based **exclusively** on archaeology. Much useful information about the native populations was written down in the sixteenth century, particularly in central Mexico, and it can help us unravel the pre-Columbian past (the time prior to the arrival of Columbus in the Americas in 1492). Although many sources exist, the single most important one to the art historian is Bernardino de Sahagún's *General History of the Things of New Spain*. A Franciscan friar (member of the Roman Catholic religious order), Sahagún recorded for posterity many aspects of pre-Hispanic life in his encyclopedia of twelve books, including history, ideology, and cosmogony (theories of the origin of the universe), as well as detailed information on the materials and methods of the skilled native craft workers. Furthermore, traditional ways of life survive among the native peoples of Mesoamerica, and scholars have increasingly found that modern practice and belief can decode the past. Remarkably, some scholars have even turned this process around, teaching ancient writing to modern peoples who may use it to articulate their identity in the twenty-first century.

5. The word "**exclusively**" in the passage is closest in meaning to

    Ⓐ exactly
    Ⓑ solely
    Ⓒ traditionally
    Ⓓ primarily

6. According to paragraph 3, why was Bernardino de Sahagún important to the study of Mesoamerican art?

    Ⓐ He recorded detailed information about native populations in the sixteenth century.
    Ⓑ He made important archaeological discoveries in central Mexico.
    Ⓒ He studied the methods and materials of skilled Mesoamerican craft workers as a basis for his own art.
    Ⓓ He encouraged native people to preserve their traditional ways of life.

7. According to paragraph 3, which of the following is true of ancient Mesoamerican writing?

    Ⓐ It is very similar to the modern writing of Mesoamerican peoples.
    Ⓑ It is not as old as originally thought.
    Ⓒ It can be used by modern peoples to express their own identities.
    Ⓓ It is most thoroughly understood by skilled native craft workers.

During the past 40 years, scholars also have made great progress in deciphering and interpreting ancient Mesoamerican writing systems, a breakthrough that has transformed our understanding of the pre-Columbian mind. Classic Maya inscriptions, for example—long thought to record only calendrical information and astrological incantations—can now be read, and we find that most of them glorify family and ancestry by displaying the right of individual sovereigns to rule. The carvings can thus be seen as portraits or public records of dynastic power. Although scholars long believed that Mesoamerican artists did not sign their works, Mayanist scholar David Stuart's 1986 deciphering of the Maya glyphs (written symbols) for "scribe" and "to write" opened a window on Maya practice; now we know at least one painter of ceramic vessels was the son of a king. Knowledge of the minor arts has also come in large part through an active art market. Thousands more small-scale objects are known now than in the twentieth century, although at a terrible cost to the ancient ruins from which they have been plundered.

8. According to paragraph 4, all of the following are true of Mayanist scholar David Stuart's 1986 discovery EXCEPT:

   (A) It reversed a belief held by earlier scholars.
   (B) It uncovered long lists of royal dynastic records.
   (C) It allowed scholars to understand two glyphs for the first time.
   (D) It revealed that at least one Maya painter was a king's son.

The process of discovery often shapes what we know about the history of Mesoamerican art. New finds are just as often made accidentally as intentionally. **(A)** In 1971 workers installing sound and light equipment under the Pyramid of the Sun at Teotihuacán stumbled upon a remarkable cave that has since been interpreted by some scholars as a royal burial chamber. **(B)** Archaeology has its own fashions too: the isolation of new sites may be the prime goal in one decade and the excavation of pyramids the focus in the next. In a third decade, outlying structures rather than principal buildings may absorb archaeologists' energies. **(C)** Nor should one forget that excavators are vulnerable to local interests. **(D)** At one point, reconstruction of pyramids to attract tourism may be desired; at another, archaeologists may be precluded from working at what has already become a tourist attraction. Also, modern construction often determines which ancient sites can be excavated. In Mexico City, for example, the building of the subway initiated the excavations there and renewed interest in the old Aztec capital.

9. Look at the part of the passage that is displayed above. The letters **(A)**, **(B)**, **(C)**, an **(D)** indicate where the following sentence could be added.

   This chance discovery has done as much for our understanding of the pyramid as any systematic study would have.

   Where would the sentence best fit?
   (A) Choice A
   (B) Choice B
   (C) Choice C
   (D) Choice D

10. **Directions:** An introductory sentence for a brief summary of the passage is provided below. Complete the summary by selecting the THREE answer choices that express the most important ideas in the passage. Some sentences do not belong in the summary because they express ideas that are not presented in the passage or are minor ideas in the passage. **This question is worth 2 points.**

> **Our knowledge of Mesoamerican art has grown since explorers first began searching for ruins of ancient Mesoamerica.**
>
> ●
>
> ●
>
> ●

Answer Choices

A   John Lloyd Stephens and Frederick Catherwood used the ruins of Maya cities in the jungle as evidence that the Maya civilization was older than the Olmec civilization.

B   Often discovered accidentally, Mesoamerican pyramids not only contain numerous samples of native art but also attract tourism.

C   Classic Maya inscriptions primarily recorded calendrical information, astrological incantations, and signatures of artists.

D   Accidental discoveries, fashions in archaeology, and local interests have shaped our knowledge of Mesoamerican art.

E   Much information about Mesoamerican art exists in sixteenth-century writings and in surviving traditions and practices in Mesoamerica.

F   Progress in deciphering ancient writing systems and active art markets have contributed to knowledge of Mesoamerican art.

Directions: Read the passage. Then answer the questions. You have 18 minutes on average to answer the questions.

WHAT IS A COMMUNITY?

The Black Hills forest, the prairie riparian forest, and other forests of the western United States can be separated by the distinctly different combinations of species they comprise. It is easy to distinguish between prairie riparian forest and Black Hills forest—one is a broad-leaved forest of ash and cottonwood trees; the other is a coniferous forest of ponderosa pine and white spruce trees. One has kingbirds; the other, juncos (birds with white outer tail feathers). The fact that ecological communities are indeed recognizable clusters of species led some early ecologists, particularly those living in the beginning of the twentieth century, to claim that communities are highly integrated, precisely balanced assemblages. This claim harkens back to even earlier arguments about the existence of a balance of nature, where every species is there for a specific purpose, like a vital part in a complex machine. Such a belief would suggest that to remove any species, whether it be plant, bird, or insect, would somehow disrupt the balance, and the habitat would begin to deteriorate. Likewise, to add a species may be equally disruptive.

One of these pioneer ecologists was Frederick Clements, who studied ecology extensively throughout the Midwest and other areas in North America. He held that within any given region of climate, ecological communities tended to slowly converge toward a single endpoint, which he called the "climatic climax." This "climax" community was, in Clements's mind, the most well-balanced, integrated grouping of species that could occur within that particular region. Clements even thought that the process of ecological succession—the replacement of some species by others over time—was somewhat akin to the development of an organism, from embryo to adult. Clements thought that succession represented discrete stages in the development of the community (rather like infancy, childhood, and adolescence), terminating in the climatic "adult" stage, when the community became self-reproducing and succession ceased. Clements's view of the ecological community reflected the notion of a precise balance of nature.

Clements was challenged by another pioneer ecologist, Henry Gleason, who took the opposite view. Gleason viewed the community as largely a group of species with similar tolerances to the stresses imposed by climate and other factors typical of the region. Gleason saw the element of chance as important in influencing where species occurred. His concept of the community suggests that nature is not highly integrated. Gleason thought succession could take numerous directions, depending upon local circumstances.

Who was right? Many ecologists have made precise measurements designed to test the assumptions of both the Clements and Gleason models. For instance, along mountain slopes, does one life zone, or habitat type, grade sharply or gradually into another? If the divisions are sharp, perhaps the reason is that the community is so well integrated, so holistic, so like Clements viewed it, that whole clusters of species must remain together. If the divisions are gradual, perhaps, as Gleason suggested, each species is responding individually to its environment, and clusters of species are not so integrated that they must always occur together.

It now appears that Gleason was far closer to the truth than Clements. The ecological community is largely an accidental assemblage of species with similar responses to a particular climate. Green ash trees are found in association with plains cottonwood trees because both can survive well on floodplains and the competition between them is not so strong that only one can persevere. One ecological community often flows into another so gradually that it is next to impossible to say where one leaves off and the other begins. Communities are individualistic.

This is not to say that precise harmonies are not present within communities. Most flowering plants could not exist were it not for their pollinators—and vice versa. Predators, disease organisms, and competitors all influence the abundance and distribution of everything from oak trees to field mice. But if we see a precise balance of nature, it is largely an artifact of our perception, due to the illusion that nature, especially a complex system like a forest, seems so unchanging from one day to the next.

Directions: Now answer the questions.

PARAGRAPH 1

The Black Hills forest, the prairie riparian forest, and other forests of the western United States can be separated by the distinctly different combinations of species they comprise. It is easy to distinguish between prairie riparian forest and Black Hills forest—one is a broad-leaved forest of ash and cottonwood trees; the other is a coniferous forest of ponderosa pine and white spruce trees. One has kingbirds; the other, juncos (birds with white outer tail feathers). The fact that ecological communities are indeed recognizable clusters of species led some early ecologists, particularly those living in the beginning of the twentieth century, to claim that communities are highly integrated, precisely balanced assemblages. This claim harkens back to even earlier arguments about the existence of a balance of nature, where every species is there for a specific purpose, like a vital part in a complex machine. Such a belief would suggest that to remove any species, whether it be plant, bird, or insect, would somehow disrupt the balance, and the habitat would begin to deteriorate. Likewise, to add a species may be equally disruptive.

11. In paragraph 1, why does the author distinguish between prairie riparian forest and Black Hills forest?

    Ⓐ To highlight the difference between the views of various ecologists about the nature of ecological communities

    Ⓑ To illustrate why some ecologists tended to view ecological communities as highly integrated

    Ⓒ To demonstrate that one forest has a greater variety of species than the other

    Ⓓ To show how these two forests differ from others in the United States

12. According to paragraph 1, what was a common claim about ecological communities before the early twentieth century?

    Ⓐ Every species in a community has a specific role in that community.

    Ⓑ It is important to protect communities by removing certain species.

    Ⓒ A precise balance is difficult to maintain in an ecological community.

    Ⓓ It is necessary for new species to be added quickly as ecological communities develop.

13. According to paragraph 1, the belief in a balance of nature suggests that removing a species from an ecological community would have which of the following effects?

   Ⓐ It would reduce competition between the remaining species of the community.

   Ⓑ It would produce a different, but equally balanced, community.

   Ⓒ It would lead to a decline in the community.

   Ⓓ It would cause more harm than adding a species to the community.

PARAGRAPH 2

One of these pioneer ecologists was Frederick Clements, who studied ecology extensively throughout the Midwest and other areas in North America. He held that within any given region of climate, ecological communities tended to slowly converge toward a single endpoint, which he called the "climatic climax." This "climax" community was, in Clements's mind, the most well-balanced, integrated grouping of species that could occur within that particular region. Clements even thought that the process of ecological succession—the replacement of some species by others over time—was somewhat akin to the development of an organism, from embryo to adult. Clements thought that succession represented discrete stages in the development of the community (rather like infancy, childhood, and adolescence), terminating in the climatic "adult" stage, when the community became self-reproducing and succession ceased. Clements's view of the ecological community reflected the notion of a precise balance of nature.

14. Which of the following best represents the view of ecological communities associated with Frederick Clements in paragraph 2 ?

   Ⓐ Only when all species in a community are at the reproductive stage of development is an ecological community precisely balanced.

   Ⓑ When an ecological community achieves "climatic climax," it begins to decline.

   Ⓒ All climates have similar climax communities.

   Ⓓ Ecological communities eventually reach the maximum level of balance that is possible for their region.

PARAGRAPH 3

Clements was challenged by another pioneer ecologist, Henry Gleason, who took the opposite view. Gleason viewed the community as largely a group of species with similar tolerances to the stresses imposed by climate and other factors typical of the region. Gleason saw the element of chance as important in influencing where species occurred. His concept of the community suggests that nature is not highly integrated. Gleason thought succession could take numerous directions, depending upon local circumstances.

15. According to Gleason in paragraph 3, the occurrence of a species in a particular community is influenced by

   Ⓐ unpredictable events

   Ⓑ how individualistic the species is

   Ⓒ the number of other species present

   Ⓓ the tolerance of other species to stresses

PARAGRAPH 4

Who was right? Many ecologists have made precise measurements, designed to test the assumptions of both the Clements and Gleason models. For instance, along mountain slopes, does one life zone, or habitat type, grade sharply or gradually into another? If the divisions are sharp, perhaps the reason is that the community is so well integrated, so holistic, so like Clements viewed it, that whole clusters of species must remain together. If the divisions are gradual, perhaps, as Gleason suggested, each species is responding individually to its environment, and clusters of species are not so integrated that they must always occur together.

16. What did the ecologists in paragraph 4 hope to determine with their measurements?

   (A) Whether different species compete for the same environments
   (B) Whether habitats are sharply separated or gradually flow into each other
   (C) Whether succession differs in different types of habitats
   (D) Whether integrated communities survive better than independent communities

PARAGRAPH 5

It now appears that Gleason was far closer to the truth than Clements. The ecological community is largely an accidental assemblage of species with similar responses to a particular climate. Green ash trees are found in association with plains cottonwood trees because both can survive well on floodplains and the competition between them is not so strong that only one can **persevere**. One ecological community often flows into another so gradually that it is next to impossible to say where one leaves off and the other begins. Communities are individualistic.

17. The word "**persevere**" in the passage is closest in meaning to

   (A) reproduce
   (B) fail
   (C) expand
   (D) continue

PARAGRAPH 6

This is not to say that precise harmonies are not present within communities. Most flowering plants could not exist were it not for their pollinators—and vice versa. Predators, disease organisms, and competitors all influence the abundance and distribution of everything from oak trees to field mice. **But if we see a precise balance of nature, it is largely an artifact of our perception, due to the illusion that nature, especially a complex system like a forest, seems so unchanging from one day to the next.**

18. Which of the sentences below best expresses the essential information in the highlighted sentence in paragraph 6 ? Incorrect choices change the meaning in important ways or leave out essential information.

   (A) We see nature as precisely balanced because nature is unchanging.
   (B) A precise balance of nature is not possible because of the complexity of natural systems.
   (C) Our sense that nature is precisely balanced results from the illusion that it is unchanging.
   (D) Because nature is precisely balanced, complex systems do not seem to change.

PARAGRAPH 4

(A) Who was right? **(B)** Many ecologists have made precise measurements designed to test the assumptions of both the Clements and Gleason models. **(C)** For instance, along mountain slopes, does one life zone, or habitat type, grade sharply or gradually into another? **(D)** If the divisions are sharp, perhaps the reason is that the community is so well integrated, so holistic, so like Clements viewed it, that whole clusters of species must remain together. If the divisions are gradual, perhaps, as Gleason suggested, each species is responding individually to its environment, and clusters of species are not so integrated that they must always occur together.

19. Look at the part of the passage that is displayed above. The letters **(A)**, **(B)**, **(C)**, and **(D)** indicate where the following sentence could be added.

    Their research has helped to decide between the two views because it has focused on questions to which Clements and Gleason would give opposing answers.

    Where would the sentence best fit?
    - (A) Choice A
    - (B) Choice B
    - (C) Choice C
    - (D) Choice D

20. **Directions:** An introductory sentence for a brief summary of the passage is provided below. Complete the summary by selecting the THREE answer choices that express the most important ideas in the passage. Some sentences do not belong in the summary because they express ideas that are not presented in the passage or are minor ideas in the passage. **This question is worth 2 points.**

Write your answer choices in the spaces where they belong. You can either write the letter of your answer choice or you can copy the sentence.

Over time, many views have been formed on the structure of ecological communities.

-
-
-

Answer Choices

A Clements held that ecological communities were like organisms that compete with each other for dominance in a particular climatic region.

B Clements saw the community as a collection of thoroughly interdependent species progressing toward a single climax community.

C Gleason held that within a single climatic region, differing local factors would cause ecological communities to develop in different ways.

D Gleason believed that sharp divisions would exist between species in different habitats.

E Today's ecologists recognize that ecological communities must be precisely and permanently balanced.

F The current thinking is that communities are individualistic and largely accidental collections of species with similar needs and tolerances.

LISTENING

In this section, you will be able to demonstrate your ability to understand conversations and lectures in English.

In the actual test, the section is divided into two separately timed parts. You will hear each conversation or lecture only one time. A clock will indicate how much time remains. The clock will count down only while you are answering questions, not while you are listening. You may take up to 16.5 minutes to answer the questions.

In this practice test, there is no time limit for answering questions.

You may take notes while you listen. You may use your notes to help you answer the questions. Your notes will not be scored.

Answer the questions based on what is stated or implied by the speakers.

In some questions, you will see this icon: 🎧. This means that you will hear, but not see, part of the question.

In the actual test, you must answer each question. You cannot return to previous questions.

At the end of this practice test, you will find an answer key.

Directions: Listen to Track 52.

ekphrastic

William Carlos Williams
Pieter Bruegel

Directions: Now answer the questions.

1. Why does the woman want to talk with the man?

   (A) To give him information he needs to become a docent
   (B) To discuss his role in an upcoming writing competition
   (C) To get his opinion about a competition she is planning
   (D) To find out what he knows about the Art of India exhibit

2. What was the focus of the newspaper advertisement that the woman mentions?

   (A) An ekphrastic poetry course that she helped develop
   (B) A new collection of Indian art at the museum
   (C) A student teaching position at a local high school
   (D) A part-time volunteer position at the art museum

3. What does the woman say about William Carlos Williams' poem "The Hunter in the Snow"?

   (A) It inspired an artist to paint a snowy scene.
   (B) It was inspired by an old landscape painting.
   (C) It is Williams' longest poem.
   (D) It is Williams' best-known poem.

4. What is indicated about the paintings that students will write about for the poetry contest?

   (A) Each student may select up to three paintings.
   (B) Students may write more than one poem about a single painting.
   (C) All the paintings are associated with one specific exhibit.
   (D) All the paintings are by Pieter Bruegel.

5. What is the man's attitude when he learns that he will be giving an hour-long tour in the Art of India exhibit?

   (A) Nervous, because he is not familiar with most of the paintings there
   (B) Disappointed, because the exhibit is not one of his favorites
   (C) Enthusiastic, because he can choose which paintings to talk about
   (D) Surprised, because the Art of India exhibit is relatively small

Directions: Listen to Track 53.

Directions: Now answer the questions.

6. What is the lecture mainly about?

    (A) Ways to limit the expansion of international trade
    (B) How restrictions on international trade can cause economic harm
    (C) Factors that influence the distribution of exports
    (D) Why international trade has expanded in recent years

7. According to the professor, why do many people want imports to be regulated?

    (A) To allow for price increases in domestic products
    (B) To make the prices of exports more competitive
    (C) To protect against domestic unemployment
    (D) To encourage the economic growth of certain industries

8. According to the professor, what is a negative result of limiting imports?

    Ⓐ The pace of technological innovation slows down.

    Ⓑ The number of domestic low-paying jobs decreases.

    Ⓒ People move to areas where income is lower.

    Ⓓ The potential income from exports is reduced.

9. What does the professor imply about the sugar industry in Florida?

    Ⓐ It is a good source of high-paying jobs.

    Ⓑ It should not be protected from competition from imports.

    Ⓒ It is a good example of the effect of international specialization.

    Ⓓ It is managed cost effectively.

10. What does the professor imply about the effect of increasing imports?

    Ⓐ It will eventually result in a decrease in exports.

    Ⓑ It is not necessarily bad for the economy.

    Ⓒ It creates domestic economic problems that are easily solved.

    Ⓓ Its impact on the economy is immediately apparent.

11. What is the professor's opinion of retraining and relocating unemployed people?

    Ⓐ It is more expensive over time than blocking imports.

    Ⓑ It can sometimes have unintended consequences.

    Ⓒ It is one possible way to adapt to an increase in imports.

    Ⓓ It maintains the production levels of inefficient industries.

Directions: Listen to Track 54.

Directions: Now answer the questions.

12. Why does the student go to see her advisor, Professor Anderson?

   Ⓐ She wants Professor Anderson's help with her research.
   Ⓑ She is responding to Professor Anderson's invitation.
   Ⓒ She has a complaint about another professor.
   Ⓓ She wants to get a letter of recommendation to law school.

13. Why does the student mention Professor Connelly's class?

   Ⓐ She was not happy with the grade she received in the class.
   Ⓑ She might be able to expand the research she did in the class.
   Ⓒ It was the most difficult class she ever took.
   Ⓓ Professor Connelly took the class on a trip to Venezuela.

14. What does the student tell Professor Anderson she will do before their next meeting?

   Ⓐ Register for Professor Connelly's class
   Ⓑ Begin to write her honors thesis
   Ⓒ Turn in her honors project to Professor Connelly
   Ⓓ Talk to Professor Connelly about doing an honors project

15. *Listen to Track 55 to answer the question.*

   What does Professor Anderson imply when he says this?

   Ⓐ Very few students are asked to consider writing an honors thesis.
   Ⓑ The woman has shown poor research skills in the past.
   Ⓒ An honors thesis could help the woman get into law school.
   Ⓓ The woman should write a proposal outlining her research skills.

16. *Listen to Track 56 to answer the question.*

   What does the woman imply when she says this?

   Ⓐ She is uncertain about her ability to write an honors thesis.
   Ⓑ She does not think an honors thesis would be useful to her.
   Ⓒ She considers herself to be a good writer.
   Ⓓ She has only written one research paper before.

Directions: Listen to Track 57.

Journalism

Directions: Now answer the questions.

17. What is the lecture mainly about?

    Ⓐ Why some newspapers do not improve their services

    Ⓑ What newspapers can do to increase their readership

    Ⓒ Why local newspapers cannot compete with major newspapers

    Ⓓ How the topics that interest readers have changed over the years

18. According to the professor, what topics are newspaper readers most interested in?
Select 2 answers.

    Ａ Political issues

    Ｂ Entertainment and weather

    Ｃ Natural disasters and accidents

    Ｄ Ordinary people

19. According to the professor, how can newspapers attract readers to serious stories?

    Ⓐ By including photos that provide background information

    Ⓑ By making minor revisions to the content of the story

    Ⓒ By making the format more appealing to readers

    Ⓓ By gradually increasing the number of serious stories

20. What does the professor imply about the use of colors in newspapers?

    Ⓐ It has been greatly influenced by reader preferences.

    Ⓑ It is more effective than early research indicated.

    Ⓒ It has not resulted in significant increases in the number of readers.

    Ⓓ It has been neglected in the study of journalism.

21. *Listen to Track 58 to answer the question.*

    What does the student imply when he says this?

    Ⓐ He agrees with the professor completely.
    Ⓑ He is surprised by the professor's point of view.
    Ⓒ He is not familiar with the topic the professor is discussing.
    Ⓓ He can offer a solution to the problem being discussed.

22. *Listen again to part of the lecture by playing Track 59.* *Then answer the question.*

    What does the professor imply when he says this?

    Ⓐ He fully supports the student's statement.
    Ⓑ His experience this morning was unexpected.
    Ⓒ He was not affected by what happened this morning.
    Ⓓ The student should not complain.

Directions: Listen to Track 60.

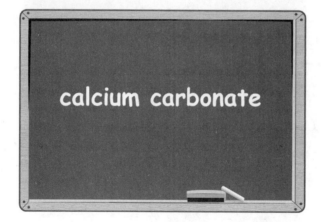

Directions: Now answer the questions.

23. What aspect of the Earth 750 million years ago is the lecture mainly about?

   Ⓐ The changes in locations of the continents
   Ⓑ The effect of greenhouse gases on the atmosphere
   Ⓒ Factors that influenced the ocean currents
   Ⓓ Factors that contributed to a global freeze

24. According to the professor, how do geologists interpret the presence of erratics in the tropics?

   Ⓐ It indicates that carbon-dioxide levels were once higher there.
   Ⓑ It is evidence of global glaciation.
   Ⓒ It indicates that the Earth may cool off at some point in the future.
   Ⓓ It is evidence that some glaciers originated there.

25. What is the ice-albedo effect?

   Ⓐ Global warming is balanced by carbon dioxide in the oceans.
   Ⓑ Solar radiation retained in the atmosphere melts ice.
   Ⓒ Large amounts of carbon dioxide are removed from the atmosphere.
   Ⓓ Reflection of heat by glaciers contributes to their growth.

26. What is the relationship between carbon dioxide and silicate rocks?

   Ⓐ Silicate rocks are largely composed of carbon dioxide.
   Ⓑ Silicate rocks contribute to the creation of carbon dioxide.
   Ⓒ The erosion of silicate rocks reduces carbon-dioxide levels in the atmosphere.
   Ⓓ The formation of silicate rocks removes carbon dioxide from the oceans.

27. What was one feature of the Earth that contributed to the runaway freeze 750 million years ago?

    Ⓐ Carbon-dioxide levels in the oceans were low.

    Ⓑ The continents were located close to the equator.

    Ⓒ The movement of glaciers carried away large quantities of rock.

    Ⓓ The level of greenhouse gases in the atmosphere was high.

28. *Listen to Track 61 to answer the question.*

    Why does the professor say this?

    Ⓐ To compare an unfamiliar object to a familiar one

    Ⓑ To reveal evidence that contradicts his point

    Ⓒ To indicate uncertainty as to what deposits from glaciers look like

    Ⓓ To encourage students to examine rocks in streams

SPEAKING

In this section, you will be able to demonstrate your ability to speak about a variety of topics.

In the actual test, the Speaking section will last approximately 16 minutes. You will answer four questions by speaking into the microphone. You may take notes while you listen. You may use your notes to help you answer the questions. Your notes will not be scored. For each question, you will have time to prepare before giving your response. You should answer the questions as completely as possible in the time allowed.

For this practice test, you may want to use a personal recording device to record and play back your responses.

For each question, play the audio track listed and follow the directions to complete the task.

At the end of this practice test, you will find important points about each question.

1. You will now give your opinion about a familiar topic. After you hear the question, you should give yourself 15 seconds to prepare and 45 seconds to speak.

    Listen to Track 62.

    > When some people visit a city or country for the first time, they prefer to take an organized tour. Other people prefer to explore new places on their own. Which do you prefer and why?
    >
    > | **Preparation Time: 15 seconds** |
    > |---|
    > | **Response Time: 45 seconds** |

2. Now you will read a passage about a campus situation and then listen to a conversation about the same topic. You will then answer a question, using information from both the reading passage and the conversation. You should give yourself 30 seconds to prepare and 60 seconds to speak.

    Listen to Track 63.

Reading Time: 45 seconds

    > **Professor Fox Accepts New Position**
    >
    > We are happy to announce that Professor Fox will be filling the vacant dean of students position. Strong organizational skills are important for this position. Professor Fox has demonstrated such skills in her role as head of the philosophy department, where she has coordinated department affairs for five years. Additionally, the dean of students must be someone who is able to work well with students, since responsibilities include counseling and advising students who are dealing with personal problems. As our head women's soccer coach, Professor Fox has proven to be a supportive role model for team members, always offering assistance when they ask for personal guidance.

Listen to Track 64.

The woman expresses her opinion about the change described in the article. Briefly summarize the change. Then state her opinion about the change and explain the reasons she gives for holding that opinion.

Preparation Time: 30 seconds
Response Time: 60 seconds

3. Now you will read a passage about an academic subject and then listen to a lecture on the same topic. You will then answer a question, using information from both the reading passage and the lecture. You should give yourself 30 seconds to prepare and 60 seconds to speak.

Listen to Track 65.

Reading Time: 45 seconds

Critical Period

It is generally believed that for many organisms, there is a specific time period, a so-called "window of opportunity," during which the organism must receive crucial input from its environment in order for normal development to occur. This period is called the *critical period*. If the needed environmental input is not received during this period, the normal development of certain physical attributes or behaviors may never occur. In other words, if the organism is not provided with the needed stimulus or influence during the critical period, it may permanently lose the capacity to ever obtain a particular physical attribute or behavior.

Listen to Track 66.

Using the examples of kittens and geese, explain the idea of a critical period.

Preparation Time: 30 seconds
Response Time: 60 seconds

4. Now you will listen to a lecture. You will then be asked to summarize the lecture. You should give yourself 20 seconds to prepare and 60 seconds to speak.

Listen to Track 67.

Using the example of the vacuum cleaner, explain when it is legally acceptable to use exaggeration in advertising and when it is not.

Preparation Time: 20 seconds
Response Time: 60 seconds

WRITING

In this section, you will be able to demonstrate your ability to use writing to communicate in an academic environment. There will be two writing tasks.

At the end of this practice test, you will find topic notes for each question.

Turn the page to see the directions for the first writing task.

Writing Based on Reading and Listening

For this task, you will read a passage about an academic topic. Then you will listen to a lecture about the same topic. You may take notes while you listen.

In your response, provide a detailed summary of the lecture and explain how the lecture relates to the reading passage.

In the actual test, you will have 3 minutes to read the passage and 20 minutes to write your response. While you write, you will be able to see the reading passage. If you finish your response before time is up, you may go on to the second writing task.

Reading Time: 3 minutes

Many people dream of owning their own business but are afraid of the risks. Instead of starting a new business, however, one can buy a franchise. A franchise is a license issued by a large, usually well-known, company to a small business owner. Under the license, the owner acquires the right to use the company's brand name and agrees to sell its products. In return, the franchising company receives a percent of the sales.

A major problem for first-time business owners is finding reliable suppliers of the goods and services they need: equipment, raw materials, maintenance, etc. It is easy to choose the wrong supplier, and doing so can be costly. Buying a franchise eliminates much of this problem. Most franchising companies have already found reliable suppliers, and franchise contracts typically specify which suppliers are to be used. This protects franchise owners from the risk of serious losses.

Another advantage of a franchise is that it can save a new business a lot of money on advertising. Advertising one's product to potential customers is a crucial factor in a business's success. A franchise owner, however, sells an already popular and recognized brand and also gets the benefit of sophisticated and expensive advertising paid by the parent company.

Finally, a franchise offers more security than starting an independent (nonfranchise) business. The failure rate for starting independent businesses is very high during the first few years; the failure rate for starting franchises is much lower. Finding one's own way in today's competitive business environment is difficult, and buying a franchise allows an inexperienced business owner to use a proven business model.

Listen to Track 68.

Directions: You have 20 minutes to plan and write your response. Your response will be judged on the basis of the quality of your writing and on how well your response presents the points in the lecture and their relationship to the reading passage. Typically, an effective response will contain a minimum of 150 words.

Listen to Track 69.

Response Time: 20 minutes

Question 1

Summarize the points made in the lecture, being sure to explain how they challenge specific points made in the reading passage.

_____

_____

_____

_____

_____

_____

_____

_____

_____

_____

Writing for an Academic Discussion

For this task, you will read an online discussion. A professor has posted a question about a topic, and some classmates have responded with their ideas.

In the actual test, you will have 10 minutes to write a response that contributes to the discussion.

Question 2

Your professor is teaching a class on sociology. Write a post responding to the professor's question.

In your response, you should do the following.

- Express and support your opinion.
- Make a contribution to the discussion in your own words.

An effective response will contain at least 100 words.

Dr. Diaz

As we discuss rules that societies expect their members to follow, let's focus specifically on how young people perceive those rules. Sometimes young people consider those rules to be too strict or unfair, and they take action to try to loosen the rules or change them. How important is it for young people to try to change rules that they consider to be unfair?

Kelly

It is so easy for some young people to get into trouble with illegal things. Parents should create rules to prevent that, and kids should not challenge those rules. Kids do not have the life experience to understand how, for example, their parents' rules about not staying out late at night are helping them stay out of trouble.

Paul

As a young person, I think the society I live in has certain rules that are in many respects unwise and unfair; for example, the rules in my country do not allow teachers to discuss certain controversial subjects in school that are important to young people. Young people should challenge those rules.

Response Time: 10 minutes

ANSWERS

Reading Section

1. D
2. C
3. B
4. B
5. B
6. A
7. C
8. B
9. B
10. D, E. F

11. B
12. A
13. C
14. D
15. A
16. B
17. D
18. C
19. C
20. B, C, F

Listening Section

1. B
2. D
3. B
4. C
5. A
6. B
7. C
8. D
9. B
10. B
11. C
12. B
13. B
14. D

15. C
16. A
17. B
18. B, D
19. C
20. C
21. B
22. A
23. D
24. B
25. D
26. C
27. B
28. A

Speaking Section

1.   To respond to this particular question, you should clearly state what your opinion is: do you prefer to take an organized tour when visiting a place for the first time, or do you prefer to explore the new place on your own? There is no "correct" answer to this question. Whichever option you prefer, your answer should be supported with examples.

   If you think that it is better to take an organized tour, you could say that a tour is better, especially if you do not know much about the new place. You might not know where to go or what to see. Plus, the guide will have more knowledge than you do. You might give a specific example of a tour that you have been on yourself.

   If you prefer to explore a place on your own, you might say that a tour would limit you, because you would be told where to go. There might be a situation where you want to stay in one place for a longer time, but the tour would not allow this. In this case, you could also give a specific example of a time when you explored a place on your own and why this was good.

   It is important to make sure that you state your opinion and develop your response with good examples and relevant details.

   Your response should be intelligible, should demonstrate effective use of grammar and vocabulary, and should be well-developed and coherent. Your response is scored using the Independent Speaking Rubric (see Appendix A).

2.   To respond to this particular question, you should state the woman's opinion of the university's decision to give the position of dean of students to Professor Fox. In this case, the woman disagrees with the decision.

   After stating that the woman disagrees with the decision, you should convey the two main reasons she gives for holding that opinion. You will need to connect information from the conversation to the reading in order for the response to be complete. The woman says that the first reason given for appointing Professor Fox—that she has strong organizational skills—is not valid. You should provide as her explanation either that some classes were cancelled because Professor Fox did not organize enough teaching assistants or that she missed a philosophy course in Europe because Professor Fox did not sign her paperwork in time.

   Your response should also convey the woman's second reason for not agreeing with the university's decision to make Professor Fox the dean of students. The woman disagrees that Professor Fox works well with students. As support, she says that Professor Fox has an aggressive coaching style. She also gives an example of her friend who was criticized by Professor Fox when she was looking for emotional support. This shows that, in the woman's opinion, Professor Fox would not be a good dean of students.

   As you need to discuss *both* of the woman's reasons for disagreeing with the university's decision, you should not include too much detail from the reading or concentrate too much on one of the reasons. Give yourself enough time to discuss both reasons.

   Your response should be intelligible, should demonstrate effective use of grammar and vocabulary, and should be well-developed and coherent. Your response is scored using the Integrated Speaking Rubric (see Appendix A).

3.   To respond to this particular question, you should first explain the idea of a critical period as it was presented in the reading. The critical period is a specific time period for many organisms. Organisms must receive external or environmental input during this critical period in order to develop normally. Do not spend too much time summarizing all of the content of the reading.

   You should then use the examples given by the professor to explain critical periods. In the first example, the professor discusses a critical period that affects a physical attribute. Vision in kittens will not develop normally if they are not exposed to light within the first four months of life. In the second example, the professor discusses a critical period affecting a behavior. Baby geese will adopt whatever large moving object they first see within the first two days of their lives as their parent. They will follow this "parent" even if it's a different species. That behavior cannot be changed even if a real goose reappears.

You do not need to repeat all of the details from the reading and the lecture, but instead integrate points from both to answer the question completely. For this question, you need to give yourself enough time to talk about both examples.

Your response should be intelligible, should demonstrate effective use of grammar and vocabulary, and should be well-developed and coherent. Your response is scored using the Integrated Speaking Rubric (see Appendix A).

4.	This particular question requires you to summarize the contents of a lecture you hear. In your response, you should talk about exaggeration in advertising, including the examples of when it is legal to use exaggeration and when it is not legal to use exaggeration.

You should begin with a general statement about the lecture, such as that exaggeration in advertising has to be so extreme that nobody will believe it. If it isn't, this advertising may be illegal. You would then talk about the first example that the professor gives. An advertiser that wanted

to make the point that its vacuum cleaner is very light showed it in a television ad floating in the air. This kind of advertisement was legal because no one would really believe that a vacuum cleaner floated in the air.

You should then talk about the professor's second example. The professor says that if the company showed the vacuum cleaner cleaning a big dirty carpet in just a few seconds, then this would be considered an unacceptable exaggeration because someone might actually believe it. We can imagine someone buying the vacuum cleaner and being disappointed that it didn't work that well.

You should read the question carefully and respond with the appropriate information. This question clearly directs you to talk about a time when it is acceptable to use exaggeration and a time when it is not acceptable. You should budget your time so that you are able to talk about both examples.

Your response should be intelligible, should demonstrate effective use of grammar and vocabulary, and should be well-developed and coherent. Your response is scored using the Integrated Speaking Rubric (see Appendix A).

Writing Section

1.	What is important to understand from the lecture is that the professor disagrees with the advantages of buying franchises presented in the reading, namely that a franchise owner does not have to look for suppliers; that a franchise owner gets the benefit of advertising done by the parent company; and that franchises provide more security than other types of business.

In your response, you should convey the reasons presented by the professor for why buying a franchise is not the best way of becoming a business owner. A high-scoring response will include the following points made by the professor that cast doubt on the points made in the reading.

Point made in the reading	Counterpoint made in the lecture
Since franchising companies have already selected reliable suppliers for franchise owners to use, a new franchise owner does not run the risk of working with unreliable suppliers.	A franchise owner is forced to use the suppliers identified by the parent company. Such suppliers often charge too much for their goods and services. A franchise owner cannot use cheaper suppliers that may be available.
Franchise owners save money on advertising because they sell well-known brands and because they get the benefit of advertising paid for by the parent companies.	In fact, franchise owners have to pay a portion of their income to the parent company in return for advertising services. However, advertising by the parent company focuses on the brand and not on the owner's individual business. Owners would get greater benefit for less money if they did their own advertising.
Buying a franchise offers very good security. The failure rate of starting franchises is much lower than the failure rate of starting independent businesses.	There is in fact an option for starting business owners that is more secure than buying a franchise: buying an already-existing independent business. Independent businesses bought from previous owners have twice as much chance of success as new franchises.

Your response is scored using the Integrated Writing Rubric (see Appendix A). A response that receives a score of 5 clearly conveys all three of the main points in the table using accurate sentence structure and vocabulary.

2. To earn a top score, you should develop a response that contributes to the discussion about the importance of young people changing societal rules. An effective response will contain at least 100 words.

One discussion participant argues that young people should not change rules because these rules were set by parents, who are more experienced than young people, for reasons that include preventing young people from getting in trouble. Another discussion participant argues that many rules set by society are unfair and should therefore be challenged by young people. You might seize on the ideas already stated and develop them in greater detail or introduce entirely new ideas. You may argue, for example, that rules should be changed by young people because the world is always in flux, and as times change, rules should change as well.

You should make sure that your ideas are well-supported by reasons and examples and are expressed clearly. Since your response represents an online post, it does not need to be organized into separate paragraphs. However, your ideas need to be well-connected, coherent, and clear. Your response is scored using the Writing for an Academic Discussion Rubric (see Appendix A).

TOEFL iBT® Test 5

READING

In this section, you will be able to demonstrate your ability to understand academic passages in English. You will read and answer questions about **two passages**.

In the actual test, you will have 36 minutes total to read both passages and answer the questions. A clock will indicate how much time remains.

Some passages may include one or more notes explaining words or phrases. The words or phrases are marked with footnote numbers, and the notes explaining them appear at the end of the passage.

Most questions are worth 1 point, but the last question for each passage is worth 2 points.

You may review and revise your answers in this section as long as time remains.

At the end of this practice test, you will find an answer key.

Directions: Read the passage. Then answer the questions. You have 18 minutes on average to answer the questions.

HABITATS AND CHIPMUNK SPECIES

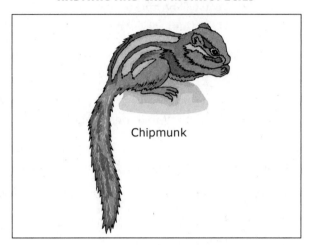

Chipmunk

There are eight chipmunk species in the Sierra Nevada mountain range, and most of them look pretty much alike. But eight different species of chipmunks scurrying around a picnic area will not be found. Nowhere in the Sierra do all eight species occur together. Each species tends strongly to occupy a specific habitat type, within an elevational range, and the overlap among them is minimal.

The eight chipmunk species of the Sierra Nevada represent but a few of the fifteen species found in western North America, yet the whole of eastern North America makes do with but one species: the Eastern chipmunk. Why are there so many very similar chipmunks in the West? The presence of tall mountains interspersed with vast areas of arid desert and grassland makes the West ecologically far different from the East. The West affords much more opportunity for chipmunk populations to become geographically isolated from one another, a condition of species formation. Also, there are more extremes in western habitats. In the Sierra Nevada, high elevations are close to low elevations, at least in terms of mileage, but ecologically they are very different.

Most ecologists believe that ancient populations of chipmunks diverged genetically when isolated from one another by mountains and unfavorable ecological habitat. These scattered populations first evolved into races—adapted to the local ecological conditions—and then into species, reproductively isolated from one another. This period of evolution was relatively recent, as evidenced by the similar appearance of all the western chipmunk species.

Ecologists have studied the four chipmunk species that occur on the eastern slope of the Sierra and have learned just how these species interact while remaining separate, each occupying its own elevational zone. The sagebrush chipmunk is found at the lowest elevation, among the sagebrush. The yellow pine chipmunk is common in low to mid-elevations and open conifer forests, including piñon and ponderosa and Jeffrey pine forests. The lodgepole chipmunk is found at higher elevations, among the lodgepoles, firs, and high-elevation pines. The alpine chipmunk is higher still, venturing among the talus slopes, alpine meadows, and high-elevation pines and junipers. Obviously, the ranges of each species overlap. Why don't sagebrush chipmunks move into the pine zones? Why don't alpine chipmunks move to lower elevations and share the conifer forests with lodgepole chipmunks?

The answer, in one word, is aggression. Chipmunk species actively defend their ecological zones from encroachment by neighboring species. The yellow pine chipmunk is more aggressive than the sagebrush chipmunk, possibly because it is a bit larger. It successfully bullies its smaller evolutionary cousin, excluding it from the pine forests. Experiments have shown that the sagebrush chipmunk is physiologically able to live anywhere in the Sierra Nevada, from high alpine zones to the desert. The little creature is apparently restricted to the desert not because it is specialized to live only there but because that is the only habitat where none of the other chipmunk species can live. The fact that sagebrush chipmunks tolerate very warm temperatures makes them, and only them, able to live where they do. The sagebrush chipmunk essentially occupies its habitat by default. In one study, ecologists established that yellow pine chipmunks actively exclude sagebrush chipmunks from pine forests; the ecologists simply trapped all the yellow pine chipmunks in a section of forest and moved them out. Sagebrush chipmunks immediately moved in, but yellow pine chipmunks did not enter sagebrush desert when sagebrush chipmunks were removed.

The most aggressive of the four eastern-slope species is the lodgepole chipmunk, a feisty rodent indeed. It actively prevents alpine chipmunks from moving downslope and yellow pine chipmunks from moving upslope. There is logic behind the lodgepole's aggressive demeanor. It lives in the cool, shaded conifer forests, and of the four species, it is the least able to tolerate heat stress. It is, in other words, the species of the strictest habitat needs: it simply must be in those shaded forests. However, if it shared its habitat with alpine and yellow pine chipmunks, either or both of these species might outcompete it, taking most of the available food. Such a competition could effectively eliminate lodgepole chipmunks from the habitat. Lodgepoles survive only by virtue of their aggression.

Directions: Now answer the questions.

**P
A
R
A
G
R
A
P
H

2**

The eight chipmunk species of the Sierra Nevada represent but a few of the fifteen species found in western North America, yet the whole of eastern North America makes do with but one species: the Eastern chipmunk. Why are there so many very similar chipmunks in the West? The presence of tall mountains interspersed with vast areas of arid desert and grassland makes the West ecologically far different from the East. The West affords much more opportunity for chipmunk populations to become geographically isolated from one another, a condition of species formation. Also, there are more extremes in western habitats. In the Sierra Nevada, high elevations are close to low elevations, at least in terms of mileage, but ecologically they are very different.

1. In paragraph 2, the author indicates that a large variety of chipmunk species exist in western North America because of

    Ⓐ a large migration of chipmunks from eastern North America in an earlier period

    Ⓑ the inability of chipmunks to adapt to the high mountainous regions of eastern North America

    Ⓒ the ecological variety and extremes of the West that caused chipmunks to become geographically isolated

    Ⓓ the absence of large human populations that discouraged species formation among chipmunks in the East

PARAGRAPH 3

Most ecologists believe that ancient populations of chipmunks **diverged** genetically when isolated from one another by mountains and unfavorable ecological habitat. These scattered populations first evolved into races—adapted to the local ecological conditions—and then into species, reproductively isolated from one another. This period of evolution was relatively recent, as evidenced by the similar appearance of all the western chipmunk species.

2. The word "**diverged**" in the passage is closest in meaning to

    (A) declined
    (B) competed
    (C) progressed
    (D) separated

PARAGRAPH 4

Ecologists have studied the four chipmunk species that occur on the eastern slope of the Sierra and have learned just how these species interact while remaining separate, each occupying its own elevational zone. The sagebrush chipmunk is found at the lowest elevation, among the sagebrush. The yellow pine chipmunk is common in low to mid-elevations and open conifer forests, including piñon and ponderosa and Jeffrey pine forests. The lodgepole chipmunk is found at higher elevations, among the lodgepoles, firs, and high-elevation pines. The alpine chipmunk is higher still, venturing among the talus slopes, alpine meadows, and high-elevation pines and junipers. Obviously, the ranges of each species overlap. Why don't sagebrush chipmunks move into the pine zones? Why don't alpine chipmunks move to lower elevations and share the conifer forests with lodgepole chipmunks?

3. Which of the sentences below best expresses the essential information in the highlighted sentence in paragraph 4 ? Incorrect choices change the meaning in important ways or leave out essential information.

    (A) Ecologists studied how the geographic characteristics of the eastern slope of the Sierra influenced the social development of chipmunks.
    (B) Ecologists learned exactly how chipmunk species separated from each other on the eastern slope of the Sierra relate to one another.
    (C) Ecologists discovered that chipmunks of the eastern slope of the Sierra invade and occupy higher elevational zones when threatened by another species.
    (D) Ecologists studied how individual chipmunks of the eastern slope of the Sierra avoid interacting with others of their species.

4. Where does paragraph 4 indicate that the yellow pine chipmunk can be found in relationship to the other species of the eastern slope of the Sierra?

    (A) Below the sagebrush chipmunk
    (B) Above the alpine chipmunk
    (C) At the same elevation as the sagebrush chipmunk
    (D) Below the lodgepole chipmunk

P
A
R
A
G
R
A
P
H

5

The answer, in one word, is aggression. Chipmunk species actively defend their ecological zones from **encroachment** by neighboring species. The yellow pine chipmunk is more aggressive than the sagebrush chipmunk, possibly because it is a bit larger. It successfully bullies its smaller evolutionary cousin, excluding it from the pine forests. Experiments have shown that the sagebrush chipmunk is physiologically able to live anywhere in the Sierra Nevada, from high alpine zones to the desert. The little creature is apparently restricted to the desert not because it is specialized to live only there but because that is the only habitat where none of the other chipmunk species can live. The fact that sagebrush chipmunks tolerate very warm temperatures makes them, and only them, able to live where they do. The sagebrush chipmunk essentially occupies its habitat by default. In one study, ecologists established that yellow pine chipmunks actively exclude sagebrush chipmunks from pine forests; the ecologists simply trapped all the yellow pine chipmunks in a section of forest and moved them out. Sagebrush chipmunks immediately moved in, but yellow pine chipmunks did not enter sagebrush desert when sagebrush chipmunks were removed.

5. The word "**encroachment**" in the passage is closest in meaning to

    (A) complete destruction
    (B) gradual invasion
    (C) excessive development
    (D) substitution

6. Paragraph 5 mentions all of the following as true of the relationship of sagebrush chipmunks to their habitats EXCEPT:

    (A) Sagebrush chipmunks are able to survive in any habitat of the Sierra Nevada.
    (B) Sagebrush chipmunks occupy their habitat because of the absence of competition from other chipmunks.
    (C) Sagebrush chipmunks are better able to survive in hot temperatures than other species of chipmunks.
    (D) Sagebrush chipmunks spend the warm season at the higher elevations of the alpine zone.

7. Which of the following statements is supported by the results of the experiment described at the end of paragraph 5 ?

    (A) The habitat of the yellow pine chipmunk is a desirable one to other species, but the habitat of the sagebrush chipmunk is not.
    (B) It was more difficult to remove sagebrush chipmunks from their habitat than it was to remove yellow pine chipmunks from theirs.
    (C) Yellow pine chipmunks and sagebrush chipmunks require the same environmental conditions in their habitats.
    (D) The temperature of the habitat is not an important factor to either the yellow pine chipmunk or the sagebrush chipmunk.

The most aggressive of the four eastern-slope species is the lodgepole chipmunk, a feisty rodent indeed. It actively prevents alpine chipmunks from moving downslope and yellow pine chipmunks from moving upslope. There is logic behind the lodgepole's aggressive demeanor. It lives in the cool, shaded conifer forests, and of the four species, it is the least able to tolerate heat stress. It is, in other words, the species of the strictest habitat needs: it simply must be in those shaded forests. However, if it shared its habitat with alpine and yellow pine chipmunks, either or both of these species might outcompete it, taking most of the available food. Such a competition could effectively eliminate lodgepole chipmunks from the habitat. Lodgepoles survive only by virtue of their aggression.

8. According to paragraph 6, why is the lodgepole chipmunk so protective of its habitat from competing chipmunks?

    Ⓐ It has specialized food requirements.
    Ⓑ It cannot tolerate cold temperatures well.
    Ⓒ It requires the shade provided by forest trees.
    Ⓓ It prefers to be able to move between areas that are downslope and upslope.

Ecologists have studied the four chipmunk species that occur on the eastern slope of the Sierra and have learned just how these species interact while remaining separate, each occupying its own elevational zone. The sagebrush chipmunk is found at the lowest elevation, among the sagebrush. The yellow pine chipmunk is common in low to mid-elevations and open conifer forests, including piñon and ponderosa and Jeffrey pine forests. The lodgepole chipmunk is found at higher elevations, among the lodgepoles, firs, and high-elevation pines. The alpine chipmunk is higher still, venturing among the talus slopes, alpine meadows, and high-elevation pines and junipers. **(A)** Obviously, the ranges of each species overlap. **(B)** Why don't sagebrush chipmunks move into the pine zones? **(C)** Why don't alpine chipmunks move to lower elevations and share the conifer forests with lodgepole chipmunks? **(D)**

9. Look at the part of the passage that is displayed above. The letters **(A)**, **(B)**, **(C)**, and **(D)** indicate where the following sentence could be added.

    Yet each species remains within a fairly well-defined elevational zone.

    Where would the sentence best fit?

    Ⓐ Choice A
    Ⓑ Choice B
    Ⓒ Choice C
    Ⓓ Choice D

10. **Directions**: An introductory sentence for a brief summary of the passage is provided below. Complete the summary by selecting the THREE answer choices that express the most important ideas in the passage. Some sentences do not belong in the summary because they express ideas that are not presented in the passage or are minor ideas in the passage. **This question is worth 2 points.**

Write your answer choices in the spaces where they belong. You can either write the letter of your answer choice or you can copy the sentence.

A variety of chipmunk species inhabit western North America.

-
-
-

Answer Choices

A Ecological variation of the Sierra Nevada resulted in the differentiation of chipmunk species.

B Only one species of chipmunk inhabits eastern North America.

C Although some chipmunk species of the Sierra Nevada have the ability to live at various elevations, each species inhabits a specifically restricted one.

D Chipmunks aggressively defend their habitats from invasion by other species of chipmunks.

E Experimental studies indicate that sagebrush chipmunks live in the desert because of their physiological requirements.

F The most aggressive of the chipmunk species is the lodgepole chipmunk.

Directions: Read the passage. Then answer the questions. You have 18 minutes on average to answer the questions.

A MODEL OF URBAN EXPANSION

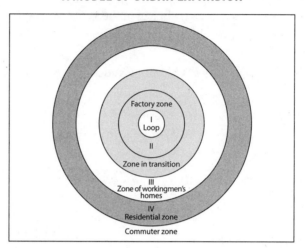

In the early twentieth century, the science of sociology found supporters in the United States and Canada partly because the cities there were growing so rapidly. It often appeared that North American cities would be unable to absorb all the newcomers arriving in such large numbers. Presociological thinkers like Frederick Law Olmsted, the founder of the movement to build parks and recreation areas in cities, and Jacob Riis, an advocate of slum reform, urged the nation's leaders to invest in improving the urban environment, building parks and beaches, and making better housing available to all. These reform efforts were greatly aided by sociologists who conducted empirical research on the social conditions in cities. In the early twentieth century, many sociologists lived in cities like Chicago that were characterized by rapid population growth and serious social problems. It seemed logical to use empirical research to construct theories about how cities grow and change in response to major social forces as well as more controlled urban planning.

The founders of the Chicago school of sociology, Robert Park and Ernest Burgess, attempted to develop a dynamic model of the city, one that would account not only for the expansion of cities in terms of population and territory but also for the patterns of settlement and land use within cities. They identified several factors that influence the physical form of cities. As Park stated, among them are "transportation and communication, tramways and telephones, newspapers and advertising, steel construction and elevators—all things, in fact, which tend to bring about at once a greater mobility and a greater concentration of the urban populations."

Park and Burgess based their model of urban growth on the concept of "natural areas"— that is, areas such as occupational suburbs or residential enclaves in which the population is relatively homogeneous and land is used in similar ways without deliberate planning. Park and Burgess saw urban expansion as occurring through a series of "invasions" of successive zones or areas surrounding the center of the city. For example, people from rural areas and other societies "invaded" areas where housing was inexpensive. Those areas tended to be close to the places where they worked. In turn, people who could afford better housing and the cost of commuting "invaded" areas farther from the business district.

Park and Burgess's model has come to be known as the "concentric-zone model" (represented by the figure). Because the model was originally based on studies of Chicago, its center is labeled "Loop," the term commonly applied to that city's central commercial zone. Surrounding the central zone is a "zone in transition," an area that is being invaded by business and light manufacturing. The third zone is inhabited by workers who do not want to live in the factory or business district but at the same time need to live reasonably close to where they work. The fourth or residential zone consists of upscale apartment buildings and single-family homes. And the outermost ring, outside the city limits, is the suburban or commuters' zone; its residents live within a 30- to 60-minute ride of the central business district.

Studies by Park, Burgess, and other Chicago-school sociologists showed how new groups of immigrants tended to be concentrated in separate areas within inner-city zones, where they sometimes experienced tension with other ethnic groups that had arrived earlier. Over time, however, each group was able to adjust to life in the city and to find a place for itself in the urban economy. Eventually many of the immigrants moved to unsegregated areas in outer zones; the areas they left behind were promptly occupied by new waves of immigrants.

The Park and Burgess model of growth in zones and natural areas of the city can still be used to describe patterns of growth in cities that were built around a central business district and that continue to attract large numbers of immigrants. But this model is biased toward the commercial and industrial cities of North America, which have tended to form around business centers rather than around palaces or cathedrals, as is often the case in some other parts of the world. Moreover, it fails to account for other patterns of urbanization, such as the rapid urbanization that occurs along commercial transportation corridors and the rise of nearby satellite cities.

Directions: Now answer the questions.

PARAGRAPH 1

In the early twentieth century, the science of sociology found supporters in the United States and Canada partly because the cities there were growing so rapidly. It often appeared that North American cities would be unable to absorb all the newcomers arriving in such large numbers. Presociological thinkers like Frederick Law Olmsted, the founder of the movement to build parks and recreation areas in cities, and Jacob Riis, an advocate of slum reform, urged the nation's leaders to invest in improving the urban environment, building parks and beaches, and making better housing available to all. These reform efforts were greatly aided by sociologists who conducted empirical research on the social conditions in cities. In the early twentieth century, many sociologists lived in cities like Chicago that were characterized by rapid population growth and serious social problems. It seemed logical to use empirical research to construct theories about how cities grow and change in response to major social forces as well as more controlled urban planning.

11. Which of the following can be inferred from paragraph 1 about what Olmsted and Riis had in common?

Ⓐ Both constructed theories based on empirical research on cities.
Ⓑ Both were among a large number of newcomers to North American cities.
Ⓒ Both wanted to improve the conditions of life in cities.
Ⓓ Both hoped to reduce the rapid growth of large cities.

12. Which of the following best states the relationship that Olmsted and Riis had to the study of sociology?

   Ⓐ Their goals were supported by the research conducted later by sociologists.
   Ⓑ Their approach led them to oppose empirical sociological studies.
   Ⓒ They had difficulty establishing that their work was as important as sociological research.
   Ⓓ They used evidence from sociological research to urge national leaders to invest in urban development.

PARAGRAPH 2

The founders of the Chicago school of sociology, Robert Park and Ernest Burgess, attempted to develop a dynamic model of the city, one that would account not only for the expansion of cities in terms of population and territory but also for the patterns of settlement and land use within cities. They identified several factors that influence the physical form of cities. As Park stated, among them are "transportation and communication, tramways and telephones, newspapers and advertising, steel construction and elevators—all things, in fact, which tend to bring about at once a greater mobility and a greater concentration of the urban populations."

13. Which of the sentences below best expresses the essential information in the highlighted sentence in paragraph 2 ? Incorrect choices change the meaning in important ways or leave out essential information.

   Ⓐ The Chicago school of sociology founded by Park and Burgess attempted to help the population of growing cities protect the land around them.
   Ⓑ The model that Park and Burgess created was intended to explain both why the population and area of a city like Chicago grew and in what way urban land was used or settled.
   Ⓒ The founders of the Chicago school of sociology wanted to make Chicago a dynamic model for how other cities should use and settle their land.
   Ⓓ Park and Burgess were concerned that cities like Chicago should follow a model of good land use as the population grew and settled new areas.

14. The author includes the statement by Robert Park in paragraph 2 in order to

   Ⓐ establish the specific topics about which Park and Burgess may have disagreed
   Ⓑ identify the aspects of Chicago's development that required careful planning
   Ⓒ specify some of the factors that contributed to the pattern of development of cities
   Ⓓ compare the definitions given by Park and Burgess for the physical form of cities

PARAGRAPH 3

Park and Burgess based their model of urban growth on the concept of "natural areas"—that is, areas such as occupational suburbs or residential enclaves in which the population is relatively homogeneous and land is used in similar ways without deliberate planning. Park and Burgess saw urban expansion as occurring through a series of "invasions" of successive zones or areas surrounding the center of the city. For example, people from rural areas and other societies "invaded" areas where housing was inexpensive. Those areas tended to be close to the places where they worked. In turn, people who could afford better housing and the cost of commuting "invaded" areas farther from the business district.

15. Paragraph 3 indicates that all of the following are true of "natural areas" as conceived by Park and Burgess EXCEPT:

   Ⓐ Use of the land in natural areas follows a consistent pattern but is generally unplanned.
   Ⓑ People living in natural areas tend to have much in common.
   Ⓒ Natural areas are usually protected from "invasion" by people in other areas.
   Ⓓ Natural areas are an important basic component of the model Park and Burgess developed.

PARAGRAPH 4

Park and Burgess's model has come to be known as the "concentric-zone model" (represented by the figure). Because the model was originally based on studies of Chicago, its center is labeled "Loop," the term commonly applied to that city's central commercial zone. Surrounding the central zone is a "zone in transition," an area that is being invaded by business and light manufacturing. The third zone is inhabited by workers who do not want to live in the factory or business district but at the same time need to live reasonably close to where they work. The fourth or residential zone consists of upscale apartment buildings and single-family homes. And the outermost ring, outside the city limits, is the suburban or commuters' zone; its residents live within a 30- to 60-minute ride of the central business district.

16. According to paragraph 4, why is the term "Loop" used in the concentric-zone model?

   Ⓐ It indicates the many connections between each of the zones in the model.
   Ⓑ It indicates that zones are often in transition and frequently changing.
   Ⓒ It reflects the fact that the model was created with the city of Chicago in mind.
   Ⓓ It emphasizes the fact that populations often returned to zones in which they used to live.

PARAGRAPH 5

Studies by Park, Burgess, and other Chicago-school sociologists showed how new groups of immigrants tended to be concentrated in separate areas within inner-city zones, where they sometimes experienced tension with other ethnic groups that had arrived earlier. Over time, however, each group was able to adjust to life in the city and to find a place for itself in the urban economy. Eventually many of the immigrants moved to unsegregated areas in outer zones; the areas they left behind were **promptly** occupied by new waves of immigrants.

17. The word "**promptly**" in the passage is closest in meaning to

   Ⓐ quickly
   Ⓑ usually
   Ⓒ eventually
   Ⓓ easily

PARAGRAPH 6

The Park and Burgess model of growth in zones and natural areas of the city can still be used to describe patterns of growth in cities that were built around a central business district and that continue to attract large numbers of immigrants. But this model is biased toward the commercial and industrial cities of North America, which have tended to form around business centers rather than around palaces or cathedrals, as is often the case in some other parts of the world. Moreover, it fails to account for other patterns of urbanization, such as the rapid urbanization that occurs along commercial transportation corridors and the rise of nearby satellite cities.

18. Paragraph 6 indicates which of the following about the application of the Park and Burgess model to modern North American cities?

   Ⓐ It is especially useful for those cities that have been used as models for international development.
   Ⓑ It remains useful in explaining the development of some urban areas but not all cities.
   Ⓒ It can be applied equally well to cities with commercial centers and those with palaces and cathedrals at their center.
   Ⓓ It is less applicable to modern cities because of changes in patterns of immigration.

PARAGRAPHS 5 & 6

Studies by Park, Burgess, and other Chicago-school sociologists showed how new groups of immigrants tended to be concentrated in separate areas within inner-city zones, where they sometimes experienced tension with other ethnic groups that had arrived earlier. Over time, however, each group was able to adjust to life in the city and to find a place for itself in the urban economy. **(A)** Eventually many of the immigrants moved to unsegregated areas in outer zones; the areas they left behind were promptly occupied by new waves of immigrants.

   The Park and Burgess model of growth in zones and natural areas of the city can still be used to describe patterns of growth in cities that were built around a central business district and that continue to attract large numbers of immigrants. **(B)** But this model is biased toward the commercial and industrial cities of North America, which have tended to form around business centers rather than around palaces or cathedrals, as is often the case in some other parts of the world. **(C)** Moreover, it fails to account for other patterns of urbanization, such as the rapid urbanization that occurs along commercial transportation corridors and the rise of nearby satellite cities. **(D)**

19. Look at the part of the passage that is displayed above. The letters **(A)**, **(B)**, **(C)**, and **(D)** indicate where the following sentence could be added.

   Typical of this kind of urban growth is the steel-producing center of Gary, Indiana, outside of Chicago, which developed because massive heavy industry could not be located within the major urban center itself.

   Where would the sentence best fit?

   Ⓐ Choice A
   Ⓑ Choice B
   Ⓒ Choice C
   Ⓓ Choice D

20. **Directions**: An introductory sentence for a brief summary of the passage is provided below. Complete the summary by selecting the THREE answer choices that express the most important ideas in the passage. Some sentences do not belong in the summary because they express ideas that are not presented in the passage or are minor ideas in the passage. **This question is worth 2 points.**

Write your answer choices in the spaces where they belong. You can either write the letter of your answer choice or you can copy the sentence.

> **Two sociologists, Robert Park and Ernest Burgess, developed the "concentric-zone model" of how cities use land and grow.**
>
> ●
>
> ●
>
> ●

Answer Choices

A The model was developed to explain how the city of Chicago was developing around centrally located transportation and communication systems.

B The model arose out of concern for the quality of life in the rapidly growing cities of early twentieth-century America.

C The founders of the model did not believe in formal city planning and instead advocated growth through the expansion of so-called "natural areas."

D According to the model, a group new to the city tends to live together near the center and over time moves to outer areas that are more diverse ethnically and occupationally.

E The model is applicable to cities that grow by attracting large numbers of workers to centrally located businesses.

F The model predicts that eventually the inner city becomes so crowded that its residents move to new satellite cities outside the city limits.

LISTENING

In this section, you will be able to demonstrate your ability to understand conversations and lectures in English.

In the actual test, the section is divided into two separately timed parts. You will hear each conversation or lecture only one time. A clock will indicate how much time remains. The clock will count down only while you are answering questions, not while you are listening. You may take up to 16.5 minutes to answer the questions.

In this practice test, there is no time limit for answering questions.

You may take notes while you listen. You may use your notes to help you answer the questions. Your notes will not be scored.

Answer the questions based on what is stated or implied by the speakers.

In some questions, you will see this icon: 🎧 . This means that you will hear, but not see, part of the question.

In the actual test, you must answer each question. You cannot return to previous questions.

At the end of this practice test, you will find an answer key.

Directions: Listen to Track 70.

Directions: Now answer the questions.

1. What are the speakers mainly discussing?

    Ⓐ Getting financial aid for college
    Ⓑ Planning a student's course schedule for the next four years
    Ⓒ Taking courses during the summer session
    Ⓓ Differences in admissions requirements between Hooper University and two other schools

2. Why does the student want to take classes at City College?

    Ⓐ Because Hooper University does not offer the classes he wants
    Ⓑ Because City College classes cost less money than ones at Hooper University
    Ⓒ So that he can take classes on the weekend
    Ⓓ So that he can graduate from Hooper University early

3. Why will the man probably take only two courses?

    Ⓐ Students are limited to two summer courses.
    Ⓑ He can attend classes only on Saturday and Sunday.
    Ⓒ His financial aid will pay for only two courses.
    Ⓓ His summer job will keep him from taking more than two courses.

4. What will Ms. Brinker probably do for the man? *Select 2 answers.*

    Ⓐ Give the man a student ID number
    Ⓑ Give the man a financial aid form
    Ⓒ Help the man figure out which classes to take
    Ⓓ Help the man apply to Hooper University
    Ⓔ Put the man's information into the City College admission system

5. Listen to Track 71.

    (A) The man waited too long to apply to City College.

    (B) The man should not attend Hooper University.

    (C) The man will be able to do what he wants to do.

    (D) The man is very unlucky.

Directions: Listen to Track 72.

Directions: Now answer the questions.

6. What is the main purpose of the lecture?

    Ⓐ To compare the study of world history to the study of United States history

    Ⓑ To explain to the students their next assignment

    Ⓒ To explain different approaches to the study of world history

    Ⓓ To explain the origins of history as an academic discipline

7. Why does the professor mention the Western-Heritage Model used in her high school?

    Ⓐ To explain why she prefers using the model

    Ⓑ To emphasize that the model was widely used in the past

    Ⓒ To correct an error in a student's description of the model

    Ⓓ To compare high school history courses to college history courses

8. According to the professor, what is an advantage of the Different-Cultures Model?

    Ⓐ It focuses on the history of the United States.

    Ⓑ It is based upon the most widely researched theories.

    Ⓒ It includes the history of a variety of cultural groups.

    Ⓓ It makes thematic connections across different cultural groups.

9. What aspect of Islamic civilization will the professor likely discuss in the course?

    Ⓐ A succession of Islamic rulers

    Ⓑ The ancient origins of Islamic architecture

    Ⓒ The isolation of European cultures from Islamic influence

    Ⓓ Islamic elements in African cultures

10. Match each of the topics below with the type of world history course in which it would most likely be discussed.

Write your answer choices in the spaces where they belong.

The Western-Heritage Model	The Different-Cultures Model	The Patterns-of-Change Model

Answer Choices

A The contributions of Native American art to United States culture

B The independent discovery of printing techniques in Asia and Europe

C Ancient Roman foundations of the United States legal system

11. *Listen again to part of the lecture by playing Track 73.* *Then answer the question.*

What is the professor's attitude?

A She doubts that the course will fulfill the students' expectations.

B She hopes that the students selected the course because of their interest.

C She is pleased that the course will fulfill the requirements.

D She is worried that the students might not be familiar with the course requirements.

Directions: Listen to Track 74.

Directions: Now answer the questions.

12. Why does the man go to see the woman?

    Ⓐ To ask her to talk to his professor about an exam

    Ⓑ To get help completing an assignment

    Ⓒ To get help understanding why he is having trouble in his classes

    Ⓓ To ask her opinion about which class he should take

13. What does the man imply about his Spanish class?

    Ⓐ He helps other students in the class.

    Ⓑ He is doing well in the class.

    Ⓒ He cannot complete all the assignments.

    Ⓓ He needs to study more for the class.

14. What problem does the man have with his reading assignments?

   Ⓐ He is not interested in what he reads.
   Ⓑ He cannot memorize definitions of terms.
   Ⓒ He is overwhelmed by the amount he has to read.
   Ⓓ He has difficulty identifying what is important information.

15. Why does the woman tell the man about her own experience as a student?

   Ⓐ To make him aware that other students have similar problems
   Ⓑ To encourage him to spend more time studying at the library
   Ⓒ To explain the importance of remembering details
   Ⓓ To convince him to take a study-skills course

16. What recommendations does the woman make about what the man should do?
Select 2 answers.

   Ⓐ Underline definitions in the text as he reads
   Ⓑ Write a summary of what he reads
   Ⓒ Read the text twice
   Ⓓ Find additional texts on his own

Directions: Listen to Track 75.

Astronomy

nebulae

Directions: Now answer the questions.

17. What is the lecture mainly about?
    (A) How astronomers found the correct interpretation for a certain observation
    (B) How astronomers distinguish between two kinds of nebulae
    (C) Various improvements to the telescope over the last 300 years
    (D) An old problem in astronomy that remains unsolved

18. According to the lecture, how did distant galaxies appear to eighteenth-century astronomers?
    (A) Like the moons of planets
    (B) Like small clouds
    (C) Like variable stars
    (D) Like bright points of light

19. What could astronomers better estimate once they knew what nebulae really were?
    (A) The diameter of variable stars
    (B) The density of cosmic dust
    (C) The size of the universe
    (D) The average number of planets in a galaxy

20. According to the professor, what did a 1920s telescope allow astronomers to do for the first time?
    (A) Study the moons of Jupiter
    (B) Observe gamma-ray bursters
    (C) Reject the dust theory of nebulae
    (D) Prove that galaxies are surprisingly small

21. What did eighteenth-century astronomers have in common with astronomers today?
    (A) They could not explain everything they detected with their instruments.
    (B) They knew the correct distances of objects they could not identify.
    (C) Their instruments were not powerful enough to detect spiral nebulae.
    (D) They argued over the natural brightness of variable stars.

22. *Listen again to part of the lecture by playing Track 76.* *Then answer the question.*

    What can be inferred about the student when she says this?
    (A) She is certain about the correct answer.
    (B) She is now aware that her original idea had a weakness.
    (C) She is not convinced that the professor is right.
    (D) She thinks that the professor misunderstood what she said earlier.

Art History

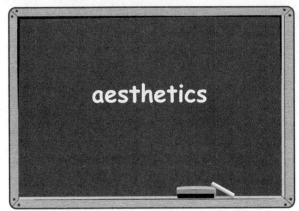

aesthetics

Directions: Now answer the questions.

23. What is the lecture mainly about?

    (A) Various painting techniques

    (B) Ways to determine the purpose of a piece of art

    (C) How moral values are reflected in art

    (D) How to evaluate a piece of art

24. According to the professor, what did ancient Greek philosophers value in a work of art?

    (A) An accurate imitation of life

    (B) An unusual perspective on life

    (C) The expression of complex emotions

    (D) The use of symbolism

25. Why does the professor talk about personal taste?

    (A) To point out its importance in the evaluation of art

    (B) To help students understand the meaning of aesthetics

    (C) To show that personal taste and aesthetics are the same

    (D) To help explain art from different cultures

26. Why does the professor mention wheels and spheres?

    (A) To illustrate how movement can be expressed in a piece of art

    (B) To demonstrate that objects are more important than colors in a piece of art

    (C) To give an example of objects that have symbolic significance

    (D) To explain why some objects rarely appear in works of art

27. The professor mentions four formal steps used in examining a piece of art. Place the steps in order from first to last.

    Write your answer choices in the spaces where they belong. You can either write the letter of your answer choice or you can copy the sentence.

1	
2	
3	
4	

Answer Choices

A Give an opinion about the piece of art.
B Identify possible symbols.
C Describe the piece of art.
D Determine the artist's meaning.

28. *Listen to Track 78 to answer the question.*

    What does the professor imply when he says this?

    Ⓐ He will assign twelve pieces of art to evaluate.
    Ⓑ He is organizing a class trip to the art museum.
    Ⓒ It takes a lot of time to evaluate a piece of art.
    Ⓓ Students will now be able to evaluate art quickly.

SPEAKING

In this section, you will be able to demonstrate your ability to speak about a variety of topics.

In the actual test, the Speaking section will last approximately 16 minutes. You will answer four questions by speaking into the microphone. You may take notes while you listen. You may use your notes to help you answer the questions. Your notes will not be scored. For each question, you will have time to prepare before giving your response. You should answer the questions as completely as possible in the time allowed.

For this practice test, you may want to use a personal recording device to record and play back your responses.

For each question, play the audio track listed and follow the directions to complete the task.

At the end of this practice test, you will find important points about each question.

1. You will now give your opinion about a familiar topic. After you hear the question, you should give yourself 15 seconds to prepare and 45 seconds to speak.

    Listen to Track 79.

    > Some people enjoy watching movies or television in their spare time. Others prefer reading books or magazines. State which you prefer and explain why.
    >
    > | **Preparation Time: 15 seconds** |
    > | :---: |
    > | **Response Time: 45 seconds** |

2. Now you will read a passage about a campus situation and then listen to a conversation about the same topic. You will then answer a question, using information from both the reading passage and the conversation. You should give yourself 30 seconds to prepare and 60 seconds to speak.

    Listen to Track 80.

Reading Time: 45 seconds

    > **Plans for Campus Gym**
    >
    > The recreational services department will receive special funding from this year's budget to increase the number of exercise machines in the campus gym. The increase is in response to numerous student complaints regarding the insufficient number of machines available. Recreational services agrees that due to an increase in university enrollment, more students are using the gym. They therefore welcomed the proposal, adding that it would encourage even more students to exercise and would help to promote a healthier lifestyle among students.

Listen to Track 81.

The woman expresses her opinion about the plan described in the announcement. Briefly summarize the plan. Then state her opinion about the plan and explain the reasons she gives for holding that opinion.

Preparation Time: 30 seconds
Response Time: 60 seconds

3.   Now you will read a passage about an academic subject and then listen to a lecture on the same topic. You will then answer a question, using information from both the reading passage and the lecture. You should give yourself 30 seconds to prepare and 60 seconds to speak.

Listen to Track 82.

Reading Time: 50 seconds

Keystone Species

Within a habitat, each species depends on other species and contributes to the overall stability of that ecosystem. However, some species do more than others by providing essential services. Without the influence of these key species, the habitat changes significantly. Scientists refer to these important players in an ecosystem as *keystone species*. When a keystone species disappears from its habitat, the habitat changes dramatically. Their disappearance can then trigger the loss of other species. As some species vanish, others move in or become more abundant. The new mix of species changes the habitat's appearance and character.

Listen to Track 83.

The professor gives examples of the effects of elephants on the African grasslands habitat. Using the examples from the talk, explain why elephants are considered a keystone species.

Preparation Time: 30 seconds
Response Time: 60 seconds

4. Now you will listen to a lecture. You will then be asked to summarize the lecture. You should give yourself 20 seconds to prepare and 60 seconds to speak.

Listen to Track 84.

Using the examples mentioned by the professor, describe two ways that writers create emphasis when writing dialogue.

Preparation Time: 20 seconds
Response Time: 60 seconds

WRITING

In this section, you will be able to demonstrate your ability to use writing to communicate in an academic environment. There will be two writing tasks.

At the end of this practice test, you will find topic notes for each question.

Turn the page to see the directions for the first writing task.

Writing Based on Reading and Listening

For this task, you will read a passage about an academic topic. Then you will listen to a lecture about the same topic. You may take notes while you listen.

In your response, provide a detailed summary of the lecture and explain how the lecture relates to the reading passage.

In the actual test, you will have 3 minutes to read the passage and 20 minutes to write your response. While you write, you will be able to see the reading passage. If you finish your response before time is up, you may go on to the second writing task.

Reading Time: 3 minutes

Soon technology will provide smart cars: cars that virtually drive themselves. A computer in the car determines the speed and route to the desired destination. The computer is in continuous contact with a global positioning system and other technologies that will provide extremely accurate information about the location of the car, other cars on the road, congestion, accidents, and so forth. The human driver will be little more than a passenger. Smart cars promise to make driving safer, quicker, and less expensive.

First of all, smart cars will prevent many accidents, thereby saving lives. The cars will be equipped with a variety of sensors that very accurately detect cars and other obstacles in their path, and they will have automatic programs that control braking and turning to avoid collisions. Given the hundreds of accidents that occur on highways daily, it is clear that humans do a poor job of avoiding accidents and that computer control would be a great improvement.

Second, with the wide use of smart cars, traffic problems will practically disappear. These computer-controlled cars can follow each other closely, even at high speeds. This ability will result in increased highway speeds. Today commuting by car can take hours a day. So the increased speed of smart cars will be a great benefit, welcomed by the many people who commute by car.

Finally, smart cars will bring a reduction in the costs of driving. Because smart cars are programmed to drive the most direct routes, car owners will have to spend less money on repairs and replacement parts. Expensive items such as brakes, tires, and transmissions will last much longer in smart cars than in other cars.

Listen to Track 85.

Directions: You have 20 minutes to plan and write your response. Your response will be judged on the basis of the quality of your writing and on how well your response presents the points in the lecture and their relationship to the reading passage. Typically, an effective response will contain a minimum of 150 words.

Listen to Track 86.

Response Time: 20 minutes

Question 1

Summarize the points made in the lecture, being sure to explain how they challenge specific points made in the reading passage.

_____

_____

_____

_____

_____

_____

_____

_____

_____

Writing for an Academic Discussion

For this task, you will read an online discussion. A professor has posted a question about a topic, and some classmates have responded with their ideas.

In the actual test, you will have 10 minutes to write a response that contributes to the discussion.

Question 2

Your professor is teaching a class on child development. Write a post responding to the professor's question.

In your response, you should do the following.

- Express and support your opinion.
- Make a contribution to the discussion in your own words.

An effective response will contain at least 100 words.

Dr. Achebe

Next week, we'll begin discussing the effect of parental monitoring on child development. We'll start by looking specifically at parental monitoring of children's access to the Internet. Some parents believe that they need to closely watch and restrict their children's online activity. Do you agree with this approach? Do you think it is important for parents to monitor and limit their children's access to the Internet? Why or why not?

Claire

In my opinion, this kind of parental monitoring is essential. If parents are aware of what their children are doing online, they can help them avoid making mistakes. For example, they can intervene if they see their child has accidentally made a big purchase from an online retailer.

Paul

I respectfully disagree with Claire. Parental monitoring hinders a child's growth and learning. Yes, children can make mistakes online, but making mistakes is how they learn. If parents always step in to correct these mistakes, it prevents children from learning from the consequences of their actions.

Response Time: 10 minutes

ANSWERS

Reading Section

1. C
2. D
3. B
4. D
5. B
6. D
7. A
8. C
9. B
10. A, C, D

11. C
12. A
13. B
14. C
15. C
16. C
17. A
18. B
19. D
20. B, D, E

Listening Section

1. C
2. D
3. A
4. A, E
5. C
6. C
7. B
8. C
9. D
10. C, A, B
11. B
12. C
13. B
14. D

15. A
16. B, C
17. A
18. B
19. C
20. C
21. A
22. B
23. D
24. A
25. B
26. C
27. C, B, D, A
28. C

Speaking Section

1. To respond to this particular question, you should clearly state what your opinion is: Do you prefer to watch movies or television in your spare time or do you prefer to read books or magazines? Then you should give reasons to support your opinion. If you prefer to watch movies or television, you might give the reason that you enjoy the visual nature of films, and that you particularly enjoy seeing other places shown in films. You might then describe a particular film that you have enjoyed, such as a travel film, and say that these films inspire you to do your own traveling.

   If you say that you prefer reading books or magazines, you might say that you prefer to imagine something that you read yourself, rather than seeing a movie of it. You could say that you are often disappointed when you see a movie that was based on a book because you had imagined the scenes and characters differently and this is why you prefer to read. You may develop this further by describing a particular film and book.

   Keep in mind that there is no "correct" answer to this question. Whatever your preference is, your answer should be supported with examples. It is important to make sure that you state your opinion and develop your response with good examples and relevant details.

   Your response should be intelligible, should demonstrate effective use of grammar and vocabulary, and should be well-developed and coherent. Your response is scored using the Independent Speaking Rubric (see Appendix A).

2. First, as the question states, you should provide a brief summary of the university's plan, which is to increase the number of exercise machines in the gym. You can also provide a brief summary of the reasons that they're doing this: 1) fewer machines are available because of increased student enrollment, and 2) it will encourage more students to exercise. You should not spend too much time on this summary; if you attempt to provide many details from the reading, you may not have enough time to discuss both of the woman's reasons for disagreeing with the proposal. For this item type, a brief summary is all that is necessary. You should make sure that your summary is clear enough for the listener to understand the proposal without having access to additional information.

   After the summary, you should state the woman's opinion of the university's plan to add exercise machines. In this case, the woman disagrees with the university's plan.

   You should then convey the two main reasons she gives for holding that opinion. You will need to connect information from the conversation to the reading in order for the response to be complete. The woman disagrees with the first point about fewer machines being available. She says even though she does see more people in the gym, she does not have to wait to use the equipment.

   Your response should also convey the woman's second reason for not agreeing with the university's plan. She thinks that adding new machines would not encourage more people to exercise. She says that the university already provides enough opportunities for students to exercise and have a healthy lifestyle. For example, there's a swimming pool, running paths, and sport teams.

   Your response should be intelligible, should demonstrate effective use of grammar and vocabulary, and should be well-developed and coherent. Your response is scored using the Integrated Speaking Rubric (see Appendix A).

3. To respond to this particular question, you should first explain the concept of keystone species as it was presented in the reading. You can talk about this as it relates to the elephant. Keystone species are important because the habitat they live in would change dramatically without them. Elephants living in grassland habitats in Africa are an example of a keystone species.

   You should then discuss the professor's examples. Note that you do not need to repeat all of the details from the reading and the lecture, but instead integrate points from both to answer the question completely.

   As one example of how the grasslands habitat would change without elephants, the professor says that elephants eat or destroy tree and shrub seeds and small plants, preventing many trees from growing in the grasslands. If they did not remove these trees, many trees would block sunshine, so grasses would die. The trees would eventually replace grasses, and the forest would replace the grasslands.

The professor discusses another way that the lack of elephants would impact the habitat. He says that other animals in this habitat depend on grasses for food and survival. When grasses die, these animals leave the habitat and new species move into the habitat. Both of these examples show why the elephant is a keystone species.

This is an example of a possible response. There are other effective ways to organize your answer. The most important thing is to discuss the specific information that is asked for in the question. Listeners should understand that elephants are considered a keystone species because they have an important effect on their environment and it would change greatly without them. The details you choose to discuss from the reading and the lecture should lead to this understanding.

Your response should be intelligible, should demonstrate effective use of grammar and vocabulary, and should be well-developed and coherent. Your response is scored using the Integrated Speaking Rubric (see Appendix A).

4. This particular question requires you to summarize the contents of a lecture you hear. In your response, you should talk about the two ways that writers create emphasis when writing dialogue. The professor says that exaggeration and understatement are two ways to create emphasis or impact.

After your general introduction, you should then talk about the first way that writers can create emphasis. The professor says that exaggeration can create impact or emphasis by describing something as bigger or more than it is. For example, a character in a story who is tired from a long walk might say, "I can't take another step" instead of saying "I'm tired." This exaggeration is more forceful and interesting.

You should then talk about the second way to create emphasis. The professor says that with understatement you can create emphasis by saying less than you mean. For example, the professor complimented her friend on a great meal by saying that it was "not bad." Using understatement makes for a stronger statement.

You should make sure that you leave yourself enough time to talk about the second example. You will be expected to cover both examples.

Your response should be intelligible, should demonstrate effective use of grammar and vocabulary, and should be well-developed and coherent. Your response is scored using the Integrated Speaking Rubric (see Appendix A).

Writing Section

1. What is important to understand from the lecture is that the professor disagrees with the advantages of smart cars presented in the reading, namely that smart cars will reduce the number of accidents; that smart cars will reduce commuting times; and that smart cars will save their owners money.

In your response, you should convey the reasons presented by the professor for why smart cars will not produce the benefits predicted in the reading. A high-scoring response will include the following points made by the professor that cast doubt on the points made in the reading.

Point made in the reading	Counterpoint made in the lecture
Since smart cars will be equipped with sophisticated technology to detect obstacles and control braking and turning, many accidents that human drivers cause today will be prevented.	Technologies used in smart cars will fail occasionally, as all technologies do. Since smart cars will travel at greater speeds and closer together, such technology failures will result in accidents that will be more serious than accidents caused nowadays by human drivers.
Commuting time for many people will be reduced because smart cars will be able to travel at greater speeds and closer together.	Every improvement in driving convenience usually results in more people taking to the road. The introduction of smart cars will likely result in more cars on the road, which will cause additional traffic congestion. Commuting time is therefore not likely to decrease.
Smart cars will be able to choose the most direct routes. With less distance traveled, smart car owners will save money on repair and part replacement costs.	Sophisticated technologies used by smart cars will make the cars more expensive to buy and also more expensive to repair. These added costs will offset the savings identified in the reading.

Your response is scored using the Integrated Writing Rubric (see Appendix A). A response that receives a score of 5 clearly conveys all three of the main points in the table using accurate sentence structure and vocabulary.

2. To earn a top score, you should develop a response that contributes to the discussion about the topic of whether parents should monitor and limit their children's access to the Internet. An effective response will contain at least 100 words.

One discussion participant argues that parental monitoring is essential and helps children avoid making mistakes; the other argues that parental monitoring hinders children's ability to grow and learn by making mistakes. You might expand on the ideas already stated by the discussion participants or introduce entirely new ideas. You may state that parental monitoring ensures children's online safety, provides guidance and education, and promotes a healthier balance between children's online and offline activities; conversely, you might say that parental monitoring restricts children's independence, autonomy, and privacy and erodes trust between parents and children. You could also debate the extent of parental monitoring—what level of parental monitoring might be excessive and what level might be appropriate. You might suggest other solutions, for example, that parents should work on establishing healthy, trusting relationships with their children.

You should make sure that your ideas are well-supported by reasons and examples and are expressed clearly. Since your response represents an online post, it does not need to be organized into separate paragraphs. However, your ideas need to be well-connected, coherent, and clear. Your response is scored using the Writing for an Academic Discussion Rubric (see Appendix A).

Appendix A

Speaking and Writing Scoring Rubrics

This section contains all the rubrics used by raters to score Speaking and Writing section responses. There are two different rubrics used to score the Speaking section and two different rubrics used to score the Writing section.

Speaking question 1 is scored using the Independent Speaking Rubric, while questions 2 through 4 are scored using the Integrated Scoring Rubric. Writing question 1 is scored using the Integrated Writing Rubric, while question 2 is scored using the Writing for an Academic Discussion Rubric.

The chart below shows the main features of responses that must be considered when assigning a score.

Section	Question	Rubric	Main features considered when scoring
Speaking	1	Independent Speaking	**Delivery** • How clear is your speech? Good responses are fluid and clear, have good pronunciation, a natural pace, and natural-sounding intonation patterns. • Even at the highest level, there may be some minor problems; however, they do not cause difficulty for the listener. **Language use** • How effectively do you use grammar and vocabulary to convey ideas? In a good response, there is control of both basic and more complex language structures, and appropriate vocabulary is used. • Even at the highest level, some minor or systematic errors may be noticeable; however, they do not obscure meaning. **Topic development** • How fully do you answer the question, and how coherently do you present your ideas? In a good response, the relationships between ideas are clear and easy to follow, as is the progression from one idea to the next. Good responses generally use all or most of the time allotted.

Section	Question	Rubric	Main features considered when scoring
Speaking	2–4	Integrated Speaking	**Delivery** • How clear is your speech? Good responses are fluid and clear, have good pronunciation, a natural pace, and natural-sounding intonation patterns. • Even at the highest level, there may be some minor problems; however, they do not cause difficulty for the listener. **Language use** • How effectively do you use grammar and vocabulary to convey ideas? In a good response, there is control of both basic and more complex language structures, and appropriate vocabulary is used. • Even at the highest level, some minor or systematic errors may be noticeable; however, they do not obscure meaning. **Topic development** • How fully do you answer the question, and how coherently do you present your ideas? Are you able to synthesize and summarize the information that was presented? In a good response, the relationships between ideas are clear and easy to follow, as is the progression from one idea to the next. Good responses generally use all or most of the time allotted. • Even at the highest level, a response may have minor inaccuracies about details or minor omissions of relevant details.
Writing	1	Integrated Writing	**Quality of the writing** • A good response is well organized. Use of grammar and vocabulary is appropriate and precise. **Completeness and accuracy of the content** • In a good response, important information from the lecture has been successfully selected, and it is coherently and accurately presented in relation to relevant information from the reading. • Even at the highest level, a response may have occasional language errors; however, they do not result in inaccurate or imprecise presentation of content or connections.
Writing	2	Writing for an Academic Discussion	**Quality of the writing** • A good response is a relevant and very clearly expressed contribution to the online discussion, and it demonstrates consistent facility in the use of language. • Even at the highest level, a response may have minor lexical or grammatical errors; however, they do not interfere with meaning.

TOEFL iBT® Speaking Scoring Rubric—Independent Task

Score	General Description	Delivery	Language Use	Topic Development
4	The response fulfills the demands of the task, with at most minor lapses in completeness. It is highly intelligible and exhibits sustained, coherent discourse. A response at this level is characterized by all of the following:	Generally well-paced flow (fluid expression). Speech is clear. It may include minor lapses or minor difficulties with pronunciation or intonation patterns, which do not affect overall intelligibility.	The response demonstrates effective use of grammar and vocabulary. It exhibits a fairly high degree of automaticity with good control of basic and complex structures (as appropriate). Some minor (or systematic) errors are noticeable but do not obscure meaning.	Response is sustained and sufficient to the task. It is generally well-developed and coherent; relationships between ideas are clear (or clear progression of ideas).
3	The response addresses the task appropriately, but may fall short of being fully developed. It is generally intelligible and coherent, with some fluidity of expression, though it exhibits some noticeable lapses in the expression of ideas. A response at this level is characterized by at least two of the following:	Speech is generally clear, with some fluidity of expression, though minor difficulties with pronunciation, intonation, or pacing are noticeable and may require listener effort at times (though overall intelligibility is not significantly affected).	The response demonstrates fairly automatic and effective use of grammar and vocabulary, and fairly coherent expression of relevant ideas. Response may exhibit some imprecise or inaccurate use of vocabulary or grammatical structures or be somewhat limited in the range of structures used. This may affect overall fluency, but it does not seriously interfere with the communication of the message.	Response is mostly coherent and sustained and conveys relevant ideas/information. Overall development is somewhat limited, usually lacks elaboration or specificity. Relationships between ideas may at times not be immediately clear.

TOEFL iBT® Speaking Scoring Rubric—Independent Task, *continued*

Score	General Description	Delivery	Language Use	Topic Development
2	The response addresses the task, but development of the topic is limited. It contains intelligible speech, although problems with delivery and/ or overall coherence occur; meaning may be obscured in places. A response at this level is characterized by at least two of the following:	Speech is basically intelligible, though listener effort is needed because of unclear articulation, awkward intonation, or choppy rhythm/pace; meaning may be obscured in places.	The response demonstrates limited range and control of grammar and vocabulary. These limitations often prevent full expression of ideas. For the most part, only basic sentence structures are used successfully and spoken with fluidity. Structures and vocabulary may express mainly simple (short) and/or general propositions, with simple or unclear connections made among them (serial listing, conjunction, juxtaposition).	The response is connected to the task, though the number of ideas presented or the development of ideas is limited. Mostly basic ideas are expressed with limited elaboration (details and support). At times relevant substance may be vaguely expressed or repetitious. Connections of ideas may be unclear.
1	The response is very limited in content and/or coherence or is only minimally connected to the task, or speech is largely unintelligible. A response at this level is characterized by at least two of the following:	Consistent pronunciation, stress, and intonation difficulties cause considerable listener effort; delivery is choppy, fragmented, or telegraphic; frequent pauses and hesitations.	Range and control of grammar and vocabulary severely limits (or prevents) expression of ideas and connections among ideas. Some low-level responses may rely heavily on practiced or formulaic expressions.	Limited relevant content is expressed. The response generally lacks substance beyond expression of very basic ideas. Speaker may be unable to sustain speech to complete the task and may rely heavily on repetition of the prompt.
0	Speaker makes no attempt to respond OR response is unrelated to the topic.			

TOEFL iBT® Speaking Scoring Rubric—Integrated Tasks

Score	General Description	Delivery	Language Use	Topic Development
4	The response fulfills the demands of the task with, at most, minor lapses in completeness. It is highly intelligible and exhibits sustained, coherent discourse. A response at this level is characterized by all of the following:	Speech is generally clear, fluid and sustained. It may include minor lapses or minor difficulties with pronunciation or intonation. Pace may vary at times as speaker attempts to recall information. Overall intelligibility remains high.	The response demonstrates good control of basic and complex grammatical structures that allow for coherent, efficient (automatic) expression of relevant ideas. Contains generally effective word choice. Though some minor (or systematic) errors or imprecise use may be noticeable, they do not require listener effort (or obscure meaning).	The response presents a clear progression of ideas and conveys the relevant information required by the task. It includes appropriate detail, though it may have minor errors or minor omissions.
3	The response addresses the task appropriately, but may fall short of being fully developed. It is generally intelligible and coherent, with some fluidity of expression, though it exhibits some noticeable lapses in the expression of ideas. A response at this level is characterized by at least two of the following:	Speech is generally clear, with some fluidity of expression, but it exhibits minor difficulties with pronunciation, intonation or pacing and may require some listener effort at times. Overall intelligibility remains good, however.	The response demonstrates fairly automatic and effective use of grammar and vocabulary, and fairly coherent expression of relevant ideas. Response may exhibit some imprecise or inaccurate use of vocabulary or grammatical structures or be somewhat limited in the range of structures used. Such limitations do not seriously interfere with the communication of the message.	The response is sustained and conveys relevant information required by the task. However, it exhibits some incompleteness, inaccuracy, lack of specificity with respect to content, or choppiness in the progression of ideas.

TOEFL iBT® Speaking Scoring Rubric—Integrated Tasks, *continued*

Score	General Description	Delivery	Language Use	Topic Development
2	The response is connected to the task, though it may be missing some relevant information or contain inaccuracies. It contains some intelligible speech, but at times problems with intelligibility and/or overall coherence may obscure meaning. A response at this level is characterized by at least two of the following:	Speech is clear at times, though it exhibits problems with pronunciation, intonation or pacing and so may require significant listener effort. Speech may not be sustained at a consistent level throughout. Problems with intelligibility may obscure meaning in places (but not throughout).	The response is limited in the range and control of vocabulary and grammar demonstrated (some complex structures may be used, but typically contain errors). This results in limited or vague expression of relevant ideas and imprecise or inaccurate connections. Automaticity of expression may only be evident at the phrasal level.	The response conveys some relevant information but is clearly incomplete or inaccurate. It is incomplete if it omits key ideas, makes vague reference to key ideas, or demonstrates limited development of important information. An inaccurate response demonstrates misunderstanding of key ideas from the stimulus. Typically, ideas expressed may not be well connected or cohesive so that familiarity with the stimulus is necessary in order to follow what is being discussed.
1	The response is very limited in content or coherence or is only minimally connected to the task. Speech may be largely unintelligible. A response at this level is characterized by at least two of the following:	Consistent pronunciation and intonation problems cause considerable listener effort and frequently obscure meaning. Delivery is choppy, fragmented, or telegraphic. Speech contains frequent pauses and hesitations.	Range and control of grammar and vocabulary severely limit (or prevent) expression of ideas and connections among ideas. Some very low-level responses may rely on isolated words or short utterances to communicate ideas.	The response fails to provide much relevant content. Ideas that are expressed are often inaccurate, limited to vague utterances, or repetitions (including repetition of prompt).
0	Speaker makes no attempt to respond OR response is unrelated to the topic.			

TOEFL iBT® Writing Scoring Rubric—Integrated Task

Score	Task Description
5	A response at this level successfully selects the important information from the lecture and coherently and accurately presents this information in relation to the relevant information presented in the reading. The response is well organized, and occasional language errors that are present do not result in inaccurate or imprecise presentation of content or connections.
4	A response at this level is generally good in selecting the important information from the lecture and in coherently and accurately presenting this information in relation to the relevant information in the reading, but it may have minor omission, inaccuracy, vagueness, or imprecision of some content from the lecture or in connection to points made in the reading. A response is also scored at this level if it has more frequent or noticeable minor language errors, as long as such usage and grammatical structures do not result in anything more than an occasional lapse of clarity or in the connection of ideas.
3	A response at this level contains some important information from the lecture and conveys some relevant connection to the reading, but it is marked by one or more of the following: • Although the overall response is definitely oriented to the task, it conveys only vague, global, unclear, or somewhat imprecise connection to the points made in the lecture to points made in the reading. • The response may omit one major key point made in the lecture. • Some key points made in the lecture or the reading, or connections between the two, may be incomplete, inaccurate, or imprecise. • Errors of usage and/or grammar may be more frequent or may result in noticeably vague expressions or obscured meanings in conveying ideas and connections.
2	A response at this level contains some relevant information from the lecture but is marked by significant language difficulties or by significant omission or inaccuracy of important ideas from the lecture or in the connections between the lecture and the reading; a response at this level is marked by one or more of the following: • The response significantly misrepresents or completely omits the overall connection between the lecture and the reading. • The response significantly omits or significantly misrepresents important points made in the lecture. • The response contains language errors or expressions that largely obscure connections or meaning at key junctures, or that would likely obscure understanding of key ideas for a reader not already familiar with the reading and the lecture.
1	A response at this level is marked by one or more of the following. • The response provides little or no meaningful or relevant coherent content from the lecture. • The language level of the response is so low that is difficult to derive meaning.
0	A response at this level merely copies sentences from the reading, rejects the topic or is otherwise not connected to the topic, is written in a foreign language, consists of keystroke characters, or is blank.

TOEFL iBT® Writing Scoring Rubric—Writing for an Academic Discussion Task

Score	Description
5	**A fully successful response** The response is a relevant and very clearly expressed contribution to the online discussion, and it demonstrates consistent facility in the use of language. A typical response displays the following: • Relevant and well elaborated explanations, exemplifications, and/or details • Effective use of a variety of syntactic structures and precise, idiomatic word choice • Almost no lexical or grammatical errors other than those expected from a competent writer writing under timed conditions (e.g., common typos or common misspellings or substitutions like there/their)
4	**A generally successful response** The response is a relevant contribution to the online discussion, and facility in the use of language allows the writer's ideas to be easily understood. A typical response displays the following: • Relevant and adequately elaborated explanations, exemplifications, and/or details • A variety of syntactic structures and appropriate word choice • Few lexical or grammatical errors
3	**A partially successful response** The response is a mostly relevant and mostly understandable contribution to the online discussion, and there is some facility in the use of language. A typical response displays the following: • Elaboration in which part of an explanation, example, or detail may be missing, unclear, or irrelevant • Some variety in syntactic structures and a range of vocabulary • Some noticeable lexical and grammatical errors in sentence structure, word form, or use of idiomatic language
2	**A mostly unsuccessful response** The response reflects an attempt to contribute to the online discussion, but limitations in the use of language may make ideas hard to follow. A typical response displays the following: • Ideas that may be poorly elaborated or only partially relevant • A limited range of syntactic structures and vocabulary • An accumulation of errors in sentence structure, word forms, or use
1	**An unsuccessful response** The response reflects an ineffective attempt to contribute to the online discussion, and limitations in the use of language may prevent the expression of ideas. A typical response may display the following: • Words and phrases that indicate an attempt to address the task but with few or no coherent ideas • Severely limited range of syntactic structures and vocabulary • Serious and frequent errors in the use of language • Minimal original language; any coherent language is mostly borrowed from the stimulus
0	**The response is blank, rejects the topic, is not in English, is entirely copied from the prompt, is entirely unconnected to the prompt, or consists of arbitrary keystrokes.**

TOEFL iBT®

Appendix B

Audio Track Transcripts

TRACK 1 TRANSCRIPT

Narrator

Listen to a conversation between a student and a librarian.

Librarian

Can I help you?

Student

Yeah, I need to find a review. It's for my English class. We have to find reviews of the play we're reading. But they have to be from when the play was first performed—so I need to know when that was . . . and I suppose I should start with newspaper reviews . . .

Librarian

Contemporary reviews.

Student

Sorry?

Librarian

You want contemporary reviews. What's the name of the play?

Student

It's *Happy Strangers*. It was written in 1962 and we're supposed to write about its influence on American theater—show why it's been so important.

Librarian

Well, that certainly explains why your professor wants you to read some of those old reviews. The critics really tore the play to pieces when it opened. It was just so controversial—nobody'd ever seen anything like it on the stage.

Student

Really? It was that big a deal?

Librarian

Oh sure. Of course, the critics' reaction made some people kinda curious about it; they wanted to see what was causing all the fuss. In fact, we were on vacation in New York—I had to be, oh around sixteen or so—and my parents took me to see it. That would've been about 1965.

Student

So that was the year it premiered? Great! But . . . newspapers from back then aren't online, so how do I . . .

Librarian

Well, we have copies of old newspapers in the basement, and all the *major* papers publish reference guides to their articles, reviews, etc. You'll find *them* in the reference stacks in back. But I'd start with 1964. I think the play'd been running for a little while when I saw it.

Student

Oh, how'd you like it? I mean it's just two characters onstage hanging around and basically doing nothing.

Librarian

Well, I was impressed: the actors were famous and, besides, it was my first time in a *real* theater. But you're right—it was definitely different from any plays that we'd read in high school. Of course, in a small town, the assignments are pretty traditional.

Student

I've only read it, but it doesn't seem like it'd be much fun to watch. The story doesn't progress in a, in any sort of logical manner. It doesn't have any real ending either. It just stops. Honestly, y'know, I thought it was kinda slow and boring.

Librarian

Well, I guess you might think that, but when I saw it back then it was anything but boring! Some parts were really funny—but I remember crying, too. But I'm not sure just reading it . . . You know, they've done this play at least once on campus. I'm sure there's a tape of the play in our video library. You might want to borrow it.

Student

That's a good idea. I'll have a better idea of what I *really* think of it—before I read those reviews.

Librarian

I'm sure you'll be surprised that anyone ever found it radical—but you'll see why it's still powerful— dramatically speaking.

Student

Well, there must be *something* about it or the professor wouldn't have assigned it. I'm sure I'll figure it out.

TRACK 2 TRANSCRIPT

Narrator

Listen again to part of the conversation. Then answer the question.

Student

I suppose I should start with newspaper reviews . . .

Librarian

Contemporary reviews.

Student

Sorry?

Librarian

You want contemporary reviews. What's the name of the play?

Narrator

Why does the woman say this:

Librarian

Contemporary reviews.

TRACK 3 TRANSCRIPT

Biology

Narrator

Listen to part of a lecture in a biology class. The class is discussing animal behavior.

Professor

OK, the next kind of animal behavior I want to talk about might be familiar to you. You may have seen, for example, a bird that's in the middle of a mating ritual. And, and suddenly it stops and preens—you know, it takes a few moments to straighten its feathers—and then returns to the mating ritual. This kind of behavior—this doing something that seems completely out of place—is what we call a displacement activity.

Displacement activities are activities that animals engage in when they have conflicting drives—if, if we take our example from a minute ago—if the bird is afraid of its mate, it's conflicted, it wants to mate, but it's also afraid and wants to run away, so instead it starts grooming itself. So the displacement activity, the, the grooming, the straightening of its feathers seems to be an irrelevant behavior.

So what do you think another example of a displacement activity might be?

Male student

How about an animal that, um, instead of fighting its enemy or running away, it attacks a plant or a bush?

Professor

That's a really good suggestion, Carl, but *that's* called redirecting. The animal is *redirecting* its behavior to another object, in this case, the plant or the bush. But that's not an irrelevant or inappropriate behavior—the behavior makes sense—it's appropriate under the circumstances, but what doesn't make sense is the *object* the behavior's directed towards. OK, who else? Carol?

Female student

I think I read in another class about an experiment, um, where an object that the animal was afraid of was put next to its food—next to the animal's food—and the animal, it was conflicted between confronting the object, and eating the food, so instead it just fell asleep. Like that?

Professor

That's *exactly* what I mean. Displacement occurs because the animal's got two conflicting drives, two competing urges, in this case, fear and hunger—and what happens is they *inhibit* each other—they cancel each other out in a way, and a third, seemingly *irrelevant* behavior surfaces . . . through a process that we call disinhibition.

Now, in disinhibition, the basic idea is that two drives that seem to inhibit, to hold back a third drive, well, well, they get in the way of each other in a, in a conflict situation, and somehow lose control, lose their inhibiting effect on that third behavior . . . wh-which means that the third drive surfaces . . . it-it's expressed in the animal's behavior.

Now, these displacement activities can include feeding, drinking, grooming, even sleeping. These are what we call "comfort behaviors." So why do you think displacement activities are so often comfort behaviors, such as grooming?

Male student

Maybe because it's easy for them to do—I mean, grooming is like one of the most accessible things an animal can do—it's something they do all the time, and they have the–the *stimulus* right there, on the outside of their bodies in order to do the grooming—or if food is right in front of them. Basically, they don't have to think very much about those behaviors.

Female student

Professor, isn't it possible that animals groom because they've gotten messed up a little from fighting or mating? I mean, if a bird's feathers get ruffled, or an animal's fur—maybe it's not so strange for them to stop and tidy themselves up at that point.

Professor

That's another possible reason, although it doesn't necessarily explain other behaviors such as eating, drinking, or sleeping. What's interesting is that studies have been done that suggest that the animal's *environment* may play a part in determining what kind of behavior it displays. For example, there's a bird—the wood thrush, anyway when the wood thrush is in an attack-escape conflict—that is, it's caught between the two urges to escape from or to attack an enemy—if it's sitting on a horizontal branch, it'll wipe its beak on its perch. If it's sitting on a vertical branch, it'll groom its breast feathers. The immediate environment of the bird—its immediate, um, its relationship to its immediate environment seems to play a part in which behavior it will display.

TRACK 4 TRANSCRIPT

Narrator

Listen again to part of the lecture. Then answer the question.

Professor

So what do you think another example of a displacement activity might be?

Male student

How about an animal that, uh, instead of fighting its enemy or running away, it attacks a plant or a bush?

Professor

That's a really good suggestion, Carl, but that's called redirecting.

Narrator

What does the professor mean when she says this:

Professor

That's a really good suggestion, Carl, but that's called redirecting.

TRACK 5 TRANSCRIPT

Literature

Narrator

Listen to part of a lecture in a literature class.

Professor

All right, so let me close today's class with some thoughts to keep in mind while you're doing tonight's assignment. You'll be reading one of Ralph Waldo Emerson's best-known essays, "Self-Reliance," and comparing it with his poems and other works. I think this essay has the potential to be quite meaningful for all of you—as young people who probably wonder about things like truth, and where your lives are going . . . all sorts of profound questions.

Knowing something about Emerson's philosophies will help you when you read "Self-Reliance." And basically, one of the main beliefs that he had, was about *truth*. Not that it's something that we can be taught . . . Emerson says it's found within ourselves.

So this truth . . . the idea that it's in each one of us . . . is one of the first points that you'll see Emerson making in this essay. It's a bit abstract, but he's very into, ah, into each person believing his or her own thought. Believing in yourself, the thought or conviction that's true for you.

But actually, he ties that in with a sort of universal truth, something that everyone knows but doesn't realize they know. Most of us aren't in touch with ourselves, in a way, so we just aren't *capable* of recognizing profound truths. It takes geniuses . . . people like, say, Shakespeare, who are unique because when they have a glimpse of this truth—this universal truth—they pay attention to it and express it, and don't just dismiss it like most people do.

So, Emerson is really into each individual believing in, and trusting, him- or herself. You'll see that he writes about . . . well, first, conformity. He *criticizes* the people of his time, for abandoning their own minds and their own wills for the sake of conformity and consistency. They try to fit in with the rest of the world, even though it's at odds with their beliefs and their identities. Therefore, it's best to be a *nonconformist*—to do your own thing, not worrying about what other people think. That's an important point—he really drives this argument home throughout the essay.

When you're reading I want you to think about that, and why that kind of thought would be relevant to the readers of his time. Remember, this is 1838. Self-reliance was a novel idea at the time, and United States citizens were less secure about themselves as individuals and as Americans.

The country as a whole was trying to define itself. Emerson wanted to give people something to really think about. Help them find their own way and, ah, what it meant to *be* who they were.

So, that's something that I think is definitely as relevant today as it was then . . . probably, uh . . . especially among young adults like yourselves. You know, uh, college being a time to sort of really think about who you are and where you're going.

Now, we already said that Emerson really emphasized nonconformity, right? As a way to sort of not lose your own self and identity in the world? To have your own truth and not be afraid to listen to it? Well, he takes it a step *further*. Not conforming also means, ah, not conforming with *yourself*, or your past. What does *that* mean? Well, if you've always been a certain way, or done a certain thing, but it's not working for you anymore, or you're not content—Emerson says that it'd be foolish to be consistent even with our own past. Focus on the future, he says: that's what matters more. Inconsistency is good! He talks about a ship's voyage—and this is one of the most famous bits of the essay—how the best voyage is made up of zigzag lines. Up close, it seems a little all over the place, but from farther away the true path shows, and in the end it justifies all the turns along the way.

So, don't worry if you're not sure where you're headed or what your long-term goals are—stay true to yourself and it'll make sense in the end. I mean, *I* can attest to that. Before I was a literature professor, I was an accountant. Before that, I was a newspaper reporter. My life has taken some pretty interesting turns, and here I am, very happy with my experiences and where they've brought me. If you rely on yourself and trust your own talents, your own interests, don't worry. Your path will make sense in the end.

TRACK 6 TRANSCRIPT

Narrator
Listen again to part of the lecture. Then answer the question.

Professor
Remember, this is 1838. Self-reliance was a novel idea at the time, and United States citizens were less secure about themselves as individuals and as Americans.

Narrator
Why does the professor say this:

Professor
Remember, this is 1838.

TRACK 7 TRANSCRIPT

Narrator

Listen to a conversation between a student and a professor.

Professor

Hey Jane. You look like you're in a hurry . . .

Student

Yeah, things're a little crazy.

Professor

Oh, yeah? What's going on?

Student

Oh, it's nothing . . . Well, since it's your class . . . I guess it's OK . . . it's, it's just that I'm having trouble with my group project.

Professor

Ah, yes. Due next week. What's your group doing again?

Student

It's about United States Supreme Court decisions. We're looking at the impact of recent cases on property rights, municipal land use cases, zoning disputes . . .

Professor

Right, OK . . . And it's not going well?

Student

Not really. I'm worried about the other two people in my group. They're just sitting back, not really doing their fair share of the work, and waiting for an A. It's kinda stressing me out, because we're getting close to the deadline and I feel like I'm doing everything for this project . . .

Professor

Ah, the good ole "free-rider" problem.

Student

Free rider?

Professor

Oh, it's just a term that describes this situation: when people in a group seek to get the benefits of being in the group without contributing to the work . . . Anyway, what exactly do you mean when you say they just sit back? I mean, they've been filing their weekly progress reports with me . . .

Student

Yes, but I feel like I'm doing 90 percent of the work. I hate to sound so negative here, but honestly, they're taking credit for things they shouldn't be taking credit for. Like last week in the library, we decided to split up the research into three parts, and then each of us was supposed to find sources in the library for our parts. I went off to the stacks and found some really good material for my part, but when I got back to our table they were just goofing off and talking. So I went and got material for their sections as well.

Professor

Hmm, you know you shouldn't do that.

Student

I know, but I didn't want to risk the project going down the drain.

Professor

I know Theresa and Kevin, I've had both of them in other courses . . . so I'm familiar with their work, and their work habits.

Student

I know, me too, and that's why this has really surprised me.

Professor

Do you . . . does your group like your topic?

Student

Well, I think we'd all rather focus on cases that deal with personal liberties—questions about freedom of speech, things like that—but I chose property rights . . .

Professor

You chose the topic?

Student

Yeah, I thought it would be good for us, all of us, to try something new.

Professor

Maybe that's part of the problem—maybe Theresa and Kevin aren't that excited about the topic—and since you picked it . . . Have you thought . . . talked to them at all about picking a different topic?

Student

But, we've already got all the sources. And it's due next week. We don't have time to start from scratch.

Professor

OK, well, I'll let you go 'cause I know you're so busy. But you might . . . consider talking to your group about your topic choice . . .

Student

I'll think about it. Gotta run. See you in class.

TRACK 8 TRANSCRIPT

United States
Government

Narrator

Listen to part of a discussion in a United States government class.

Professor

OK, last time we were talking about government support for the arts. Who can sum up some of the main points? Frank?

Male student

Well, I guess there wasn't *really* any, you know, *official* government support for the arts until the twentieth century. But the first attempt the United States government made to, you know, to support the arts was the Federal Art Project.

Professor

Right. So, what can you say about the project?

Male student

Um, it was started during the Depression, um, in the 1930s, to employ out-of-work artists.

Professor

So was it successful? Janet? What do you say?

Female student

Yeah, sure, it was successful—I mean, for one thing, the project established a lot of, like, community art centers and, uh, galleries in places like rural areas where people hadn't really had access to the arts.

Professor

Right.

Male student

Yeah, but didn't the government end up wasting a lot of money for art that wasn't even very good?

Professor

Uh, some people might say that, but wasn't the primary objective of the Federal Art Project to provide jobs?

Male student

That's true. I mean, it did provide jobs for thousands of unemployed artists.

Professor

Right, but then, when the United States became involved in the Second World War, unemployment was down, and it seemed that these programs weren't really necessary any longer.

So, moving on . . . we don't actually see any govern—er, well, any *real* government involvement in the arts *again* until the early 1960s, when President Kennedy and other politicians started to push for major funding to support and promote the arts. It was felt by a number of politicians that, well, that the government had a *responsibility* to . . . uh, support the arts as sort of, oh what can we say, the soul, or *spirit* of the country. The idea was that there'd be a federal *subsidy*, uh, financial *assistance* to artists and artistic or cultural institutions. And for just those reasons, in 1965, the National Endowment for the Arts was created.

So, it was through the NEA, the National Endowment for the Arts, um, that the arts would develop, would be *promoted* throughout the nation. And then, individual states throughout the country started to establish their *own* state arts councils to help support the arts. There was kind of a cultural explosion—and by the mid-1970s, by 1974, I think, all 50 states had their own arts agencies, their own state arts councils that worked with the federal government, with corporations, artists, performers, you name it.

Male student

Did you just say corporations? How were they involved?

Professor

Well, you see, corporations aren't always altruistic, they might not support the arts unless . . . well, unless the government made it attractive for them to do so, by offering corporations tax incentives to support the arts—that is by letting corporations pay less in taxes if they were patrons of the arts. Uh, the Kennedy Center in Washington, D.C., you may, maybe you've been there, or Lincoln Center in New York. Both of these were built with substantial financial support from corporations. And the Kennedy and Lincoln Centers aren't the only examples—many of your cultural establishments in the United States will have a plaque somewhere acknowledging the support, the money, they've received from whatever corporation. Yes, Janet?

Female student

But aren't there a lot of people who don't think it's the government's role to support the arts?

Professor

Well, as a matter of fact, a lot of politicians who did not believe in government support for the arts, they wanted to do away with the agency entirely for that very reason—to get rid of governmental support—but they only succeeded in taking away about half the annual budget. And as far as the public goes . . . well, there are about as many individuals who disagree with government support as there are those who agree—in fact, with artists in particular, you have lots of artists who support— and who have benefitted from—this agency, although it seems that just as many artists oppose a government agency being involved in the arts for many different reasons—reasons like they don't want the government to control what they create. In other words . . . the arguments both for and against government funding of the arts are as many and, and as varied as the individual styles of the artists who hold them.

TRACK 9 TRANSCRIPT

Narrator

Listen again to part of the discussion. Then answer the question.

Male student

Yeah, but didn't the government end up wasting a lot of money for art that wasn't even very good?

Professor

Uh, *some* people might say that, but wasn't the *primary* objective of the Federal Art Project to *provide jobs*?

Narrator

What does the professor imply when she says this:

Professor

Uh, *some* people might say that, but wasn't the *primary* objective of the Federal Art Project to *provide jobs*?

TRACK 10 TRANSCRIPT

Narrator

Many universities now offer academic courses over the Internet. However, some people still prefer learning in traditional classrooms. Which do you think is better? Explain why.

TRACK 11 TRANSCRIPT

Narrator

The computer department is considering making a scheduling change. You will have 45 seconds to read an article in the campus newspaper about the change. Begin reading now.

TRACK 12 TRANSCRIPT

Narrator

Now listen to two students discussing the article.

Male student

I just don't think this will work.

Female student

Why not?

Male student

Because it's not gonna solve the problem. Students are busy at night . . . I mean, we have jobs, families, clubs, social events. Most of us already have something to do every single night of the week.

Female student

I see your point. I sure couldn't fit anything into my schedule during the week—I've got swimming practice most nights.

Male student

Right. And as far as expense goes, I think they're going about it the wrong way. I mean, it costs money to hire more teachers and keep the academic building open later. Which is a lot more expensive than just simply buying more computers.

Female student

More computers?

Male student

That's right. Computer prices have come way down the past few years, so the department won't have to spend as much now as they did in the past. Besides, the computer department classrooms, you know, the rooms themselves, they're actually very big . . . there's plenty of space to add more computers.

Narrator

The man expresses his opinion about the proposal described in the article. Briefly summarize the proposal. Then state his opinion about the proposal and explain the reasons he gives for holding that opinion.

TRACK 13 TRANSCRIPT

Narrator

Now read a passage from a psychology textbook. You have 45 seconds to read the passage. Begin reading now.

TRACK 14 TRANSCRIPT

Narrator

Now listen to part of a lecture on this topic in a psychology course.

Professor

Last month my favorite uncle paid me a surprise visit. I hadn't seen him in many years . . . The doorbell rang, I opened the door, and there was Uncle Pete. Now, I'm sure when I saw him I said something like: "Uncle Pete! What a surprise! How nice to see you!" Anyway, my wife was standing next to me and according to her—I wasn't really aware of this—my eyes got really wide and I broke into a huge big smile. She said I was actually jumping up and down, like a little boy. Well, anyway, later that evening Uncle Pete told me how very, very good he felt when he saw how happy I was to see him.

But compare that with this: my daughter . . . she's six . . . We were building a birdhouse together last week. And I was showing her how to use a hammer and nail. And of course, stupid me, I wasn't being very careful and I smashed my thumb with the hammer. Boy, did it hurt! I almost felt like screaming, but I didn't want to upset my daughter, so I said, "Don't worry, honey. It's nothing." Meanwhile, I was shaking my hand, as if that would stop my thumb from hurting, and my face was contorted in pain. My voice was trembling too. So even though I told my daughter I was OK, I'm sure she didn't believe me. Because she kept asking me if I was OK.

Narrator

Explain how the examples from the professor's lecture illustrate the relationship between verbal and nonverbal communication.

TRACK 15 TRANSCRIPT

Narrator

Listen to part of a talk in an art appreciation class.

Professor

In order for art to communicate—to appeal to the emotions or the intellect—it has to combine various *visual elements* to express meaning . . . or emotion. It's really the visual components of the work—things like color, texture, shape, lines—and how these elements work together that tell *us* something about the work. Artists combine and manipulate these visual elements to express a message or to create a mood.

Think about how a painter might use *color,* for example. You all know from experience that different colors appeal in different ways to the senses and can convey different meanings. An artist chooses certain colors to evoke a particular mood and make powerful statements. The color red, for example, is a strong color and can conjure up strong emotions . . . such as extreme joy, or excitement . . . or even anger. Blue, on the other hand, is considered a cool color. Blue colors tend to have a calming effect on viewers.

Another visual element important to art is texture. By texture, I mean the surface quality or "feel" of the work . . . its smoothness, or roughness, or softness. . . . Now, of course, in some types of art, the texture is physical—it can actually be touched by the fingers. But in painting, for example, texture can be visual. The way an artist paints certain areas of a painting can create the illusion of texture . . . an object's smoothness, or roughness, or softness. A rough texture can evoke stronger emotions and strength while a smooth texture is more calming and less emotional.

As I said earlier, artists often combine elements to convey a message about the work. Take a painting that, say, uses a lot of strong colors like reds and oranges and . . . and uses brushstrokes that are broad—wide, sweeping brushstrokes that suggest a rough texture. Well, these elements together can convey a wilder, more chaotic emotion in the viewer than, more than in, say . . . a painting with tiny, smooth brushstrokes and soft or pale colors. Artists use these visual effects and the senses they arouse to give meaning to their work.

Narrator
Using points and examples from the lecture, explain the importance of visual elements in painting.

TRACK 16 TRANSCRIPT

Narrator
Now listen to part of a lecture on the topic you just read about.

Professor
Many scientists have problems with the arguments you read in the passage. They don't think those arguments prove that dinosaurs were endotherms.

Take the polar dinosaur argument. When dinosaurs lived, even the polar regions where dinosaur fossils have been found were much warmer than today—warm enough during part of the year for animals that were not endotherms to live. And during the months when the polar regions were cold, the so-called polar dinosaurs could have migrated to warmer areas or hibernated like many modern reptiles do. So the presence of dinosaur fossils in polar regions doesn't prove the dinosaurs were endotherms.

Well, what about the fact that dinosaurs had their legs placed under their bodies, not out to the side, like a crocodile's? That doesn't necessarily mean dinosaurs were high-energy endotherms built for running. There's another explanation for having legs under the body: this body structure supports more weight. So with the legs under their bodies, dinosaurs could grow to a very large size. Being large had advantages for dinosaurs, so we don't need the idea of endothermy and running to explain why dinosaurs evolved to have their legs under their bodies.

OK, so how about bone structure? Many dinosaur bones do have Haversian canals, that's true, but dinosaur bones also have growth rings. Growth rings are a thickening of the bone that indicates periods of time when the dinosaurs weren't rapidly growing. These growth rings are evidence that dinosaurs stopped growing or grew more slowly during cooler periods. This pattern of periodic growth—ya know, rapid growth followed by no growth or slow growth and then rapid growth again—is characteristic of animals that are not endotherms. Animals that maintain a constant body temperature year round, as true endotherms do, grow rapidly even when the environment becomes cool.

TRACK 17 TRANSCRIPT

Narrator

Summarize the points made in the lecture, being sure to explain how they challenge the specific points made in the reading passage.

TRACK 18 TRANSCRIPT

Narrator

Listen to a conversation between a student and a counselor at the university counseling center.

Student

Hi, thanks for seeing me on such short notice.

Counselor

No problem. How can I help?

Student

Well, I think I might've made a mistake coming to this school.

Counselor

What makes you say that?

Student

I'm a little overwhelmed by the size of this place. I come from a small town. There were only 75 of us in my high school graduating class. Everyone knew everyone; we all grew up together.

Counselor

So it's a bit of a culture shock for you, being one of 15,000 students on a big campus in an unfamiliar city.

Student

That's an understatement. I just can't get comfortable in class, or in the dorms, you know, socially.

Counselor

Hmm, well—let's start with your academics. Tell me about your classes.

Student

I'm taking mostly introductory courses, and some are taught in these huge lecture halls.

Counselor

And you're having trouble keeping pace with the material?

Student

No, in fact, I got an A on my first economics paper. It's just that, it's so impersonal. I'm not used to it.

Counselor

Are all your classes impersonal?

Student

Nah . . . It's just that, for example, in sociology yesterday, the professor asked a question. So I raised my hand . . . several of us raised our hands . . . and I kept my hand up because I did the reading and knew the answer. But the professor just answered his own question and continued with the lecture.

Counselor

Well, in a big room, it's possible he didn't notice you. Maybe he was trying to save time. In either case, I wouldn't take it personally.

Student

I suppose. But I just don't know how to, you know, *distinguish* myself.

Counselor

Why not stop by his office during office hours?

Student

That wouldn't seem right, y'know . . . taking time from other students who need help.

Counselor

Don't say that. That's what office hours are for. There's no reason you couldn't pop in to say hi, to, uh, to make yourself known. If you're learning a lot in class, let the professor know. Wouldn't *you* appreciate positive feedback if *you* were a professor?

Student

You're right. That's a good idea.

Counselor

OK, uh, let's turn to your social life. How's it going in the dorms?

Student

I don't have much in common with my roommate or anyone else I've met so far. Everyone's into sports, and I'm more artsy, you know, into music. I play the cello.

Counselor

Ahhh. Have you been playing long?

Student

Since age 10. It's a big part of my life. At home, I was the youngest member of our community orchestra.

Counselor

You're not going to *believe* this! There's a string quartet on campus—all students. And it so happens the cellist graduated last year. They've been searching high and low for a replacement, someone with experience. Would you be interested in auditioning?

Student

Absolutely! I wanted to get my academic work settled before pursuing my music here, but I think this would be a good thing for me. I guess if I really want to fit in here, I should find people who love music as much as I do. Thank you!

Counselor

My pleasure.

TRACK 19 TRANSCRIPT

Sociology

Narrator

Listen to part of a lecture in a sociology class.

Professor

Have you ever heard the one about alligators living in New York sewers? The story goes like this: a family went on vacation in Florida, and bought a couple of baby alligators as presents for their children, then returned from vacation to New York, bringing the alligators home with them as pets. But the alligators would escape and find their way into the New York sewer system where they started reproducing, grew to huge sizes and now strike fear into sewer workers. Have you heard this story? Well, it isn't true and it never happened, but despite that, the story's been around since the 1930s.

Or how about the song "Twinkle, twinkle, little star"? You know "Twinkle, twinkle, little star, how I wonder what you are . . ." Well, we've all heard this song. Where am I going with this? Well, both the song and the story are examples of memes, and that's what we'll talk about, the theory of memes.

A meme is defined as a piece of information copied from person to person. By this definition, most of what you know . . . ideas, skills, stories, songs . . . are memes. All the words you know, all the scientific theories you've learned, the rules your parents taught you to observe . . . all are memes that have been passed on from person to person.

So what? . . . you may say. Passing on ideas from one person to another is nothing new . . . Well, the whole point of defining this familiar process as transmission of memes is so that we can explore its analogy with the transmission of *genes*.

As you know, all living organisms pass on biological information through the genes. What's a gene? A gene is a piece of biological information that gets copied, or replicated, and the copy, or replica, is passed on to the new generation. So genes are defined as replicators . . .

Genes are replicators that pass on information about properties and characteristics of organisms. By analogy, *memes* also get replicated and in the process pass on cultural information from person to person, generation to generation. So memes are also replicators. To be a successful replicator, there are three key characteristics: longevity, fecundity, and fidelity. Let's take a closer look . . .

First, longevity. A replicator must exist long enough to be able to get copied and transfer its information. Clearly, the longer a replicator survives, the better its chances of getting its message copied and passed on. So longevity is a key characteristic of a replicator. If you take the alligator story, it can exist for a long time in individual memory—let's say my memory. I can tell you the story now, or ten years from now. The same with the "Twinkle, twinkle" song. So these memes have longevity, because they're memorable, for one reason or another.

Next, fecundity. Fecundity is the ability to reproduce in large numbers. For example, the common housefly reproduces by laying several thousand eggs. So each fly gene gets copied thousands of times. Memes? Well, they can be reproduced in large numbers as well. How many times have you sung the "Twinkle, twinkle" song to someone? Each time you replicated the song—and maybe passed it along to someone who didn't know it yet, a small child maybe.

And finally, fidelity. Fidelity means accuracy of the copying process. We know fidelity is an essential principle of genetic transmission. If a copy of a gene is a bit different from the original, that's called a *genetic* mutation, and mutations are usually bad news. An organism often cannot survive with a mutated gene—and so a gene usually cannot be passed on unless it's an exact copy. For *memes*, however, fidelity is not always so important. For example, if you tell someone the alligator story I told you today, it probably won't be word for word exactly as I said it. Still, it will be basically the same story, and the person who hears the story will be able to pass it along. Other memes are replicated with higher fidelity, though—like the "Twinkle, twinkle" song? It had the exact same words twenty years ago as it does now. Well, that's because we see songs as something that has to be performed accurately each time. If you change a word, the others will usually bring you in line. They'll say, "That's not how you sing it," right?

So, you can see how looking at pieces of cultural information as replicators, as memes, and analyzing them in terms of longevity, fecundity, and fidelity, we can gain some insight about how they spread, persist, or change.

TRACK 20 TRANSCRIPT

Narrator
Why does the professor say this:

Professor
If you change a word, the others will usually bring you in line. They'll say, "That's not how you sing it," right?

TRACK 21 TRANSCRIPT

Earth Science

Narrator

Listen to part of a discussion in an earth science class.

Professor

OK. So much for sand. But before we go on to other elements of soil . . . any questions so far?

Female student

Yeah. One time we were walking down the beach, kinda sliding our feet . . . and with each step, we heard this . . . sort of squeaking sound coming from the sand . . . almost like the barking of a dog. What was that all about?

Professor

Well, when you slide your foot along the surface of the sand, there's some resistance—some friction. And that causes a vibration in the layer of sand just below—what you hear as a short squeak or bark.

Professor

But that reminds me . . . Have you ever heard of "singing" sand dunes?

Female student

Singing? Oh, come on . . .

Professor

No, really.

Male student

Are you trying to pull our leg?

Professor

Not at all. These sand dunes really exist, over 40 of 'em. They're basically big piles of sand, ranging in height from less than 30 meters high to over 300. They're found in deserts all over the world: in California, Africa, Asia . . . Marco Polo even saw one on his travels to China 700 years ago.

Female student

But give me a break—they actually sing?

Professor

Well, their "song" has also been described as sounding like a long, drawn-out bass-note on a musical instrument . . . or even an airplane—the sound of a low-flying airplane. But yes, it's clearly audible . . . sometimes even from several kilometers away.

Male student

You mean . . . OK, I play the bass in the university orchestra . . . . So one of these sand dunes sounds like when I play a low note on my bass?

Professor

Yes. Especially when you use a bow. When you're drawing that bow across a string, there's friction and you're causing that string to vibrate, right? And the instrument resonates with a long, deep bass-note.

Male student

Uh-huh. . . .

Professor

OK, imagine the wind piles up a large amount of new sand up along the top of a dune, and that sand gives way all of a sudden. . . . Now you've got this avalanche of sand sliding down the face of the dune, right? . . . Just like your bow slides across the string on your bass. But here, it's not a string that's vibrating, but the dune . . . actually, a layer of sand at the surface of the dune . . . that's vibrating and resonating to make this low droning sound . . . as the avalanche slides over it.

Male student

A dune has layers? Isn't it just one big hill of sand?

Professor

Well, the sand got blown there by the wind, so the stuff on top is still pretty loosely packed . . . and dry. Underneath, it's not so loose, mostly due to moisture. . . . Even in deserts where it hasn't rained in years, there's some moisture trapped in the layer below. Now the outer layer has to be really dry or else you won't hear much of anything. But the wetter sand underneath has really different sound properties from those of the dry layer above. And the boundary between the layers acts like a mirror, in a way, to reflect sound . . . and so does the very outer surface of the dune. So the sound reflects back and forth inside that dry outer layer, and one particular pitch gets amplified—a monotone, just about, that grows louder and louder and then keeps on reverberating . . . long after the avalanche of sand has slid down to the bottom of the slope.

Female student

Oh, like . . . the stairways in my dormitory are enclosed in concrete stairwells. And if you sing one particular note, it'll echo back and forth between the walls in there, . . . really loud, even after you stop singing.

Professor

Exactly. That note, or pitch, is the frequency that resonates best in a space of those particular dimensions.

Male student

And the pitch of the sound the sand dune makes? How high or low that is depends on the size of the dune, right? Like, . . . the bass I play is a lot bigger than a violin, so the sounds that resonate the loudest from it are a lot deeper than the higher pitches you get from a violin.

Professor

Hmm. There's a certain logic to that comparison. Actually, though, it's not the height or size of the dune . . . but rather, it's the thickness of that outer layer of sand. In other words, it's the distance between those reflecting surfaces we talked about . . . the top and bottom surfaces of that layer of dry sand—the pitch depends on how far apart they are.

TRACK 22 TRANSCRIPT

Narrator

After a student compares different stringed instruments to sand dunes, what does the professor imply when he says this:

Professor

Hmm. There's a certain logic to that comparison.

TRACK 23 TRANSCRIPT

Narrator

Listen to a conversation between a student and a professor.

Student

Hi. I was wondering if could talk with you about the assignment in the Film Theory class?

Professor

Of course, Jill.

Student

It seems that pretty much everyone else in the class gets what they're supposed to be doing, but *I'm* not so sure.

Professor

Well, the class *is* for students who are really serious about film. You must have taken film courses before?

Student

Yeah, in high school, Film Appreciation.

Professor

Hmm, I wouldn't think that'd be enough. Did you concentrate mainly on form, or content?

Student

Oh, definitely content. We'd watch, say, *Lord of the Flies*, and then discuss it.

Professor

Oh, *that* approach . . . treating film as literature, ignoring what makes it unique . . .

Student

I liked it, though . . .

Professor

Sure, but *that* kind of class . . . well, I'm not surprised you're feeling a little lost. Y'know, we have two introductory courses that are supposed to be taken before you get to *my* course—one in film art, techniques . . . technical stuff . . . and another in film history. So students in the class *you're* in should be pretty far along in film studies. In fact, usually the system blocks anyone trying to sign up for a class they shouldn't be taking, who hasn't taken the courses you're required to do *first*, as *prerequisites*.

Student

Well, I did have a problem with that, but I discussed it with one of your office staff and she gave me permission.

Professor

Of course. No matter how many times I tell them, they just keep on . . . Well, for your own good, I'd really suggest dropping back and starting at the usual place . . .

Student

Yes, but . . . I've already been in this class for four weeks! I'd hate to just drop it now, especially since I find it so different, so interesting.

Professor

I guess *so*—frankly, I can't believe you've lasted this long! These are pretty in-depth theories we've been discussing, and you've been doing OK so far, I guess. But, still, the program's been designed to progress through certain stages. Like any other professional training, we build on previous knowledge.

Student

Then maybe you could recommend some extra reading I can do, to catch up?

Professor

Well, are you intending to study film, as your main concentration?

Student

No. No, I—I'm just interested; I'm actually in marketing, but there seems to be a connection . . .

Professor

Oh, well, in *that* case . . . if you're taking the course just out of *interest* . . . I mean, I'd still highly recommend signing up for the introductory courses at *some* point. But in the *meantime*, there's no harm, I guess, in trying to keep up with *this* class. The interest is clearly there. Uh, instead of any extra reading just now, though, you *could* view some of the *old* introductory lectures—we have 'em on video—*that'd* give you a better handle on the subject. It's still a pretty tall order, and we'll be moving right along, so you'll really need to stay on top of it.

Student

OK, I've been warned. Now, could I tell you about my idea for the assignment . . .?

TRACK 24 TRANSCRIPT

Literature

Narrator

Listen to part of a lecture in a literature class.

Professor

Now, we can't really talk about fairy tales without first talking about *folk* tales . . . because there's a strong connection between these two genres, these two types of stories. In fact, many fairy tales started out as folktales.

So, what's a *folk* tale? How would you characterize them? Jeff?

Male student

Well, they're old stories, traditional stories. They were passed down orally within cultures, from generation to generation, so they changed a lot over time; I mean, every storyteller, or maybe every town, might have had a slightly different version of the same folktale.

Professor

That's right, there's *local difference,* and that's why we say folktales are communal.

By "communal," we mean they reflect the traits and the concerns of a particular community at a particular time. So essentially the same tale could be told in different communities, with certain aspects of the tale adapted to fit the specific community. Um, *not* the plot . . . the details of what *happens* in the story would remain constant; that was the thread that held the tale together. But all the other elements, like the location or characters, might be modified for each audience.

OK, so what about *fairy* tales? They also are found in most cultures, but how are they different from folktales? I guess the first question is what is a fairy tale? And don't anyone say, "a story with a fairy in it." Because we all know that very few fairy tales actually have those tiny magical creatures in them. But what else can we say about them? Mary?

Female student

Well, they seem to be less realistic than folktales. Like they have something improbable happening—a frog turning into a prince, say. Oh, that's another common element, royalty . . . a prince or princess. And fairy tales all seem to take place in a location that's nowhere and everywhere at the same time.

Professor

What's the line, ah—how do all those stories start? "Once upon a time, in a faraway land . . ." In the case of *folk* tales, each storyteller would specify a particular location and time, though the time and location would differ for different storytellers. With *fairy* tales, however, the location is generally unspecified, no matter who the storyteller is . . . that "land faraway . . ." We'll come back to this point in a few minutes.

Male student

Um, I thought a fairy tale was just the written version of an oral folktale.

Professor

Well, not exactly, though that is how many fairy tales developed. For example, in the late eighteenth century, the Grimm brothers traveled throughout what's now Germany recording local *folk* tales. These were eventually published—as *fairy* tales—but not before undergoing a process of evolution.

Now, a number of things happen when an oral tale gets written down. First, the language changes, it becomes more formal, more standard—some might say less colorful. It's like the difference in your language depending on whether you're talking to someone or writing them a letter.

Second, when an orally transmitted story is written down, an authoritative version, with a recognized author is created. The communal aspect gets lost; the tale no longer belongs to the community; it belongs to the world, so to speak. Because of this, elements like place and time can no longer be tailored to suit a particular audience, so they become less identifiable, more generalizable to any audience.

On the other hand, descriptions of characters and settings can be developed more completely. In *folk* tales, characters might be identified by a name, but you wouldn't know anything more about them. But in *fairy* tales, people no longer have to remember plots—they're written down, right? So more energy can be put into other elements of the story, like character and setting. So you get more details about the characters, and about where the action takes place, what people's houses were like, whether they're small cabins or grand palaces . . . And it's worth investing that energy because the story, now in book form, isn't in danger of being lost, those details won't be forgotten. If a *folk* tale isn't repeated by each generation, it may be lost for all time. But with a fairy tale, it's always there in a book, waiting to be discovered again and again.

Another interesting difference involves the change in audience—who the stories are meant for. Contrary to what many people believe today, folktales were originally intended for adults, not for children. So why is it that fairy tales seem targeted toward children nowadays?

TRACK 25 TRANSCRIPT

Narrator
Listen again to part of the lecture. Then answer the question.

Female student
And fairy tales all seem to take place in a location that's nowhere and everywhere at the same time.

Professor
What's the line, ah—how do all those stories start? "Once upon a time, in a faraway land . . ."

Narrator
Why does the professor say this:

Professor
What's the line, ah—how do all those stories start? "Once upon a time, in a faraway land . . ."

TRACK 26 TRANSCRIPT

Narrator
Do you agree or disagree with the following statement? Why or why not? Use details and examples to explain your answer.

It is more important to study math or science than it is to study art or literature.

TRACK 27 TRANSCRIPT

Narrator
The university has announced a new policy regarding dining services. Read an article about it in the student newspaper. You have 50 seconds to read the article. Begin reading now.

TRACK 28 TRANSCRIPT

Narrator

Now listen to two students discussing the article.

Female student

Did you see that article?

Male student

Yeah—and it sounds like a great idea. It's really good for the students in that program.

Female student

Don't they cook in class anyway?

Male student

Well, yeah, they do . . . but my cousin was in the program a few years ago, and she said that it's very different to cook for a lot of people in that kind of atmosphere than to cook for classmates.

Female student

Why is that?

Male student

Well, in class you can take your time. But, cooking for more people, there's more pressure—I mean, you're in a rush, people are waiting . . . and it might be easy to make a mistake with all that stress . . .

Female student

Then they'll think you're a bad chef, right?

Male student

Absolutely!

Female student

So, OK, it's good practice. But what about the extra cost?

Male student

Well, look at it this way. You've eaten at some of the fancier restaurants in town, right?

Female student

Yeah, there are some great places to eat around here.

Male student

Well, these students . . . they'll be making fantastic meals. And it's gonna be cheaper than going out to one of those restaurants.

Female student

Much cheaper actually . . .

Male student

So, you know, it'll be worth it. The meals will be as good as the ones in those expensive restaurants.

Narrator

The man expresses his opinion about the plan described in the article. Briefly summarize the plan. Then state his opinion about the plan and explain the reasons he gives for holding that opinion.

TRACK 29 TRANSCRIPT

Narrator

Read the passage about target marketing. You will have 45 seconds to read the passage. Begin reading now.

TRACK 30 TRANSCRIPT

Narrator

Now listen to part of a lecture on this topic in a marketing class.

Professor

Nowadays, something you notice more and more is television commercials that are made specifically for certain television programs. So, let's say a company wants to sell a telephone . . . a cell phone. Now, during TV shows that young people watch—you know, shows with pop music or teen serials—they create a commercial that emphasizes how fun the phone is. You know, the phone has bright colors, and they show kids having a good time with their friends. And, well, the company wants the kids watching TV at this time to want to buy this phone—this phone that's made especially for them.

But, the same company will make a different commercial to be shown during, say, a program about business or a business news show. Now, for this group of people, businesspeople, the company will have to show how efficient their phone is, how it can handle all business easily and maybe even save money. And here's the thing—it's basically the same phone; the company has just made two different commercials to appeal to different groups of people.

Narrator

Using the professor's examples, explain the advertising technique of target marketing.

TRACK 31 TRANSCRIPT

Narrator

Now listen to part of a lecture in a psychology class.

Professor

Why do we do the things we do? What drives us to participate in certain activities . . . to buy a certain car . . . or even to choose a certain career? In other words, what motivates us to do what we do?

Well, in studies of motivation, psychologists distinguish between two very different types. Our reasons for doing something, our motivations, can be *extrinsic*—in other words, based on some kind of *external* reward like praise or money . . . or they can be *intrinsic* . . . meaning we engage in the activity because it pleases us *internally*. Both create strong forces that lead us to behave in certain ways; however, intrinsic motivation is generally considered to be more long-lasting than the other.

As I said, extrinsic motivation is . . . *external*. It's the desire to behave in a certain way in order to obtain some kind of external reward. A child, for example, who regularly does small jobs around the house does them not because she enjoys taking out the garbage or doing the dishes but because she knows if she does these things, she'll be given a small amount money for doing them. But how motivated would the child be to continue doing the work if her parents suddenly stopped giving her money for it?

With intrinsic, or internal, motivation we want to do something because we enjoy it, or get a sense of accomplishment from it. Most people who are internally motivated get pleasure from the activity . . . so they just feel good about doing it. For example, I go to the gym several times a week. I don't go because I'm training for a marathon or anything. I just enjoy it. I have more energy after I exercise and I know it's good for my health so it makes me feel good about myself. And that's what's kept me going there for the past five years.

Narrator
Using points and examples from the talk, explain the two types of motivation.

TRACK 32 TRANSCRIPT

Narrator
Now listen to part of a lecture on the topic you just read about.

Professor
Unfortunately, none of the arguments about what the Chaco great houses were used for is convincing.

First—sure, *from the outside* the great houses look like later Native American apartment buildings, but the *inside* of the great houses casts serious doubt on the idea that many people lived there. I'll explain. If hundreds of people were living in the great houses, then there would have to be many *fireplaces* where each family did its daily cooking. But there're very *few* fireplaces. In one of the largest great houses there were fireplaces for only around ten families. Yet there are enough *rooms* in the great house for more than a *hundred* families. So the primary function of the houses couldn't have been residential.

Second, the idea that the great houses were used to store grain maize is unsupported by evidence. It may *sound* plausible that large, empty rooms were used for storage, but excavations of the great houses have *not* uncovered many traces of maize *or* maize containers. If the great houses were used for storage, why isn't there more spilled maize on the floor? Why aren't there more remains of big containers?

Third, the idea that the great houses were ceremonial centers isn't well supported either. Ya know that mound at Pueblo Alto? It contains lots of other materials besides broken pots, stuff you wouldn't expect from ceremonies. For example, there're large quantities of building materials—sand, stone, even construction tools. This suggests that the mound is a just a *trash heap* of construction material, stuff that was thrown away or not used up when the house was being built. The pots in the pile could be regular trash, too, left over from the meals of the construction workers. So the Pueblo Alto mound is *not* good evidence that the great houses were used for special ceremonies.

TRACK 33 TRANSCRIPT

Narrator

Summarize the points made in the lecture, being sure to explain how they cast doubt on the specific theories discussed in the reading passage.

TRACK 34 TRANSCRIPT

Narrator

Listen to a conversation between a student and an employee in the university's career services office.

Student

Hi. Do you have a minute?

Administrator

Sure. How can I help you?

Student

I have a couple of questions about the career fair next week.

Administrator

OK, shoot.

Student

Um, well, are seniors the only ones who can go? I mean, you know, they're finishing school this year and getting their degrees and everything . . . and, well, it seems like businesses would want to talk to them and not first-year students like me . . .

Administrator

No, no. The career fair is open to all our students and we encourage anyone who's interested to go check it out.

Student

Well, that's good to know.

Administrator

You've seen the flyers and the posters around campus, I assume.

Student

Sure! Can't miss 'em. I mean, they all say where and when the fair is . . . just not who should attend.

Administrator

Actually, they do. But it's in the small print. We should probably make that part easier to read, shouldn't we? I'll make a note of that right now. So, do you have any other questions?

Student

Yes, actually I do now. Um, since I'd only be going to familiarize myself with the process—you know, "check it out"—I was wondering if there's anything you'd recommend that I do to prepare.

Administrator

That's actually a very good question. As you know, the career fair is generally an opportunity for local businesses to recruit new employees and for soon-to-be graduates to have interviews with several companies they might be interested in working for. Now, in your case, even though you wouldn't be looking for employment right now, it still wouldn't hurt for you to prepare much like you would if you were looking for a job.

Student

You mean like get my résumé together and wear a suit?

Administrator

That's a given. I was thinking more along the lines of doing some research. The flyers and posters list all the businesses that are sending representatives to the career fair. Um, what's your major, or do you have one yet?

Student

Well, I haven't declared a major yet but I'm strongly considering accounting. See, that's part of the reason I want to go to the fair . . . to help me decide if that's what I really want to study . . .

Administrator

That's very wise. Well, I suggest that you get on the computer and learn more about the accounting companies, in particular, that will be attending. You can learn a lot about companies from their Internet Web sites. Then prepare a list of questions.

Student

Questions . . . hmm. So in a way I'll be interviewing them?

Administrator

That's one way of looking at it. Think about it for a second. What do you want to know about working for an accounting firm?

Student

Well, there's the job itself . . . and salary, of course . . . and, um, working conditions . . . I mean, would I have an office or would I work in a big room with a zillion other employees? And . . . um . . . and maybe about opportunities for advancement . . .

Administrator

See? Those are all important things to know. After you do some research you'll be able to tailor your questions to the particular company you're talking to.

Student

Wow, I'm glad I came by here! So, it looks like I've got some work to do.

Administrator

And if you plan on attending future career fairs, I recommend you sign up for one of our interview workshops.

Student

I'll do that.

TRACK 35 TRANSCRIPT

Narrator

Why does the student say this:

Student

So, it looks like I've got some work to do.

TRACK 36 TRANSCRIPT

Narrator

Listen to part of a lecture in a biology class.

Professor

OK, I have an interesting plant species to discuss with you today. Uh, it's a species of a *very* rare tree that grows in Australia—*Eidothea hardeniana*—but it's better known as the Nightcap Oak.

Now, it was discovered only very recently, just a few years ago. Uh, it remained hidden for so long because it's so rare, there're only about, oh, two hundred of 'em in existence. They grow in a rain forest, in a mountain range in the north part of New South Wales, which is, uh, a state in Australia. So just two hundred individual trees in all.

Now, another interesting thing about the Nightcap Oak is that it is . . . it represents . . . a-a very old . . . *type*, a kind of a tree that grew . . . a hundred million years ago. Uh, we found fossils that old that bear a remarkable resemblance to the tree. So, it's a *primitive* tree, a living fossil, you might say. It's a relic from earlier times, and it has survived all these years without much change. And . . . it-it's probably a kind of tree from which other trees that grow in Australia today evolved. Just-just to give you an idea of what we're talking about, here's a picture of the leaves of the tree and its flowers.

I dunno how well you can see the flowers; they're those little clusters sitting at the base of the leaves.

OK, what have we tried to find out about the tree since we've discovered it? Hmm, well, how . . . why is . . . is it so rare is one of the first questions. Uh, how is it, uh, how does it reproduce, is another question. Uh, maybe those two questions are actually related? Jim.

Male student

Hmm, I dunno, but I can imagine that . . . for instance . . . uh, seed dispersal might be a factor—I mean, if the, uh, y'know if the seeds cannot really disperse in a wide area then you know the tree may not, uh, *colonize* new areas, it-it can't spread from the area where it's growing.

Professor

Right, that's-that's actually a very good answer. Uh, of course, you might think there might not be many areas where the tree could spread *into*, uh, because, uh, well it's-it's very specialized in terms of the habitat. But that's not really the case here, uh, the-the suitable habitat-habitat that is the actual rain forest is much larger than-than the few hectares where the Nightcap Oak grows. Now, this tree is a flowering tree as I showed you, uh, uh, it-it produces a fruit, much like a plum, on the inside there's a seed with a hard shell. Uh, it-it appears that the shell has to crack open or break down somewhat to allow the seed to soak up water. If the Nightcap Oak remains, if their seeds remain locked inside their shell, they will not germinate. Now actually the seeds, uh, they don't retain the power to germinate for very long, maybe two years, so there's actually quite a short window of opportunity for the seed to germinate. So the shell somehow has to be broken down before this, uh, germination ability expires. And-and then there's a kind of rat that likes to feed on the seeds as well. So, given all these limitations, not many seeds that the tree produces will actually germinate. So this is a possible explanation for why the tree does not spread. It doesn't necessarily explain how it *became* so rare but it explains why it doesn't increase.

OK, so it seems to be the case that this species, uh this Nightcap Oak, is not very good at spreading. However, it seems, though we can't be sure, that it's very good at *persisting* as a population. Uh, uh, we, uh, there-there're some indications to suggest that the population of the Nightcap Oak has not declined over the last, uh, y'know, many hundreds of years. So, it's stayed quite stable; it-it's not a remnant of some huge population that has dwindled in the last few hundred years for some reason. It's not *necessarily* a species in retreat. OK, so it cannot spread very well but it's good at maintaining itself. It's rare but it's not disappearing. OK, the next thing we might wanna ask about a plant like that is what chances does it have to survive into the future. Let's look at that.

TRACK 37 TRANSCRIPT

Narrator

Listen again to part of the lecture. Then answer the question.

Professor

OK, what have we tried to find out about the tree since we've discovered it? Hmm, well, how . . . why is . . . is it so rare is one of the first questions. Uh, how is it, uh, how does it reproduce, is another question. Uh, maybe those two questions are actually related?

Narrator

Why does the professor say this:

Professor

Maybe those two questions are actually related?

TRACK 38 TRANSCRIPT

Narrator

Listen to a conversation between a student and a professor.

Student

Professor Martin?

Professor

Hi, Lisa—what can I do for you?

Student

Well, I've been thinking about, you know, what you were saying in class last week? About how we shouldn't wait until the last minute to find an idea and get started working on our term paper?

Professor

Good, good. And have you come up with anything?

Student

Well, yeah, sort of—see, I've never had a linguistics class before, so I was sort of . . . I mean, I was looking over the course description, and a lot of the stuff you've described there, I just don't know what it's talking about, you know? Or what it means. But there was one thing that really did jump out at me . . .

Professor

Yes . . .?

Student

The section on dialects? 'Cause, like, that's the kind of thing that's always sort of intrigued me, you know?

Professor

Well, that's certainly an *interesting* topic, but you may not realize, I mean, the *scope* . . .

Student

Well, especially now, 'cause I've got, like, *one* roommate who's from the South, and *another* one from New York, and we all talk, like, *totally* different, you know?

Professor

Yes, I understand, but . . .

Student

But then I was noticing, like, we don't really get into this till the end of the semester, you know? So I . . .

Professor

So you want some pointers where to go for information on the subject? Well, you could always *start* by reading the chapter in the book on sociolinguistics; that would give you a basic understanding of the key issues involved here.

Student

Yeah, that's what *I* thought! So I started reading the chapter, you know—about how everyone speaks some dialect of their language? And I'm wondering, like, well, how do we even manage to understand each other at all?

Professor

Ah! Yes, an interesting question. You see . . .

Student

So then I read the part about "dialect accommodation"—you know, the idea that people tend to adapt their speaking to make it closer to the speech of whoever they're talking to. And I'm thinking, yeah, *I* do that when I talk with my roommates! And without even thinking about it or anything, you know?

Professor

OK, all right—"dialect accommodation" is a more manageable sort of topic . . .

Student

So I was thinking, like, I wonder just how much other people do the same thing? I mean, there's students here from all over the place; does everyone change the way they talk to some degree, depending on who they're talking to?

Professor

You'd be surprised!

Student

So, anyway, my question is, do you think it'd be OK if I did a project like that for my term paper? You know, find students from different parts of the country, record them talking to each other in different combinations, report on how they accommodate their speech or not, that kind of thing?

Professor

Tell you what, Lisa: Write me up a short proposal for this project—how you're going to carry out the experiment and everything, a-a design plan—and I think this'll work out just fine!

TRACK 39 TRANSCRIPT

Narrator

Listen again to part of the conversation. Then answer the question.

Student

The section on dialects? 'Cause, like, that's the kind of thing that's always sort of intrigued me, you know?

Professor

Well, that's certainly an *interesting* topic, but you may not realize, I mean, the *scope* . . .

Narrator

What can be inferred about the professor when he says this:

Professor

Well, that's certainly an *interesting* topic, but you may not realize, I mean, the *scope* . . .

TRACK 40 TRANSCRIPT

Creative Writing

Narrator

Listen to part of a lecture in a creative writing class.

Professor

All right everybody. The topic for today is, well . . . we're gonna take a look at how to start creating the characters for the stories you're writing. One way of doing that is to come up with what's called a character sketch. I don't mean a sketch like a drawing. I guess that's obvious. It's, um . . . a sketch is a way of getting started on defining your characters' personalities.

To begin, how do we create fictional characters? We don't just pull them from thin air, do we? I mean, we don't create them out of nothing. We base them—consciously or unconsciously—we base them on real people. Or, we, um . . . blend several people's traits . . . their attributes . . . into one character.

But when people think fiction, they may assume the characters come from the author's imagination. But the writer's imagination is influenced by . . . by real people. Could be anyone, so pay attention to the people you meet . . . someone in class, at the gym, that guy who's always sitting in the corner at the coffeehouse . . . uh, your cousin who's always getting into dangerous situations. We're pulling from reality . . . gathering bits and pieces of real people. You use these people . . . and the bits of behavior or characteristics as a starting point as you begin to sketch out your characters.

Here's what you should think about doing first. When you begin to formulate a story, make a list of interesting people you know or have observed. Consider *why* they're unique . . . or annoying. Then make notes about their unusual or dominant attributes. As you create fictional characters, you'll almost always combine characteristics from several different people on your list to form the identity and personality of just one character.

Keeping this kind of character sketch can help you solidify your character's personality . . . so that it remains consistent throughout your story. You need to define your characters . . . know their personalities so that you can have them acting in ways that're predictable . . . consistent with their personalities. Get to know them like a friend. You know your friends well enough to know how they'll act in certain situations, right?

Say you have three friends, their car runs out of gas on the highway. John gets upset, Mary remains calm, Teresa takes charge of handling the situation. And, let's say . . . both John and Mary defer to her leadership. They call you to explain what happened. And when John tells you he got mad, you're not surprised because he always gets frustrated when things go wrong. Then he tells you how Teresa took charge, calmed him down, assigned tasks for each person, and got them on their way. Again you're not surprised. It's exactly what you'd expect. Well, you need to know your characters like you know your friends . . . if you know a lot about a person's character, it's easy to predict how they'll behave. So if your characters' personalities are well defined, it'll be easy for you as the writer to portray them realistically . . . believably in any given situation.

While writing character sketches, *do* think about *details*. Ask yourself questions, even if you don't use the details in your story . . . uh, what does each character like to eat, what setting does each prefer . . . the mountains? The city? What about educational background? Their reactions to success . . . or defeat? Write it all down.

But here I need to warn you about a possible pitfall. Don't make your character into a stereotype. Remember, the reader needs to know how your character is different from other people who might fall in the same category. Maybe your character loves the mountains and has lived in a remote area for years. To make sure he's not a stereotype, ask yourself how he sees life differently from other people who live in that kind of setting. Be careful not to make him into the cliché of the rugged mountain dweller.

OK. Now I'll throw out a little terminology . . . it's easy stuff. *Major* characters are sometimes called *round* characters. *Minor* characters are sometimes called . . . well, just the opposite. *Flat*. A round character is fully developed. A flat character isn't—character development is fairly limited. The flat character tends to serve mainly as a, um, a motivating factor. For instance, you introduce a flat character who has experienced some sort of defeat . . . and then your round . . . your main character, who loves success and loves to show off, comes and boasts about succeeding . . . and jokes about the flat character's defeat in front of others . . . humiliates the other guy. The flat character is introduced solely for the purpose of allowing the round character to show off.

TRACK 41 TRANSCRIPT

Narrator
Listen again to part of the lecture. Then answer the question.

Professor
One way of doing that is to come up with what's called a character sketch. I don't mean a sketch like a drawing. I guess that's obvious. It's, um . . . a sketch is a way of getting started on defining your characters' personalities.

Narrator
Why does the professor say this:

Professor
I don't mean a sketch like a drawing.

TRACK 42 TRANSCRIPT

Earth Science

Narrator

Listen to part of a lecture in an earth science class.

Professor

We're really just now beginning to understand how *quickly drastic* climate change can take place. We can see past occurrences of climate change that took place over just a few hundred years. Take, uh, the Sahara desert . . . in Northern Africa.

The Sahara was really different 6,000 years ago. I mean, you wouldn't call it a tropical paradise or anything—ah, or maybe you *would* if you think about how today in some parts of the Sahara it only rains about once a century. Um, but basically, you had greenery and you had water. And what *I* find *particularly* interesting, amazing, really what *really* indicates how *un*-desert-like the Sahara was thousands of years ago, was something painted on a rock: prehistoric art—*hippopotamuses*. As you know, hippos need a lot of water, and hence . . . Hence what?

Female student
They need to live near a large source of water year-round.

Professor
That's right.

Male student
But how's that proof that the Sahara used to be a lot wetter? I mean, the people who painted those hippos . . . well, couldn't they have seen them on their travels?

Professor

OK, in principle they could, Carl. But the rock paintings aren't the only evidence. Beneath the Sahara are huge *aquifers*, basically a sea of fresh water that's perhaps a million years old, filtered through rock layers. And, ah, and-and then there's fossilized pollen from low shrubs and grasses that once grew in the Sahara. In fact these *plants* still grow, ah, but hundreds of miles away in more vegetated areas. Anyway, it's this fossilized pollen, along with the aquifers, *and* the rock paintings—these three things are all evidence that the Sahara was once much greener than it is today, that there were hippos and probably elephants, and giraffes, and so on.

Male student

So, what happened?

Professor

How did it happen? Well now we're so used to hearing about how human activities are affecting the climate, right; but that takes the focus away from the natural variations in the Earth's climate. Like the Ice Age, right? The planet was practically covered in ice just a few thousand years ago. Now, as far as the Sahara goes, there's some recent literature that points to the migration of the monsoon in that area.

Male/Female students

Huh?

Professor

What do I mean? OK. A monsoon is a seasonal wind that can bring in a large amount of rainfall. Now, if the monsoon *migrates*, well *that* means the rains move to another area, right?

So what *caused* the monsoon to migrate? Well, the answer is the dynamics of Earth's motions—the same thing that caused the Ice Age, by the way. The Earth's *not always* the same distance from the Sun. *And* it's *not always tilting* toward the Sun at the same angle. There're slight variations in these two parameters. They're gradual variations, but their *effects* can be pretty abrupt, and *can* cause the climate to change in *just* a few hundred years.

Female student

That's abrupt?

Professor

Well, yeah, considering that other climate shifts take *thousands* of years, this one's pretty abrupt. So these changes in the planet's motions, they caused the climate to change; but it was also *compounded*. What the Sahara experienced was a sort of *runaway drying* effect.

As I said, the monsoon migrated south—so there was less rain in the Sahara. The *land* started to get *drier*—which in turn caused a huge *decrease* in the amount of *vegetation*, because vegetation doesn't grow as well in dry soil, right? And then, less vegetation means the soil can't hold water as well—the soil *loses* its ability to *retain* water when it *does* rain. So then you have less moisture to help clouds form . . . nothing to evaporate for cloud formation. And then the cycle continues—less rain, drier soil, less vegetation, fewer clouds, less rain, etcetera, etcetera.

Male student

But what about the people who made the rock paintings?

Professor

Good question. No one really knows. But there might be some connection to ancient Egypt. At about the same time that the Sahara was becoming a desert, mmm . . . 5,000 years ago, Egypt *really* began to flourish out in the Nile River Valley. And that's not that far away. So it's only *logical* to hypothesize that a lot of these people migrated to the Nile Valley when they realized that this was more than a temporary drought. And some people take this a step further—and that's OK, that's science—and they hypothesize that this migration actually provided an important impetus in the development of ancient Egypt. Well, we'll stay tuned on that.

TRACK 43 TRANSCRIPT

Narrator

Listen again to part of the lecture. Then answer the question.

Professor

I mean, you wouldn't call it a tropical paradise or anything—ah, or maybe you *would* if you think about how today in some parts of the Sahara it only rains about once a century.

Narrator

Why does the professor say this:

Professor

Or maybe you *would* if you think about how today in some parts of the Sahara it only rains about once a century.

TRACK 44 TRANSCRIPT

Narrator

Some people have one career throughout their lives. Other people do different kinds of work at different points in their lives. Which do you think is better? Explain why.

TRACK 45 TRANSCRIPT

Narrator

Now read a letter that a student has written to the university newspaper. You have 50 seconds to read the letter. Begin reading now.

TRACK 46 TRANSCRIPT

Narrator

Now listen to two students discussing the letter.

Female student

I totally disagree with Tim's proposal.

Male student

Why?

Female student

Well, look. Tim's my friend, but he's not your typical student. He stays up late partying every night—weeknights too.

Male student

If he parties every night, no wonder he can't pay attention.

Female student

Yes, and most students aren't like that. They come to class prepared and rested, and they can concentrate.

Male student

So you're saying the problem is really Tim.

Female student

Yes. He was in one of my classes last year and whenever I looked at him, he was actually sleeping.

Male student

I guess if he's sleeping, he can't really know what's happening, what other people in class are doing.

Female student

Right. And you want to know what does happen in that last hour of seminar? In a lot of seminars that I've been in, that's when things get interesting.

Male student

Really?

Female student

Yes. That's usually when students get really involved in the discussion and start exchanging important ideas. And if the history department actually did what Tim suggests, well, if they did that, what would happen is you'd lose what might be the most worthwhile part of a seminar.

Narrator

The woman expresses her opinion about the proposal described in the letter. Briefly summarize the proposal. Then state her opinion about the proposal and explain the reasons she gives for holding that opinion.

TRACK 47 TRANSCRIPT

Narrator

You have 45 seconds to read a passage from a psychology textbook. Begin reading now.

TRACK 48 TRANSCRIPT

Narrator

Now listen to part of a lecture on this topic in a psychology class.

Professor

OK, the first kind of memory, we're all very familiar with this, right? You probably remember what you had for dinner last night. You have a conscious memory of last night's dinner, so, um, if I ask you "What did you eat last night?" you could tell me.

But these other kind of memories—implicit memories. They work differently.

Let's take an example from the world of advertising. When you're driving along a highway, you see plenty of billboards—you know, roadside advertisements. You certainly don't remember them all. But they still affect you. Marketing researchers have shown . . . well, to be specific, let's say there's a billboard on the highway advertising a car called "the Panther." The ad shows a big picture of the car. And above the car in huge letters is the name of the car: "Panther." A lot of people drive by the billboard. But . . . ask those drivers later if they saw any advertisements for cars, and, well, they'll think about it, and a lot of them will say no. They honestly don't remember seeing any. They have no conscious memory of the "Panther" billboard. So you ask these same people a different question: You ask, um, OK, ah, you ask them to name an animal starting with the letter P. What do you think they will answer? Do they say "pig"? Pig is the most common animal that starts with the letter P. But they don't say "pig." They say "panther." The billboard had an effect, even though the drivers don't remember ever seeing it.

Narrator

Using the example of the car advertisement, explain what is meant by implicit memory.

TRACK 49 TRANSCRIPT

Narrator

Now listen to part of a talk in an education class.

Professor

One of the hardest parts of teaching is keeping your students' attention. Now, the key to doing this is understanding the *concept* of attention.

Basically, there are two types of attention. The first type is active. Active attention is voluntary—it's when you intentionally make yourself focus on something. And since it requires effort, it's hard to keep up for a long time. OK, so, um, let's say you're teaching a . . . a biology class. And today's topic is frogs. All right, you're standing at the front of the room and lecturing: "A frog is a type of animal known as an amphibian . . ." Well, this isn't necessarily going to keep the students' interest. But most of them will force themselves to pay active attention to your lecture . . . but it's only a matter of time before they get distracted.

Now, the other type of attention is *passive* attention—when it's involuntary. Passive attention requires no effort, because it happens naturally. If something's really interesting, students don't have to *force* themselves to pay attention to it—they do it without even thinking about it. So back to our biology lecture. You start talking about frogs, and then you pull a live frog out of your briefcase. You're describing it while you hold it up . . . show the students how long its legs are and how they're used for jumping, for example. Then maybe you even let the frog jump around a bit on the desk or the floor. In this case, by doing something unexpected . . . something more engaging, you can tap into their passive attention. And it can last much longer than active attention; as long as the frog's still there, your students will be interested.

Narrator

Using points and examples from the talk, explain the difference between active and passive attention.

TRACK 50 TRANSCRIPT

Narrator

Now listen to part of a lecture on the topic you just read about.

Professor

The communal online encyclopedia will probably never be perfect, but that's a small price to pay for what it *does* offer. The criticisms in the reading are largely the result of prejudice against and ignorance about how far communal online encyclopedias have come.

First, errors. It's hardly a fair criticism that communal online encyclopedias have errors. Traditional encyclopedias have *never* been *close* to perfectly accurate. If you're looking for a *really* comprehensive reference work without *any* mistakes, you're not going to find it—on- *or* off-line. The real point is that it's easy for errors in factual material to be corrected in a communal online encyclopedia—but with the traditional encyclopedia, the errors remain for decades.

Second, hacking. Communal online encyclopedias have recognized the importance of protecting their articles from malicious hackers. One strategy they started using is to put the crucial facts in the articles that nobody disputes in a "*read-only*" format, which is a format that no one can make changes to. That way you're making sure that the crucial facts in the articles are reliable. Another strategy that's being used is to have special editors whose job is to monitor all changes made to the articles and eliminate those changes that are clearly malicious.

Third, about trivial or popular topics. The problem for traditional encyclopedias is that they have limited space, so they have to decide what's important and what's not. And in practice, the judgments of the group of academics that make these decisions don't reflect the great range of interests that people really have. But space is definitely *not* an issue for online encyclopedias. The academic articles are still represented in communal online encyclopedias, but there can be a great variety of articles and topics that accurately reflect the great diversity of users' interests. The diversity of views and topics that communal online encyclopedias offer is one of their strongest advantages.

TRACK 51 TRANSCRIPT

Narrator

Summarize the points made in the lecture, being sure to explain how they oppose the specific points made in the reading passage.

TRACK 52 TRANSCRIPT

Narrator

Listen to a conversation between a student and the volunteer coordinator at the university art museum.

Coordinator

Michael, do you remember the advertisement for your position here, the ad we ran in the student newspaper?

Student

Uh, yeah, vaguely.

Coordinator

It said that, in addition to leading public tours of the museum, volunteer docents might be asked to perform other duties.

Student

Oh, I do remember that. Is that what you wanted to chat with me about?

Coordinator

Yes. The museum has partnered with the local school district to run a poetry contest for high school students.

Student

A poetry contest. Cool. But, um . . . what does poetry have to do with museum tours?

Coordinator

A lot, since it's going to be an ekphrastic poetry contest.

Student

Ek-ekphrastic?

Volunteer coordinator

Yes, an ekphrastic poem is one that's inspired by a piece of artwork. Like, um, William Carlos Williams' poem *The Hunter in the Snow*. It was written in the 1960s and was inspired by a painting made by Pieter Bruegel in the 1500s.

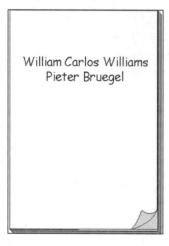

Student

I know Bruegel's work! Beautiful panoramic scenes. I can see how they'd inspire a poet.

Coordinator

Good. So the students'll be submitting poems based on paintings in our museum. We're calling the contest *The Art of Poetry*; we hope to make it an annual thing.

Student

Interesting! So can the students write about any painting they want?

Coordinator

Oh, that might get too unwieldy for the judges, y'know, and for the docents. There's also time limitations, because anyone who registers for the contest must attend a special educational tour focusing on the Art of India exhibit. And that's why we need you.

Student

OK. Eh, when will the tour take place?

Coordinator

Tours. We're setting them up for the third week in March . . . about one month from now, uh, Monday through Friday from 4 to 5 p.m. May I sign you up for one or more of those days?

Student

Sure. I guess Tuesday and Thursday would work, since I have all morning classes those days. Did you want me . . . should I just give my regular talk about the Indian art?

Coordinator

Uh, that's the thing, Michael. You'll have a whole hour. So, instead of spending ten minutes in that exhibit, as you normally do, you'll spend the entire time talking about as many Indian paintings as possible and answering questions.

Student

Wait. Eh, but I've only been trained to discuss three of those paintings! And there's gotta be at least thirty in that exhibit!

Coordinator

It's okay. I'll e-mail all the background you'll need for the rest of them, and you won't have to go into too much depth. I'll also be giving you a list of questions and scenarios for students to think about and discuss, questions like, "Who are the people in the painting?" and "Imagine yourself as one of those people." You can facilitate these discussions.

Economics

Narrator

Listen to part of a lecture in an economics class.

Professor

When attempting to understand international trade, some things seem so obvious that they can hardly be controverted, and other points that are important are invisible unless you've thought about the subject carefully.

Consider the following: if there's an increase in imports, let's say, um, let's say imports of furniture, and the domestic producers of furniture find this new competition very difficult and are cutting production and employment, then it seems obvious and easy to understand and many people conclude from this that increasing imports will cause generally greater unemployment at home.

What is not so obvious is that how much we import and how much we export . . . those are interdependent and you can't understand the one without the other. But the exports that are generated are not easily discernable, so most people don't see them. They see only the imports of furniture rising and employment in domestic furniture production falling.

So as a result, many people argue that we ought to protect jobs by limiting imports—either by tariffs, quotas, regulations, or whatever—without realizing that this also has the effect of reducing potential future exports to the rest of the world, things that we can produce very, very . . . cost effectively and therefore profitably.

The fundamental proposition in international economics is that it makes sense to import those things that we . . . that can be produced more economically abroad than at home and export things to the rest of the world that we can produce more cost effectively than produced elsewhere in the world. Therefore, if we limit imports, we put ourselves in danger of not being able to export.

The details of this relationship will take much longer to explain than I can fully go into now but the point of the matter is that gains—the benefits of gains—from international trade result from being able to get things cheaper by buying them abroad than you can make them at home. Now there're some things that we can make at home that are . . . that we can do more economically than they can do abroad.

In the case of the United States, typically high-technology products, uh . . . are things that Americans have innovated in and started firms doing that sort of thing at which they do very well. Whereas goods that produce . . . that use a lot of relatively low skill labor, like furniture production, cotton production, sugar production . . . those are things that are frequently made more inexpensively in places where wage rates are low and the cost of using capital is very high.

However, in Florida they produce a lot of sugar, but the costs are so high, if we didn't have extensive restrictions on imports of sugar, the output of sugar would decline dramatically. But the sugar industry in the U.S. doesn't produce high-paying jobs, it uses resources in ineffective ways and it blocks the import of more cost-effectively produced sugar. It, it's a very bad bargain for the people in the United States to want to protect low-paying jobs thereby halting the growth of world trading and international . . . uh, more international specialization. It would be better to remove restrictions on imports and allow other countries in the world . . . countries that can produce them more cheaply . . . let them specialize in producing those products.

Now, I agree that people who are directly affected by imports, what they focus on . . . is, is that their prospects . . . their job prospects are being reduced, and their economic circumstances are getting worse. And that's a relevant problem and an important problem; what isn't so obvious is . . . that by retraining and relocating people to places and industries where jobs are expanding rather than contracting, we can make the whole economy function more effectively and productively than by trying to block imports.

Um, what is interesting to note is that, even if there were no international trade issues, like imports, any changes that occur in a country's economy—any new technology, change in preferences, change in regulations or whatever—will lead to "adjustments" that lead some sectors of the economy to decline and others to expand.

And that's what we have to figure out, and that's a hard problem to deal with in detail, is how to facilitate people adjusting from sectors where their job prospects are not so good, and in particular where real wages aren't so high, to acquire skills that will permit them to move into higher-paying jobs in other parts of the economy either by retraining or relocating. Helping pay for the relocation of these people would be very helpful, but trying to block the changes is really counterproductive. It makes people in our country poorer, and it makes people elsewhere in the world poorer as well.

TRACK 54 TRANSCRIPT

Narrator
Listen to a conversation between a student and a professor.

Student
Hi, uh . . . Professor Anderson . . . wondering if you had a couple minutes . . .

Professor
Of course, Paula . . .

Student
Thanks . . . uh, you sent me a letter recently about doing, uh, an honors project—inviting me to come in and talk about . . .

Professor
Right, right, well, as your academic advisor, it's my job to look out for your academic interests, and based on your grades, and some very positive feedback I've heard from your professors, I wanted to formally invite you to consider doing an honors project . . .

Student
Yeah . . . well, thanks . . . uh, actually I kinda wanted to ask you . . . quite frankly—like how much work it would probably be? I mean, I'm gonna be spending a lot of time applying to law schools next semester and . . .

Professor
Well, let me tell you how it works . . . and then you can decide from there.

Student
OK.

Professor

Basically, the honors project is an opportunity to do . . . some in-depth work on a topic you're interested in before graduating college. You register for the class, but it doesn't work the same way a regular class does—you find a professor who you want to work with—you ask the professor—a sort of mentor who's knowledgeable on the topic you're interested in—the topic you're gonna write your honors thesis on . . .

Student

Writing a *thesis*? That's part of the *project*? Ah, like how many pages are we talking?

Professor

Usually about 50 . . . but it's a valuable experience, writing a thesis paper.

Student

So, basically, after I register for the class, I need to ask a professor who'll sorta help me . . .

Professor

Actually, you need to do that—a professor needs to agree to oversee your honors project—before you register.

Student

Oh, OK . . .

Professor

I mean, I know it sounds kinda daunting, but that's what the professor's there for—to help guide you through the different steps of the process and . . . uh . . . most students are very pleased with the experience . . . they're able to demonstrate advanced research skills, which is important; especially in your case, writing an honors thesis would be a big plus . . .

Student

You think so?

Professor

Absolutely. Especially considering your plans, since you're applying to law schools. It shows initiative, that you've done well as an undergraduate—to be allowed to do the honors project . . . that you're able to work independently and, of course, you would graduate with honors . . .

Student

Yeah, it *does* sound good—it's just, you know, I've never written something like that before, so . . .

Professor

Well, you choose something you're interested in—maybe you can even expand a shorter research paper from another class or . . .

Student

So, like, maybe . . . You know, I took this course from Professor Connelly—his course on Comparative Governments last semester and, uh . . . did pretty well—I wrote a paper actually, on political parties in Venezuela and—and he seemed to like my research. Anyway, he, uh, I got an A in the course.

Professor

Good, so it sounds like you do have a general idea for a topic, and you might know what professor you want to work with . . . and look, it's still a couple weeks before registration, maybe you should talk to Professor Connelly and then get back to me.

Student

Yeah, I will—thanks. I'll come by again sometime next week.

Professor

That's fine. Good luck.

TRACK 55 TRANSCRIPT

Narrator

What does Professor Anderson imply when he says this:

Professor

. . . they're able to demonstrate advanced research skills, which is important; especially in your case, writing an honors thesis would be a big plus . . .

TRACK 56 TRANSCRIPT

Narrator

What does the woman imply when she says this:

Student

Yeah, it does sound good—it's just, you know, I've never written something like that before . . . so . . .

TRACK 57 TRANSCRIPT

Journalism

Narrator

Listen to part of a lecture in a journalism class. The professor has been discussing newspapers.

Professor

About 40 years ago, half of all Americans felt they'd be lost without a daily newspaper. But today, only one in *ten* Americans say they'd be lost without a paper. In fact, today, half of all Americans say they don't need a newspaper at all. And so people in the newspaper industry are trying to figure out how they can get more people reading the newspaper more often. They're trying to crack journalism's riddle for the ages: what makes people read newspapers? OK, well, let me ask you—as a journalism student, what do *you* think is the answer to this question? Elizabeth?

Female student

Um, I would probably try to improve the content of the newspaper.

Professor

Better content. Hmm. You mean like *well-written* editorials and articles?

Female student

Well, I mean provide more *interesting* content, like, I would first try to find out what readers really want to read . . . and then put *that* into the paper.

Professor

Yes, in fact, not too long ago, there was an extensive study conducted to investigate what draws people to newspapers. Uh, they found out that there's a clear, strong link between satisfaction with *content* and overall readership. Those newspapers that contained what the readers wanted most brought in the most readers. No big surprise there, right? So, what kind of content brings in readers? The study found that *people-centered local news* ranks at the top of the list . . . stories about *ordinary* people. For example, you could write about the experiences of those who were involved in a news story, and their friends and relatives . . . The vantage points would be those of *ordinary* people, not of police or other officials . . . OK? Now the study also showed that people want more stories about movies, TV, and weather, and *fewer* stories and photos about natural disasters and accidents . . . So, to get reader satisfaction, you need to select the right topics, and within those topics, the right news events or stories to cover. Yes, James?

Male student

It seems to me that a lot of what you just mentioned doesn't line up with the principles of good journalism. Catering to readers' tastes may improve overall readership, but what about the social responsibilities that newspapers have? I mean, there are some topics that newspapers *need* to write about in order to serve the public interest. Those topics may not always be fun and interesting for the average reader, but it's still the newspaper's responsibility to make that information available to the public.

Professor

That's a good point. You need a good mix of content. You can't just rush towards an attractive topic and forget about the reporting role of newspapers. There's a danger of going soft—newspapers *do* have to perform their obligations to citizens. So what newspapers sometimes do is to combine serious journalism with a reader-friendly *presentation*. Um, let me give you an example: When the justice department opened an investigation on the local police—some pretty serious stuff that could be boring to some readers—well, one local newspaper ran a lead story on their front page, but they also simplified the format by including small breakout boxes that presented—in a nutshell—the highlights of the story. That way, they could report the serious stories they needed to report, and, and still hold their readers' attention. OK? Uh, going back to the research on readership growth we were talking about . . . Uh, the most vital step of all, the study shows, may be making the paper easier to *use*. How can we make the paper "easier to *use*"? Well, it means stories need to include information, such as phone numbers, times, dates, addresses, Web sites and the like, so that readers can "go and do" things based on what they've read.

Female student

Professor Ellington? Um, when you said we need to make the paper "easier to use," I thought you were gonna say something about use of graphics, colors, and stuff like that.

Professor

Well, I guess those things do help in a way, but it turned out that those contemporary touches, uh, such as more attractive designs, extensive use of color, and informational graphics matter much less than you'd expect. Surprising, isn't it?

Female student

Yeah, it is . . . Um, how about service? Does the study say anything about improving service? I don't think people are gonna subscribe if the paper doesn't arrive, or shows up late . . .

Professor

Or shows up wet, which by the way, happened to me this morning. Oh, absolutely. Service affects readership. In fact, improving your service is much more likely to increase your readership than making changes in your editorial content . . . Not only on-time delivery in good condition, but also things like efficient billing, affordability, um . . . Yes?

Female student

They could also, like, increase the number of sites where they sell single copies.

Professor

Certainly that's one way to improve service.

TRACK 58 TRANSCRIPT

Narrator

What does the student imply when he says this:

Male student

It seems to me that a lot of what you just mentioned doesn't line up with the principles of good journalism. Catering to readers' tastes may improve overall readership, but what about the social responsibilities that newspapers have?

TRACK 59 TRANSCRIPT

Narrator

Listen again to part of the lecture. Then answer the question.

Female student

I don't think people are gonna subscribe if the paper doesn't arrive, or shows up late . . .

Professor

Or shows up wet, which by the way, happened to me this morning. Oh, absolutely. Service affects readership.

Narrator

What does the professor imply when he says this:

Professor

Or shows up wet, which by the way, happened to me this morning. Oh, absolutely.

Geology

Narrator

Listen to part of a lecture in a geology class.

Professor

Um, beginning in the late 1960s, geologists began to uncover some evidence of a rather surprising kind when they looked . . . um . . . at various places around the world. What they found out when they examined rocks from about a . . . the period from about 750 million years ago to about 580 million years ago, they found that . . . it seemed that glaciers covered the entire surface of the Earth—from pole to pole, including the tropics.

Um . . . how did they come to this astonishing conclusion? What was the evidence for this? Especially when glaciers today are found only at the poles . . . or in the mountains.

Well, uh . . . basically when glaciers grow and move they leave behind a distinctive deposit consisting of primarily . . . of, at least on the top level, of ground up little bits of rock . . . almost . . . they almost look like rocks that have been deposited by streams, if you've ever seen those. And that's caused because, although the glacier is ice, it is actually flowing very slowly and as it moves it grinds the top layer of rock, it breaks off pieces and carries them away. So when you have glaciation you have a distinctive pattern of these pieces of rock which are called "erratics."

Erratics are rocks . . . they're the stones that are often carried long distances by glaciers.

So, in the 1960s and onward up through the 1990s, we keep finding evidence for glaciation, no matter what the latitude . . . even in tropical latitudes. Now, today there are glaciers in the tropics but only at very high elevations. But 750 million years ago, apparently there were glaciers even at sea level in the tropics.

How could this have happened?

Well, first . . . the growth of glaciers, uh, benefits, if you will, from a kind of a positive feedback loop called the "ice-albedo effect."

With the ice-albedo effect, glaciers—'cause they're white—reflect light and heat more . . . much more than does liquid water . . . or soil and rock, which are dark and absorb heat. So, the more glaciers there are, the more heat is reflected, so the climate gets cooler, and glaciers grow even more.

However . . . normally, on a global scale, there is a major process that functions to curb the growth of glaciers. And, that process involves carbon dioxide.

Now, we're all familiar with the notion that carbon dioxide is what we call a "greenhouse gas." The more carbon dioxide there is in the atmosphere, the more heat the atmosphere retains. That's what a greenhouse gas does. So, the greenhouse-gas effect is kinda the opposite of the albedo effect.

Um . . . now as it happens . . . when silicate rocks, which is a very common class of rock, when they're exposed to the air and to normal weathering, they erode. Carbon dioxide is attracted to these eroding rocks and binds to them, forming calcium carbonate.

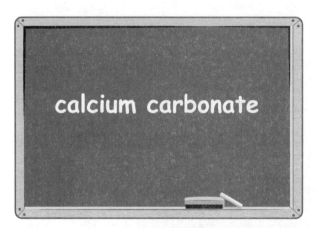

Calcium carbonate is eventually washed into the ocean where it settles to the bottom. This process, this forming of calcium carbonate, has the effect of sucking the carbon dioxide out of the air and storing it at the bottom of the ocean.

Now, follow me here. The process that's sucking carbon dioxide out of the air, keeping the greenhouse gas levels low, cannot happen if the rock is covered with ice.

So, while glaciers reflect light and heat . . . cooling the Earth, they at the same time cover rocks so there's less calcium carbonate formed . . . which leaves more carbon dioxide in the atmosphere. Higher levels of carbon dioxide keep the atmosphere warm . . . which slows the growth of glaciers. So, it's a balance, and the glacier growth remains pretty much under control.

Now, what happened 750 million years ago to upset that balance? It seems a relatively simple explanation actually . . .

750 million years ago . . . all the major continents are rocky, bare, and pretty much lined up along the equator; they hadn't yet moved to where they are today. So, what happened was, perhaps a slight cooling of . . . the very slight and temporary cooling of the Sun—which still happens from time to time—and the Earth starts to cool, the ice starts to spread on the oceans . . . starting at the poles.

Now, by the time the ice reaches about two-thirds of the way to the equator, it's too late.

See . . . because the continents are the last things to be covered by glaciers, they continue weathering . . . the rocks keep eroding and the carbon dioxide levels keep falling . . . So, the ice-albedo effect from the glaciers is increasing in strength while the atmosphere continues to lose its ability to retain heat making glacier growth unstoppable. Now you have what's called a "runaway freeze." And for perhaps as long as 50 million years, possibly with some interludes, the Earth was frozen from pole to pole, like a giant snowball.

TRACK 61 TRANSCRIPT

Narrator

Listen again to part of the lecture. Then answer the question.

Professor

Well, uh . . . basically when glaciers grow and move they leave behind a distinctive deposit consisting of primarily . . . of, at least on the top level, of ground up little bits of rock . . . almost . . . they almost look like rocks that have been deposited by streams, if you've ever seen those.

Narrator

Why does the professor say this:

Professor

. . . they almost look like rocks that have been deposited by streams, if you've ever seen those.

TRACK 62 TRANSCRIPT

Narrator

When some people visit a city or country for the first time, they prefer to take an organized tour. Other people prefer to explore new places on their own. Which do you prefer and why?

TRACK 63 TRANSCRIPT

Narrator

A university professor is switching to a new position. Read the article from the university about the professor. You will have 45 seconds to read the article. Begin reading now.

TRACK 64 TRANSCRIPT

Narrator

Now listen to two students discussing the article.

Female student

I don't like this at all.

Male student

Why not? She's done a lot for the philosophy department . . . like, well, hiring some great new teaching assistants . . . and putting together seminars.

Female student

Well, she has trouble organizing schedules.

Male student

Whadda'ya mean?

Female student

Well, she only realized last minute that she didn't have enough teaching assistants in the department, so some classes got cancelled.

Male student

Oh!

Female student

And I wanted to take a special two-week philosophy course in Europe . . . she was supposed to sign all the paperwork, but she didn't do it in time so I missed the whole trip!

Male student

Oh, wow. So organization's not her strong point, I guess.

Female student

Yeah. Besides, she's always critical. A lot of us on the team have complained to the university about her aggressive coaching style.

Male student

Oh, really? I met her . . . I mean, I thought she was nice.

Female student

Humph! Well, my friend . . . she had some serious problems in her family. She went to talk to Professor Fox and . . .

Male student

Yeah? What happened?

Female student

Well, she wanted emotional support from someone she looked up to, but instead Professor Fox made all kinds of critical comments. Maybe she's good at philosophy, but she's not a counselor. When students go to the dean, they go because they need someone to talk to, not so someone can criticize them.

Narrator

The woman expresses her opinion about the change described in the article. Briefly summarize the change. Then state her opinion about the change and explain the reasons she gives for holding that opinion.

TRACK 65 TRANSCRIPT

Narrator

Read the following paragraph from a psychology textbook. You will have 45 seconds to read the passage. Begin reading now.

TRACK 66 TRANSCRIPT

Narrator

Now listen to part of a lecture in a psychology class.

Professor

Let's start with a physical attribute, say, uh, in kittens. Adult cats have extremely good vision, especially at night. But in order for a kitten's eyesight to develop normally, the kitten must be exposed to light during the first four months of its life. Without that, its eyesight will not develop correctly, it will never be able to see as well as it should. Even if the kitten is exposed to plenty of light *after* those four months of darkness, it won't matter, its vision will *never* develop normally.

As far as behavior's concerned, well, have you ever seen how little baby geese line up and then, single-file, they follow their parent goose around? Well, what would happen if they didn't see a parent goose within the first two days of their lives?

Actually, for normal behavior to develop, they must see what to follow within these first two days. What happens is, whatever large moving object they first see during those two days, they'll adopt that object as their parent . . . forever. It can never be changed. For example, suppose after the baby geese were hatched, the only other animal around was, I don't know, say a dog. OK? So the baby geese see a dog, but no other geese. Even though the dog is a totally different species, the geese will adopt it as their parent—they'll follow it around. And even if the parent geese reappear later, it won't matter to the babies—they'll follow the dog. After two days the behavior is fixed and they'll never exhibit the normal behavior of following their real parent—a goose.

Narrator

Using the examples of kittens and geese, explain the idea of a critical period.

TRACK 67 TRANSCRIPT

Narrator

Now listen to part of a lecture in a business ethics class. The professor is discussing advertising.

Professor

Advertisers often try to sell you things by exaggerating about the quality of their products. It helps them get your attention. And exaggeration in advertising is usually considered acceptable, but not always. In the United States, there are laws to help determine what advertisers can say about their products. Basically, the law says advertisers can exaggerate as long as no one's gonna actually believe the exaggeration and take it literally. So, the exaggeration has to be very extreme. If it's not extreme enough and someone would actually buy the product because they believed the exaggeration, that advertisement may be illegal.

Take this example: a vacuum cleaner manufacturer made a vacuum cleaner that didn't weigh very much, and they wanted to get the point across about how light it was. So they made a TV commercial showing the vacuum cleaner floating in the air while cleaning the house. Well, that was a visual exaggeration. It got people's attention. And because a floating vacuum cleaner is obviously impossible, the commercial was legal because no one would actually believe the visual exaggeration and buy the vacuum cleaner because they thought it floated in the air.

But what if the company wanted to show that the vacuum cleaner was very powerful? What if it made a television commercial where a person uses the vacuum cleaner to perfectly clean this really big and really dirty carpet in, uh, just a few seconds. Well that would really grab your attention. But the thing is, even though the commercial is an exaggeration, you can imagine someone actually believing it and buying the vacuum cleaner and then being very disappointed because the vacuum cleaner couldn't do that. So advertisers can't use an exaggeration like that because it's actually not extreme enough and someone might believe it.

Narrator

Using the example of the vacuum cleaner, explain when it is legally acceptable to use exaggeration in advertising and when it is not.

TRACK 68 TRANSCRIPT

Narrator

Now listen to part of a lecture on the topic you just read about.

Professor

Many people think that if you want to go into business for yourself, it's best to buy a franchise. But recently a study looked closely at franchises, and some of the findings call that idea into question.

One interesting point was that many franchise contracts force franchise owners to . . . to buy very specific goods and services, and those goods and services tend to be overpriced. In other words, even though there are equivalent goods and services available on the market, uh, that are considerably cheaper, the owners aren't *allowed* to buy them.

Another point was about advertising. When you buy a franchise, you agree to pay up to *six percent* of your sum total in sales—that's quite a lot of money. One thing you're supposed to get in return for this money is that the company does the advertising for you. But the company doesn't advertise your business. What gets advertised is the *company's* brand, the *company's* products, which are sold by many other businesses in many other places. It turns out, individual franchise owners mostly get very little benefit—*much* less than they would get by spending even half that money to advertise their own business directly.

Finally, the biggest issue: security. Starting a franchise is not the most secure option out there. True, it's less risky than starting an independent business. But there's a *third* option that the passage didn't talk about. You can buy an *already existing independent* business from a previous owner. And the study showed that independent businesses bought from previous owners have *twice* as much chance of success during the first four years as franchises.

TRACK 69 TRANSCRIPT

Narrator

Summarize the points made in the lecture, being sure to explain how they challenge specific points made in the reading passage.

TRACK 70 TRANSCRIPT

Narrator

Listen to a conversation between a student and an admissions officer at City College.

Student

Hi. Can I ask you a few questions about starting classes during your summer session?

Admissions officer

Sure. Ask away! It starts next week, you know.

Student

Yeah, and I want to get some required courses out of the way so I can . . . maybe I can graduate one term earlier and get out into the job market sooner.

Admissions officer

That sounds like a good idea. Let me pull up the summer school database on my computer here . . .

Student

OK.

Admissions officer

OK, there it is. What's your student ID number?

Student

Oh, well, the thing is . . . I'm not actually admitted *here*. I'll be starting school upstate at Hooper University in the fall. But I'm down here for the summer, staying with my grandparents, 'cause I have a summer job near here.

Admissions officer

Oh, I see, well . . .

Student

So I'm outta luck?

Admissions officer

Well, you would be if you were starting anywhere but Hooper. But City College has a sort of special relationship with Hooper . . . a full exchange agreement . . . so our students can take classes at Hooper and vice versa. So if you can show me proof . . . um, your admissions letter from Hooper, then I can get you into our system here and give you an ID number.

Student

Oh, cool. So . . . um . . . I wanna take a math course and a science course—preferably biology. And I was also hoping to get my English composition course out of the way, too.

Admissions officer

Well all three of those courses are offered in the summer, but you've gotta understand that summer courses are condensed—you meet longer hours and all the assignments are doubled up because . . . it's the same amount of information presented and tested as in a regular term, but it's only six weeks long. Two courses are considered full time in summer term. Even if you weren't working, I couldn't let you register for more than that.

Student

Yeah, I was half expecting that. What about the schedule? Are classes only offered during the day?

Admissions officer

Well, during the week, we have some classes in the daytime and some at night, and on the weekends, we have some classes all day Saturday or all day Sunday for the six weeks.

Student

My job is pretty flexible, so one on a weekday and one on a weekend shouldn't be any problem. OK, so after I bring you my admissions letter, how do I sign up for the classes?

Admissions officer

Well, as soon as your student ID number is assigned and your information is in our admissions system, you can register by phone almost immediately.

Student

What about financial aid? Is it possible to get it for the summer?

Admissions officer

Sorry, but that's something you would've had to work out long before now. But the good news is that the tuition for our courses is about half of what you're going to be paying at Hooper.

Student

Oh, well that helps! Thank you so much for answering all my questions. I'll be back tomorrow with my letter.

Admissions officer

I won't be here then, but do you see that lady sitting at that desk over there? That's Ms. Brinker. I'll leave her a note about what we discussed, and she'll get you started.

Student

Cool.

TRACK 71 TRANSCRIPT

Narrator

Listen again to part of the conversation. Then answer the question.

Student

So I'm outta luck?

Admissions officer

Well, you would be if you were starting anywhere but Hooper.

Narrator

What does the woman mean when she says this:

Admissions officer

Well, you would be if you were starting anywhere but Hooper.

TRACK 72 TRANSCRIPT

World History

Narrator

Listen to part of a lecture in a world history class.

Professor

In any introductory course, I think it's always a good idea to step back and ask ourselves "What are we studying in this class, and why are we studying it?"

So, for example, when you looked at the title of this course in the catalog—"Introduction to World History"—what did you think you were getting into . . . what made you sign up for it—besides filling the social-science requirement?

Anyone . . .?

Male student

Well . . . just the—the history—of everything . . . you know, starting at the beginning . . . with . . . I guess, the Greeks and Romans . . . the Middle Ages, the Renaissance . . . you know, that kinda stuff . . . like what we did in high school.

Professor

OK . . . Now, what you're describing is *one* approach to world history.

In fact, there are several approaches—basic "models" or "conceptual frameworks" of what we study when we "do" history. And what you studied in high school—what I call the "Western-Heritage Model," this used to be the most common approach in U.S. high schools and colleges . . . in fact, it's the model I learned with, when I was growing up back—oh, about a hundred years ago . . .

Uh . . . at Middletown High School, up in Maine . . . I guess it made sense to *my* teachers back then—since, well, the history of western Europe *was* the cultural heritage of everyone in my class . . . and this remained the dominant approach in most U.S. schools till . . . oh, maybe . . . 30, 40 years ago . . . But it doesn't take more than a quick look around campus—even just this classroom today—to see that the student body in the U.S. is much more diverse than my little class in Middletown High . . . and this Western-Heritage Model was eventually replaced by—or sometimes combined with—one or more of the newer approaches . . . and I wanna take a minute to describe these to you today, so you can see where *this* course fits in.

OK . . . so . . . up until the mid-twentieth century, the basic purpose of most world-history courses was to learn about a set of values . . . institutions . . . ideas . . . which were considered the "heritage" of the people of Europe—things like . . . democracy . . . legal systems . . . types of social organization . . . artistic achievements . . .

Now, as I said, this model gives us a rather *limited* view of history. So, in the 1960s and '70s it was combined with—or replaced by—what I call the "Different-Cultures Model." The '60s were a period in which people were demanding more relevance in the curriculum, and there was criticism of the *European* focus that you were likely to find in all the academic disciplines. For the most part, the Different-Cultures Model didn't challenge the basic assumptions of the Western-Heritage Model. What it did was insist on representing *other* civilizations and cultural categories, *in addition* to those of western Europe . . .

In other words, the heritage of *all* people: not just what goes back to the Greeks and Romans, but also the origins of African . . . Asian . . . Native American civilizations. Though more inclusive, it's still, basically, a "heritage model" . . . which brings us to a *third* approach, what I call the "Patterns-of-Change Model."

Like the Different-Cultures Model, this model presents a wide cultural perspective. But, with this model, we're no longer *limited* by notions of fixed cultural or geographical boundaries. So, then, studying world history is not so much a question of how a particular nation or ethnic group developed, but rather it's a look at common themes—conflicts . . . trends—that cut across modern-day borders of nations or ethnic groups. In my opinion, this is the best way of studying history, to better understand current-day trends and conflicts.

For example, let's take the study of the Islamic world. Well, when I first learned about Islamic civilization, it was from the perspective of Europeans. Now, with the Patterns-of-Change Model, we're looking at the past through a wider lens. So *we* would be more interested, say, in how interactions with Islamic civilization—the religion . . . art . . . literature—affected cultures in Africa . . . India . . . Spain . . . and so on.

Or . . . let's take another example. Instead of looking at each cultural group as having a separate, *linear* development from some ancient origin, in *this* course we'll be looking for the common themes that go beyond cultural or regional distinctions. So . . . instead of studying . . . a particular succession of British kings . . . or a dynasty of Chinese emperors . . . in *this* course, we'll be looking at the broader concepts of monarchy, imperialism . . . and political transformation.

TRACK 73 TRANSCRIPT

Narrator
Listen again to part of the lecture. Then answer the question.

Professor
So, for example, when you looked at the title of this course in the catalog—"Introduction to World History"—what did you think you were getting into . . . what made you sign up for it—besides filling the social-science requirement?

Narrator
What is the professor's attitude?

TRACK 74 TRANSCRIPT

Narrator

Listen to a conversation between a student and his academic advisor.

Student

Excuse me, Ms. Chambers? Um, I don't have an appointment, but I was kinda wondering if you had a minute to help me with something.

Academic advisor

Oh, sure. Have a seat.

What's on your mind?

Student

Well, uh . . . I guess I really don't know where to start . . . It's not just one class. It's . . . I'm not doing all that great. Like on my homework assignments. And in class. And I don't know why. I mean, I just don't get it! I-I read the assignments and I do the homework and I'm still not doing too well . . .

Academic advisor

Um, which classes? You mean, like Spanish . . . you're taking Spanish, right?

Student

Oh, no, not Spanish . . . if it weren't for Spanish I'd really be in trouble . . . no, but it's really all the others, psychology and sociology especially.

Academic advisor

Is it the material, what you read in the textbooks? You don't understand it?

Student

No, that's just it—I think I understand stuff when I read it . . .

Academic advisor

You don't re . . .

Student

Remember? Well, I remember names and definitions, but . . . like, in class, when the professor asks us about the theories, what they're all about, I never have the answer.

Academic advisor

Sounds like you're trying to learn by memorizing details, instead of picking out the main points of the reading. So, tell me, how do you study?

Student

Well, I—I . . . I mean, I read the assigned chapters, and I try to underline everything . . . like all of the words I don't know, and I always memorize the definitions. But, I dunno, when I get back in class, it always seems like the other students've gotten a better handle on what was in the reading. So, maybe it's just me . . .

Academic advisor

Oh, it's not. Believe me. Lots of students . . . You know, my first year as a college student . . . I really had a hard time. I spent hours reading in the library . . . but I was just wasting time, 'cause I wasn't really studying the right things. I did the same sort of thing it sounds like you're doing, not focusing on what's really important in the reading, but on the smaller details.

Student

Yeah, maybe. But I spend so much time studying, it seems like I should be doing better.

Academic advisor

The first year of college can be a little overwhelming, I know. Point is, lots of students have trouble adjusting at first, you know, figuring out how to study, how to use their time, you know, to your best advantage. It's good that you do the assigned readings . . . but, you've . . . well, I think you're unnecessarily underlining and memorizing. That takes a lot of time, and, well, it's not the best use of your time. Here's something you can do: when you read, just read the assigned sections, and then . . . and without looking back at the text—write a summary of the key points, the main ideas in the chapter. And after you do that, it-it's good to go back and reread the text. And you look for any examples you can find to support those key points. Let me show you an example of what I mean.

Narrator

Listen to part of a lecture in an astronomy class.

Professor

I'll tell you a story about how one astronomy problem was solved. It happened many years ago, but you'll see that it's interesting and still relevant. Two, three hundred years ago, astronomers already had telescopes, but they were not as powerful as those we have now. Let's say . . . they were at the level of telescopes amateur astronomers use today. Tell me, what do you see in the night sky when you use a telescope like that? Quick, tell me.

Female student

Planets . . .

Professor

Right . . .

Male student

Even . . . like . . . the moons of Jupiter?

Professor

Right . . .

Female student

Stars.

Professor

OK . . . what else? . . . You think that's all? . . . Ever heard of nebulae? . . . I bet you have . . . Well, let's just, um, put it up anyway . . .

Nebulae are small fuzzy patches you see in the sky, they look like little clouds. Many of them have a spiral shape, and that's why we called them *spiral* nebulae . . . So astronomers in the eighteenth century . . . *eighteenth* century . . . when they looked through the telescope, they could see planets—and they knew those were planets . . . the moons of Jupiter—and they knew they were the moons of Jupiter . . . and then they saw spiral nebulae and they didn't have a clue.

What could those be? So, some of them thought—"these things are cloudy and fuzzy, so they're probably small clouds of cosmic dust, and they don't have to be very far away from us." But there were others who thought, "OK, the things *look* small and fuzzy, but *maybe* they're actually distant galaxies of stars, but we can't see the stars, because they're *so* far away and they seem so tiny that they *look* like dust, and even the whole galaxy looks like a tiny little cloud."

Which of the two theories do you think was more . . . uh, surprising?

Male student
The galaxy one.

Professor
And why?

Male student
Well, I mean it assumed that the nebulae are not what they look like at first sight. The first theory assumed that, right?

Professor
OK. And now tell me this . . . which one would have seemed more likely at the time?

Male student
Uh . . . They couldn't tell.

Professor
Right. Two morals here: first, there can be different explanations for the same observation. And second, "obvious" doesn't necessarily mean "right" . . . What happened next was . . . for a long time nothing. More than 150 years. No one could decide . . . Both hypotheses seemed plausible . . . And a lot was at stake—because if the *galaxy* theory was right, it would be proof that the universe is enormous . . . and if the *dust* theory was right . . . maybe *not* so enormous. So the size of the universe was at stake . . . Finally in the 1920s we came up with a telescope that was strong enough to tell us something new here. When we used it to look at the spiral nebulae, we saw . . . well, we were not absolutely sure . . . but it really looked like there were stars in those nebulae. So not dust after all, but stars . . .

But how far away were they, really? How would you measure that? Any ideas? Laura?

Female student

Well, how about measuring how strong those stars shine? Because, if the star is far away, then its light would be weak, right?

Professor

Yes . . . but there's a problem here. You need to know how bright the star is in the first place, because some stars are naturally much brighter than others. So, if you see a star that's weak . . . it can mean one of two things . . .

Female student

Oh . . . it's either far away or it's just a weak star.

Professor

And you can't really always tell which. But you're on the right track. There is a kind of star where you can *calculate* its natural brightness . . . and—you guessed it—we found some in the nebulae. It's called a *variable* star—or a "variable" for short—because its brightness *varies* in regular intervals. I won't go into detail here, but . . . basically . . . the longer the interval, the brighter the star, so from the *length* of those intervals we were able to calculate their natural brightness. This told us how distant they were—and many turned out to be very, very far away. So we can be sure that the spiral nebulae really *are* very distant galaxies—which is what some eighteenth-century astronomers *guessed* but didn't have the instruments to prove . . .

Now, one reason I told you this story is that *today* there are still plenty of situations when we see something out there, but we really aren't sure *what* it is. An example of one such mysterious observation would be gamma-ray bursters.

We've known about these gamma-ray bursters for a long time now, but we can't all agree on what they are.

TRACK 76 TRANSCRIPT

Narrator

Listen again to part of the lecture. Then answer the question.

Professor

But how far away were they, really? How would you measure that? Any ideas? Laura?

Female student

Well, how about measuring how strong those stars shine? Because, if the star is far away, then its light would be weak, right?

Professor

Yes . . . but there's a problem here. You need to know how bright the star is in the first place, because some stars are naturally much brighter than others. So, if you see a star that's weak . . . it can mean one of two things . . .

Female student

Oh . . . it's either far away or it's just a weak star.

Narrator

What can be inferred about the student when she says this:

Female student

Oh . . . it's either far away or it's just a weak star.

TRACK 77 TRANSCRIPT

Art History

Narrator

Listen to part of a lecture in an art history class.

Professor

Today we're going to talk about how to look at a piece of art, how to "*read*" it—what you should look for . . . what aspects of it you should evaluate. A lot of people think that if you stand in front of a work of art and gaze at it for a couple of minutes, you're evaluating it. But truly *reading* a piece of art, evaluating it *properly*, is a complex process, a process that takes *time*.

When we're confronted with a piece of art, there're several things we have to keep in mind, for example, its beauty . . . that's where aesthetics comes in.

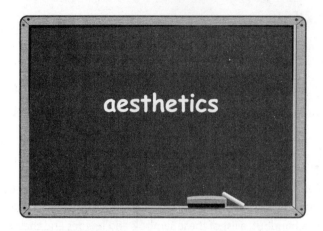

Aesthetics is the philosophy that deals with the definition of beauty, which goes all the way back to ancient Greece. They, um, the early Greek philosophers said that beauty and art are based on imitation. Their feeling about art was that it's beautiful when it imitates life; they thought that the *truthfulness* of an image, how truthful it is to life, determines its value as art. Today we have a broader definition of aesthetics.

Now *don't* identify aesthetics as personal taste. Taste is bound by time; taste is tied to a society, a given set of moral values, usually. You may not like a piece of art from a different culture—it may not be your taste—but you appreciate its beauty 'cause you recognize certain aesthetic principles. Art generally adheres to certain aesthetic principles like balance, uh, balanced proportions, contrast, movement, or rhythm.

We'll discuss aesthetics more in detail when we look at some pieces of art together. Another thing to keep in mind in evaluating art is that art has a *purpose*, generally determined by the artist. You may not know what it is, and you don't need to know what it is to appreciate a piece of art, but it helps. For example, if you know what the artist's purpose is . . . if you know that a piece of art expresses the artist's feeling about a political or social situation, you'll probably look at it differently.

Now, besides beauty and purpose, what are the other aspects of a piece of art that need to be evaluated? Very simple—you examine a piece of art following these four formal steps. The first step is *description* . . . describe physical characteristics of the piece—like this painting is large, it's oil on canvas. Describe the subject—it's a person, it's a landscape—or predominant colors like, um, earth colors . . . that's a description.

OK? So, you've described the piece. The next step is *analysis*. You're looking at the piece for any universal symbols, characters, or themes it might contain. Certain symbols are universal, and the artist counts on your understanding of symbols. Even colors have symbolic significance, as you may know. And also *objects* depicted in a piece of art are often used to represent an abstract idea. Like wheels or spheres—they look like circles, right?—so wheels and spheres represent wholeness and continuity. I have a handout, a list of these symbols and images and their interpretations, that I'll give you later. But for now, the point is that after you describe the piece of art, you *analyze* its content . . . you determine whether it contains elements that the artist is using to try to convey a certain meaning.

If it does, the next step is *interpretation*. Interpretation follows analysis very closely. You try to interpret the meaning of the symbols you identified in the piece. Almost all art has an obvious and an implied meaning. The implied meaning is hidden in the symbolic system expressed in the piece of art. What we see depicted is *one* scene, but there can be several levels of meaning. Your interpretation of these symbols makes clear what the artist is trying to tell us.

The last step is *judgment or opinion*—what do you think of the piece, is it powerful or boring?— but I give that hardly any weight. If the four steps were to be divided up into a chart, then description, analysis, and interpretation would take up 99 percent. Your opinion is not important in understanding a piece of art. It's nice to say: I like it . . . I wouldn't mind hanging it over my couch, but to evaluate a piece of art, it's not critical.

OK. Now you know what I mean by "reading" a piece of art, and what it entails. Try to keep all that in mind next time you go to an art museum. I can tell you right now that you probably won't be able to look at more than 12 pieces of art during that visit.

OK, now let's look at a slide of a piece of art and try to "read" it together.

TRACK 78 TRANSCRIPT

Narrator
What does the professor imply when he says this:

Professor
Try to keep all that in mind next time you go to an art museum. I can tell you right now that you probably won't be able to look at more than 12 pieces of art during that visit.

TRACK 79 TRANSCRIPT

Narrator

Some people enjoy watching movies or television in their spare time. Others prefer reading books or magazines. State which you prefer and explain why.

TRACK 80 TRANSCRIPT

Narrator

Read the announcement about City University's plans for the campus gym. You will have 45 seconds to read. Begin reading now.

TRACK 81 TRANSCRIPT

Narrator

Listen to two students discussing the plan.

Male student

Hey, have you read about this . . . the plans for the gym?

Female student

Yeah, but I could sure think of better things to do with the money.

Male student

You're kidding. I thought you'd be all for it. You go to the gym all the time.

Female student

Yeah, but I never have any problem. Sure there're a lot of people there but I never have to wait to use the exercise bikes, or even the weight machines. Do you?

Male student

Not really. It's not *that* busy.

Female student

The other thing is . . . well, we have all sorts of exercise programs, a terrific swimming pool that's always open, great running paths, all kinds of sports teams. I'm just saying that a bunch of new machines in the gym aren't gonna make any difference. People like to get their exercise in different ways . . . and on this campus there're already plenty of choices.

Male student

You may be right . . .

Narrator

The woman expresses her opinion about the plan described in the announcement. Briefly summarize the plan. Then state her opinion about the plan and explain the reasons she gives for holding that opinion.

TRACK 82 TRANSCRIPT

Narrator

Now read the passage about keystone species. You will have 50 seconds to read the passage. Begin reading now.

TRACK 83 TRANSCRIPT

Narrator

Now listen to part of a lecture on this topic in a biology class.

Professor

Let's take the elephant, for example. Elephants are an important species in the African grasslands. Without them, the grasslands actually stop being grasslands at all if you can believe it—they change to forests. What happens is that in the grasslands some types of seeds other than grasses can sprout and begin to grow, which . . . if they're left alone . . . they could eventually grow into shrubs or trees. But what happens is that elephants come along and eat the sprouting plants . . . or the plants get crushed under the elephants' feet. And even if a plant or two manage to survive, it won't last long because sooner or later the elephant will knock it over or pull it out of the ground.

So what if the elephants weren't there and these plants were allowed to grow to maturity? Well, pretty soon there'd be whole clusters of trees. Their branches and leaves would shade the grasses . . . and without the sunlight, the grasses won't survive. So pretty soon the grass disappears, trees grow in its place and eventually the whole grassland changes to forest.

And as you can imagine the elephant has an impact on other animal species in the habitat as well. A lot of animals in this habitat rely on the grasses for food, for example. When the grasses disappear—when their food source disappears—these animals are eventually forced to leave. Gradually, some new species come into the habitat—species that are better suited to life in the forest. These new species replace the ones that left. So you can see the influence of the elephant on the environment is significant.

Narrator

The professor gives examples of the effects of elephants on the African grasslands habitat. Using the examples from the talk, explain why elephants are considered a keystone species.

TRACK 84 TRANSCRIPT

Narrator

Now listen to part of a lecture in a creative writing class.

Professor

As writers, you want the dialogue in your story to have impact. Well, there are many ways to do that, and I'm gonna talk about two of them—exaggeration and understatement. Now, understatement is the opposite of exaggeration, but you can actually use them both to do the same thing—to create emphasis or impact. Let's compare them and see how they do that.

OK, exaggeration. When you want your characters to emphasize a point, you can have them describe things or their feelings as bigger or more extreme than they really are. For example, your main character comes back from a very long walk and she's very tired. Well, you can have her say "Boy, I'm tired." *Or* you can have her say, "I can't take another step." Well, *of course* she can take another step, but you see, if she exaggerates, she'll make her point in a more forceful and interesting way.

But you can also create emphasis with *understatement*, and like I said it's the opposite of exaggeration, but it does the same thing. With understatement you emphasize by saying, by saying *less*, by saying less than you mean. That sounds paradoxical, so I'll give you an example. From real life.

My friend Ed is a very talented cook. So last week he cooked me a delicious meal. Now, I could've said to him, "This food is really great, Ed," but that's kinda boring. Plus, Ed *knew* I thought the food was delicious. I'd eaten three servings. So instead I said, "This food's not bad, Ed." Now clearly the food was a lot *better* than *not bad*. But by understating, by describing the food as—as *less* good than it really was, I actually made a stronger statement. The characters in your stories can do this too.

Narrator

Using the examples mentioned by the professor, describe two ways that writers create emphasis when writing dialogue.

TRACK 85 TRANSCRIPT

Narrator

Now listen to part of a lecture on the topic you just read about.

Professor

Even if computerized smart cars meet all the technological expectations set for them, it's not clear that they'd produce the benefits some have predicted.

Smart cars will still get into some accidents. After all, even the most technologically advanced devices fail occasionally. And since the smart car technology will allow cars to be more tightly packed together on the roads, these accidents will be pileups that involve many more cars and so be much worse than accidents that occur today. Overall, there is little reason to believe that smart cars will save lives or reduce the number of injuries in automobile accidents.

Second, let's talk about the potential to increase highway speeds and therefore decrease commuting time. Well, history has consistently shown that when some driving convenience is introduced, more and more people decide to drive because they expect an easier driving experience. But then the increased number of drivers in the case of smart cars of the future would not decrease commuting time. This is because the traffic congestion caused by the additional cars on the road would not allow the drivers to take advantage of the smart cars' potential for higher speeds.

And finally, it's not reasonable to expect that smart cars will save drivers money. The global positioning technology required to direct smart cars to their desired destinations is very expensive, and smart cars will need other costly technologies too, such as sensors that control how far a smart car stays behind the car in front of it. Moreover, the advanced technology of smart cars will make repairs to them more expensive than repairs on conventional automobiles. These new expenses will more than offset the expected savings on the repair and replacement of traditional mechanical car parts.

TRACK 86 TRANSCRIPT

Narrator
Summarize the points made in the lecture, being sure to explain how they challenge specific points made in the reading passage.

Notes